# Think Big

'Insights from Behavioural Science are being used around the globe for a variety of purposes but never, until now, for career building – something Grace Lordan does systematically, eloquently and instructively in *Think Big*' Robert Cialdini, author of *Influence* and *Pre-Suasion*

'This is a rare self-help book that's actually informed by evidence. Drawing on her knowledge of behavioural economics and psychology, Grace Lordan shares a host of perceptive, practical tips for getting out of your own way and making progress towards your career goals' Adam Grant, *New York Times* bestselling author of *Think Again* and *Originals*, and host of the TED podcast *WorkLife*

'Want to advance your career fast without compromising personal happiness? *Think Big* can help. It provides a handy, science-driven framework to career-building that can fit around even the busiest person's daily life' Jonah Berger, Wharton Professor and bestselling author of *The Catalyst*

'On your journey to thinking big – about yourself and about the world – Grace Lordan is a wise and winning guide. She's written the ultimate primer on enlisting modest changes to achieve monumental goals' Daniel H. Pink, author of *When*, *Drive* and *To Sell is Human*

'Dr Grace Lordan has created one of the most important books anyone can read to help their working life. Anchored with behavioural science she shows how all of us can move towards our ambitions while fighting back worries and self-doubts' Bruce Daisley, author of *The Joy of Work*

'In this must-read book, Grace equips you with the know-how required to take your career to the next level. This book will not only inspire you to think bigger, but to take immediate action in turning those dreams of yours into reality. When you think big and start taking small, consistent steps forward each day, anything becomes possible!' Simon Alexander Ong

'If you know it's time to aim higher in your career, *Think Big* provides a clear and compelling behavioural science toolkit to help you realize your goals and replace your current reality with something bigger, better and more enjoyable' Dorie Clark, author of *Reinventing You* and teacher in the executive education faculty, Duke University Fuqua School of Business

'Engaging, practical and insightful. Reading *Think Big* is like having a savvy performance coach sat inside your head, helping correct your path towards the career you really want' Graham Allcott, founder of Think Productive

'In a refreshingly down-to-earth way, Grace shows how the insights from behavioural science can not only help you to build the career you want but also the career that will make you happy. This book will interest and entertain you whatever your stage of career' Professor Paul Dolan, London School of Economics, author of *Happiness by Design* and *Happy Ever After*

'*Think Big* contains a combination rare in a business book: it is both sound in theory and useful in practice. I only wish it had come out ten years ago' Rory Sutherland, Vice-Chairman, Ogilvy UK

## ABOUT THE AUTHOR

Dr Grace Lordan is the Founding Director of The Inclusion Initiative (TII), Director of the MSc in Behavioural Science and an Associate Professor in Behavioural Science at the London School of Economics. An economist by background, her research is focused on understanding why some individuals succeed in life and others don't. She is an expert on the effects of unconscious bias, discrimination and technology changes. Grace is an expert advisor to the UK government, sitting on their skills and productivity board. Her academic writings have been published in top international journals in economics and the broader social sciences. This is her first book.

# Think Big

*Take Small Steps and Build the Future You Want*

DR GRACE LORDAN

LIFE

PENGUIN LIFE

AN IMPRINT OF

PENGUIN BOOKS

PENGUIN LIFE

UK | USA | Canada | Ireland | Australia
India | New Zealand | South Africa

Penguin Life is part of the Penguin Random House group of companies whose addresses can be found at global.penguinrandomhouse.com.

Penguin Random House UK

First published 2021

005



Text Design by Couper Street Type Co.
Set in 13.5/16pt Garamond MT Std
Typeset by Jouve (UK), Milton Keynes
Printed and bound in Great Britain by Clays Ltd, Elcograf S.p.A.

The authorized representative in the EEA is Penguin Random House Ireland, Morrison Chambers, 32 Nassau Street, Dublin D02 YH68

A CIP catalogue record for this book is available from the British Library

ISBN: 978–0–241–42016–4

www.greenpenguin.co.uk

MIX
Paper | Supporting responsible forestry
FSC® C018179
FSC www.fsc.org

Penguin Random House is committed to a sustainable future for our business, our readers and our planet. This book is made from Forest Stewardship Council® certified paper.

*Dedicated to my mum, Rita.*
*Love always – Grace.*

# Contents

# CHAPTER 1

# BEGIN

It's not hard to picture someone who isn't enjoying their job . . .

Imagine Katie. Katie left university, where she'd studied history, and entered a graduate training programme at a big advertising company. She showed a particular adeptness at marketing, and at the end of her placement she was offered a full-time position. Katie seemed to thrive in this role. At the time, social media marketing was in the ascendency, and Katie quickly grasped how she could make it work for her clients – mainly large food companies. A few big coups followed: a prizewinning campaign here, a new client there, and she was promoted. Then she was promoted again. Her twenties were flying by, and Katie seemed to be flying, too. Now, at thirty-five, Katie is in charge of a global team that delivers online marketing solutions to some of the world's biggest food production companies. She is well-liked by her colleagues, has an amazing salary, and is the envy of her social circle.

But Katie hates her job. Like many others, she fell into her profession. Katie feels she should be having the time of her life, but she's totally miserable. Something has to change. But what?

Katie represents those who on the surface seem to have it all figured out, but really yearn for something different. Katie could do with disrupting her work life and thinking bigger.

And Katie isn't the only type of person that needs to think bigger . . .

Imagine Reyansh, who dropped out of university. He always intended to go back but never did, and instead bounced around a few different jobs in the service industry. He's been a barman and a waiter, but has found a niche as a barista. For the last couple of years he's been working in a coffee shop, and since joining, the coffee shop's fiercely loyal clientele has steadily grown. Reyansh makes a decent cup of coffee, but that's not why the coffee shop is doing so well. The reason people come back is because of Reyansh. He's funny, he's charming, and sometimes – because it's sunny, or he likes your coat – he gives you free coffee. (Though the owner cheerfully berates him for this.) Reyansh isn't the quickest barista on the books – he's usually too busy chatting – and there is supposed to be a loyalty card scheme to administer freebies. But everybody can see that Reyansh adds inordinate value to the business. He's a great shift supervisor, he's brilliant at teaching trainees, and even the crankiest, most difficult customers leave the shop smiling.

But Reyansh isn't satisfied. Being a barista is fine, but it was always intended as a stop gap. For one thing, the pay isn't great. For another, while making coffee and hanging out with people is fun, he craves something deeper and more meaningful from his work.

Reyansh personifies people that fail to launch within the

specific time period society expects of them. It can be daunting to launch later than your peers, particularly when you don't have a clear idea of what your passion is. Reyansh could do with thinking bigger, bringing his future self forward and identifying a more satisfying career pathway.

And Reyansh isn't the only type of person who needs to reimagine where their career is going . . .

Imagine Juan, who is working happily in an investment bank. He likes his work and his colleagues, and is perfectly fine with the 50+ hour working week. Juan now manages a team of ten people, and takes great effort to bring them along. He is a mid-level manager. Over the last five years he has seen members of his team advance within the organization relatively quickly, two of whom have been promoted over him. Juan genuinely wishes them well, but he cannot understand why his own progress has stalled. He is growing disillusioned but keeps smiling on the outside.

Juan is a good example of people who plateau despite craving advancement. He could do with rethinking how he approaches the next few years of his career, so he can move beyond his plateau.

So Katie is miserable, Reyansh has failed to launch and Juan has plateaued. Perhaps you picked up this book because you're facing a similar problem.

Maybe you know where you want to be in your career, but you don't know how to get there. Maybe you don't even know that – you simply know that you aren't where you're supposed to be right now. Or maybe you feel as though you know where you want to go, and know, on paper, how to get there, but somebody else is preventing you from doing it – a bad boss, say, or an unhelpful colleague.

Fear not.

This book is going to help you take small steps to build the career you want, and it's going to show you how to do that using insights from behavioural science.

Drawing from multiple disciplines, behavioural science seeks to understand why people make the choices they do, and also identifies easy tweaks that we can make to our environment to get different outcomes. Behavioural science can help explain why people stumble in their career journeys. It can also help explain why some aren't entering the race in the first place, and why others drop out at the first sight of failure. Behavioural science teaches us that we should think big and set a goal for our future. It also teaches us that by taking regular small steps today that support this big thinking, we can get to where we want to go.

As a professor of behavioural science at the London School of Economics, whether I am teaching masters' and executive-level students or giving talks to industry, I always want one fact to land: the research I do into human behaviour helps explain why an outcome they want is not materializing.

I'm going to do the same in this book. I will explain why the outcome you've been working towards might not have materialized yet, and I'll also show you how to *overcome* these obstacles. I will blend my own original insights with research from the frontiers of behavioural science, and draw on lessons from the fields of economics, psychology and management to empower you to build the career you want. While I have changed the names and other identifying information of the people whose stories I tell in this book, the substance of their experiences is real. You may even see yourself in some of them.

Perhaps you are starting a business, or closing a business. Perhaps you are starting university, or thinking of dropping out. Maybe you are vying for a promotion, or wishing for a lateral move across divisions in your company. You could be one of the many people who are uninspired by their working lives and in need of change.

Regardless what role, industry or stage of career you are in, I guarantee you'll find valuable lessons in these pages that will help you think big about your future and visualize a big-thinking goal. To help you achieve this goal, the book will also focus on identifying the regular small steps you will take to achieve your ambitions. And just as important are the behavioural science insights that will help you stick to taking these small steps, and to circumvent or navigate around biases and other obstacles that get in your way on your big-thinking journey.

## HOW I ENDED UP WHERE I AM TODAY

In December 2011, I moved to the LSE as a lecturer. I was full of enthusiasm, excitement and expectation. About six months into my new role, I had a conversation with a professor in my external network who I really admired and respected. As we discussed the next steps in my career, he told me that it would take at least five years to become a senior lecturer, and that even that trajectory was highly unlikely.

I was devastated to hear it would take me that long. I felt like a deflated balloon. If I were a cartoon drawing, there would have been a black cloud hanging over my head. After the shock of the news, I internalized the feedback from Professor Negativity and hit a plateau. I even started going backwards. My enthusiasm for my research waned; I couldn't work productively. I dwelled on how mediocre I was compared to others.

The professor's comments became a self-fulfilling prophecy. A prediction like this, from a respected source, causes itself to become true – because whoever is impacted by the prediction believes it, and changes their behaviour accordingly. In this case, a supposed mentor's beliefs about my abilities negatively affected my performance as I lived *down* to their expectations.

But this professor did not know me well. Actually, he did not know me at all.

That realization came to me in the middle of one sleepless night, like a slap in the face. Professor Negativity had created a narrative about me which was false. Like a fairy tale, it was based on archetypes. These archetypes were constructed from inaccurate social norms about people like 'Grace'. People can confuse my relaxed demeanour for the attitude of somebody who doesn't take their career seriously. Or perhaps my admission that I found it difficult to finish projects had caused him to label me as someone who would never finish a project. Equally, women in economics are still a rare breed in academia, and even rarer still as you advance through the ranks. Maybe my unusual path to academia – with no stop at an Ivy League institution on the way – meant he assigned a lower probability to me ever being successful. Who knows?

One thing I realized that night was that he was wrong. I was also certain that his narrative about me had been constructed because of the professor's own cognitive biases and blind spots.

But what could I do?

One simple change I could make right then and there was to get a different mentor. So I did just that. In fact, I found three. I listened carefully to what they all had to say. This process was really important, as I truly believe in listening to feedback. I also believe that if everyone says you are dead, you should lie down. If, for instance, they had all told me the same thing as Professor Negativity – that I would be very unlikely to make senior lecturer within five years – it would have been wise to listen, and up my game. But they didn't. In fact, none of Professor Negativity's sentiments were repeated. Ever.

So what happened five years later? Well, I had already been promoted to associate professor (which is a higher grade than senior lecturer), and was writing a CV that would see me promoted to professor. I had far surpassed my expectations: I had my dream job, with a clear progression path. I also avoided Professor Negativity at conferences.

Perhaps more importantly, though, I was happier. I didn't have that black cloud over my head. But things would have been very different if I had continued to internalize the first feedback I heard as a hard reality. Things would have been different if I hadn't navigated around that obstacle.

I was lucky. At the time, I was conducting research about precisely these kinds of obstacles. I used myself as a laboratory as I furthered my understanding of the study of human behaviour. I was becoming a behavioural scientist.

These days, you can find me in Connaught House at the London School of Economics, where I am an associate professor of behavioural science, well on my way to becoming a professor. I am a director of the new MSc in Behavioural Science, and also the director and founder of The Inclusion Initiative at the LSE. My research seeks to understand why people choose the jobs they do, and why some people have more success than others in getting to where they want to go. My findings demonstrate clearly that while some factors on our career journey are not within our control, a lot of others are. This has led me to advise many business leaders, helping them find ways to level the playing field for their employees, to ensure they are rewarded based on ability, skills and talent alone.

This book, though, looks at the problem from the other way around. It is about empowering individuals to think bigger, and enabling them to build the career they want through taking regular small steps.

## WHAT HOLDS US BACK?

While having big dreams is easy, making them happen is hard. Navigating working life today is tricky, and the skills we need are always changing. Advances in technology and increasing globalization are shaping the type of work that is available at a pace. More of us find ourselves working in winner-takes-all arenas. From the traditional workplace to the modern-day start-up, the people who are perceived to be the best at what they do get extraordinary rewards, while those who rank just a quarter percentile point below them get rewards that are much more ordinary.

It can feel exhausting if you are striving to get to a specific finishing line. It can be even worse if you are working really hard but have no direction or end goal in mind. Many of us sacrifice self-care in the quest for success. We miss family events, health check-ups, forget special occasions and more. If we are putting our well-being and happiness at risk, surely we should be rewarded according to our impact, skills, abilities and talent? Otherwise the risks we are taking don't have fair pay-offs.

So we put in the effort and enhance our skills. These newly acquired skills produce something amazing: breakthrough research, an innovative strategy, or a product that everyone will be better off from having. We are then rewarded in kind. Right?

Unfortunately, the process which determines who gets what reward and why is not exact, and is often unfair. Great new products fail daily, real talent goes unnoticed, and valuable innovations are cast aside. Cognitive biases are often the reason why our ideas falter and careers stall. These biases have likely impacted you and your career over and over and over again. They may even be so blatant they bring you to tears when you notice them. It is frustrating when people who can influence your career progression reveal blind spots that make the journey longer and – even worse – less enjoyable. You may grow disheartened when narratives of 'this is how we do things around here' stand in the way of your innovative ideas, or you have to waste time in endless discussions driven by bureaucracy, red tape and lobbying. You may find yourself getting grumpy when you witness biases hindering the career progression of extraordinary and intelligent people in your own workplace just because they didn't go to one of the top schools, aren't part of the right networks or don't have the right look.

But it's not just about other people – the influence of cognitive bias is not isolated to the actions (or inactions) of others. *Our own* cognitive biases hold us back, too.

You may consider yourself a good decision-maker. You always put thought into the choices that you make. You don't allow emotions to rule your head. You're pretty logical, right?

Wrong.

Behavioural science has proven beyond doubt that, most of the time, our decision-making is badly hampered by cognitive biases and blind spots, regardless of how good we think we have been in our deliberations. We often hold a belief that we are acting purposefully when we aren't. We aren't as rational as we think.

How can our own cognitive biases hold us back at work? Well, for those of you who are working for a large company, ask yourself why you aren't going for a promotion next year. Is it because you haven't fulfilled the requirements, or (as is the case most of the time) are the promotion criteria unclear and you want to make sure that you more than exceed them?

Take a step back. What is the rational decision?

If I am rational, I want to get the benefits of a promotion as soon as I can. I want the extra income, the status, and the proverbial monkey off my back. In the case of criteria being unclear, then shouldn't I go for promotion even earlier? I should take a chance, right?

But maybe I'm placing too much weight on the cost of being rejected instead.

If this applies to you, a cognitive bias is holding you back. You are overestimating the costs of getting turned down (the rejection, the pain, the embarrassment and so on) and underestimating the benefits of potentially being successful.

For most of us, the anticipation of rejection is so bad that we don't put our hat in the ring as often as we should. We anticipate the rejection as being too awful to even consider facing it. However, the actual experience of the rejection is not as bad as we anticipate. And there are silver linings, too. For me, rejection tends to involve a good glass of red wine and some chocolate to accompany the pep talk I give myself before trying again. Most importantly, we learn a lot from trying and failing. It is a life experience, in and of itself.

Let me use another example. Do you hate your current job and dream about setting up a business? Maybe you have a cool product idea, but you break out in a cold sweat when thinking about not having a regular pay cheque for the foreseeable future. So you carry on with your long commute, and worry vaguely that your true calling is passing you by.

Is this rational? Are you looking at the decision as all or nothing? Are you underestimating the cost of regret? Are you taking into account the costs of 'what if?' when you are eighty years old and haven't followed your dreams?

Our own cognitive biases hold us back. In fact, for most of us, *this is the main problem.* If I am truly self-reflective, I would put the ratio at 80 (me): 20 (others). I have stuck with projects far too long after I should have binned them. This makes me a victim of the ***sunk cost fallacy***, which is the tendency to continue only because of previously invested resources. I have also grossly underestimated how long it will take me to do some of the most basic tasks, falling victim to the ***planning fallacy***, which rears its head when we believe our pursuits will always follow the best-case scenario. At various phases in my career I have felt like an imposter when putting myself forward, despite having the credentials and the experience to make me a pretty solid bet. It is telling that even those that are aware of ***imposter syndrome*** fall into its trap. I have also procrastinated for endless periods (including when writing this book), to avoid feeling the pinch of failure or rejection.

To recognize that we are part of the cause of a prolonged career journey that stumbles, stalls, reverses and even edges near a cliff for periods of time is actually quite freeing. The acknowledgement of the possibility that *our own* biases hold us back allows us to be proactive. Looking at the above ratio, I can take control of 80 per cent of those cognitive biases. Doing so will have a huge impact on how my career progresses. And this is true for you, too – albeit your ratios may be different.

From today, I want you to take control of your career

journey, and use behavioural science insights to help you identify and pursue a new big-thinking goal, or to get across the finish line and realize a long-term dream.

## WHEN WILL I GET THERE?

When we think big, it can be tempting to put an exact deadline for completion on our new journey. I want you to avoid doing that. Everyone's journey is going to be a function of a combination of talent, effort and luck. You can put in effort and hone talent, but you cannot control luck. What I am certain of is that you are going to go on a career-transformation journey, and it is going to take years.

Yes, that's right . . . years!

For some of you it will be two years, for others five years . . . and if you are aiming to be the leader of a country, the CEO of a big company or create the next path-breaking product, it may even be ten.

But don't panic! There is plenty to enjoy along the way. You will not be waiting years to realize gains. In fact, I am certain you will experience growth almost straight away. Like a road trip from New York to San Francisco, there are key milestones, moments when you just enjoy the view, and lots of fun, exciting experiences to be had en route.

> The point of a road trip isn't simply to arrive somewhere else; the journey itself is rewarding, too.

Equally, there will be times in your career journey when you get a flat tyre or hit roads where there is nothing worth seeing. You may also choose to take a break to allow for other key life events. If you buy a book that promises you a new destination – or a major life change – in one week or one month, I hope it's refundable. We all have the potential to achieve great things, but if it were that easy, everyone would be doing it.

Unless you are in a situation where you can upend your entire life, you need to get real and realize that big thinking is a medium-term expedition. We should view this expedition as medium-term because it will take years rather than days, weeks or months, but at the same time it will not take most of your adult life to complete it. This approach also allows for a great work–life balance. It is not do-or-die; if you don't get it right every single day, it's not the end of the world. And having a good work–life balance should be central to the pursuit of any big-thinking goal.

As a thought experiment, cast your mind back to the person you were five years ago. Make a mental note of any major changes you have experienced in your life since then. The major changes do not have to be work-related; they can include relationship changes, a bereavement, moving country, having children, starting and finishing a degree, losing a significant amount of weight, running a marathon, etc. Do you think that your personality changed? Do you think that your ability to handle situations changed? Did you change how you physically dress or wear your hair? Make a list of all the notable changes you can recall. Now, make a list of the changes you think you will make in the *next* five years.

I do this exercise sometimes when I am teaching behavioural science executive students. But rather than asking the group to fill out both columns, I ask them to fill in one column or the other. Every single time, I have found that the lists written by the people who are reflecting on the last five years are much longer, and more ambitious overall, than the lists by those who are thinking forward to the next five years.

And these are people who have elected to attend a course for business leaders! By default, they are expecting major future changes, right?

So what gives?

The majority of us see ourselves as having experienced many major changes when we look backwards. However, we also imagine that the next five years will not bring any great or significant change. We assume we will stay more or less the same. But this is simply a behavioural science illusion. Regardless of age, we tend to underestimate the amount we can achieve in the medium term going forward, yet we view ourselves as having made major progress in the medium term in the past![1]

So our future selves are underachievers; and, in contrast, our past selves are overachievers. Imagine what could have been achieved if you had consciously set a big-thinking goal for the last two, five or even ten years and committed to small steps to achieve it? Rather than striving for the next pay cheque, the next pay rise or the next promotion, you could have aimed for something bigger. You could have aimed for something different. You could have been striving for something you really wanted. Believe me: thinking big and taking small steps that support your ideas can reinvent you!

But, as humans, we are impatient. We generally favour a lofty goal over short periods because we are excited to walk in the shoes of our improved selves sooner rather than later. And that's pretty understandable. But it also sets us up for failure. Very often we can't make the changes that we need to over the short term without completely restructuring our lives. Voices in your head start shouting that it's too hard, that you are unhappy and life is too short. So you quit. And when you do so, you learn a lesson: you are a quitter. Next time you plan a life change, you are reminded that you are a quitter – so why even bother starting something?

> When thinking big, it is never all or nothing. Regular small positive actions have a disproportionately large positive effect on major life outcomes.

Have you ever tried to lose weight over a short period by cutting carbs only to fall off the wagon . . . by eating a wagon loaded with pasta? It's the same phenomenon. Or maybe there is some long-standing New Year's resolution that you always make but never keep to? Quitting smoking, reading more, drinking less alcohol? Maybe every 31 December you pledge to overhaul your career, but come 31 January you are back on autopilot wishing for the weekend. All too often, by the end of January we lack the energy and motivation to follow through on our best-laid plans. That's because short-term goals set most of us up for long-term failure.

We are creatures of routine. The easiest way to ensure that you do not achieve a goal is to jump in too quickly. Of course, there are always exceptions to this rule – I'm sure you've read plenty of stories of people who turned their life around in two weeks. But we don't infer a trend from an anomaly. Besides, if you scratch the surface, you might find their story is much more complicated. Behind a spectacular two-week turnaround there's often years of structured and sustained effort. It is this effort that causes the success. It doesn't make for a neat newspaper headline or an exciting party anecdote – but it's the truth.

In most cases, the person who is deemed an overnight success has long been quietly honing their craft and creating opportunities so they can finally be recognized for their expertise.

There is real truth in the saying: 'Luck is what happens when preparation meets opportunity.'

Setting your sights on a medium-term horizon of two, five or even ten years allows for real change. It is also a sweet spot: you will not feel a significant drop in happiness if you begin with small steps that are peppered into your usual routine. Your efforts will not disrupt your schedule too aggressively, but these small steps still accumulate, and add up to something big. This is a key insight from behavioural science:

> Small changes that are actioned regularly have disproportionate effects on our life outcomes.

This brings me back to Katie, Reyansh and Juan. Though the outcomes in their scenarios are totally different, the problem is the same. Reyansh hasn't been back to university because he's told himself he isn't organized enough. But being organized is a basic administrative skill that can be learned. If you can make a cup of coffee and cash up a till, you can learn how to organize your time. Similarly, his failure to commit to anything is symptomatic of a fear of failure. Despite being clever and capable, Reyansh has held himself back by never pushing himself outside his comfort zone. He doesn't believe change is possible.

Katie, on the other hand, has never asked what she wants for herself. It goes without saying that she is also very capable and clever, but she's internalized a story of what success looks like, and – even though it isn't right for her – she has doggedly stuck to it. 'What will happen if I try to do something else?' she thinks. 'What will my friends say? My parents? What if I can't pay my mortgage?'

Juan is stuck because of ***status quo bias***. He has hit a plateau and has not yet taken the time to discover what he can control in order to get himself out of it. His job is like a comfort blanket, and while he craves change, needing this comfort is holding him back.

What might happen if Katie, Reyansh and Juan worked to overcome their biases and took a medium-term approach towards changing their career?

A two-year journey is enough time for Katie to set up a boutique marketing consultancy of her own. Why? Well, that two-year window would give Katie enough time to disentangle the tasks in her job that she likes from those she does not, register a new company, hire her first members of staff and pivot to a happier working life.

A seven-year journey is enough time for Reyansh to become a practising psychotherapist. How? By tracking backwards and looking at the things he's liked doing in his different jobs, Reyansh can identify talents – like his people skills – and, with this discovery under his belt, choose a university course that leverages those talents. Seven years is sufficient for him to complete university while holding on to his barista job part-time, and then he can make the transition to full-time practice.

A four-year journey is enough time for Juan to work on the things that are holding him back so he can progress to managing director. What is holding him back? Well, for one, the tendency for others in the organization to misinterpret his easy-going manner as a lack of senior leadership potential. Once the biases of others are recognized, they can be tackled effectively. In a four-year window, Juan can invest in honing his confidence and authority so he can make his added value clearer to senior colleagues in a series of regular catch-ups he takes the liberty of scheduling. Juan is up to that challenge.

What will happen if *you* go on a medium-term journey and think big?

When we go on a journey, we need a map. For the journey you are about to embark on, this book is your map. It will help you plan out and navigate your medium-term expedition. Because we are all unique in our ambitions, you will each have a different journey length. However, the process that all of you go through will essentially be the same. You're going to set intentions to unlock new abilities and skills, and gain access to new opportunities.

You will take the time to identify the obstacles that are standing in your way. We often put obstacles in our own way. Obstacles are also, either consciously or unconsciously, caused by the actions of others. These others could be your colleagues, your friends or your family – or a combination of all three. New abilities may be needed to allow you to successfully navigate around such obstacles.

Most of us face both of these barriers. We hold ourselves back, and we are held back. This book uses cutting-edge behavioural science research to help circumvent these obstacles.

I have personally taken the time to think big. This has led me to realize that there are a number of distinct topics that need to be tackled, and there is a systematic way of doing so. The creation and maintenance of a big-thinking goal has six steps that you need to work through to give yourself the best chance of completing it.

First, there must be something well-defined to aim for. You need a big-thinking **goal**. This is what you visualize when you think big. What is your goal? What does your future self look like? When deciding what this goal is, you will also need to identify the activities that allow you to achieve it. These activities are like stepping stones across a lake (or pond, depending on how ambitious you plan to be), and they are the small steps that you will take in order to realize your big-thinking goal.

Second, you need to find **time** to take those small steps. More than that, you need to recognize that humans have a tendency to be impatient – we favour spending time engaged in activities that bring us immediate gratification. In contrast, the activities that move you forward have pay-offs that are in the future. Tools from behavioural science can help you prioritize your journey and stick to your intended path, giving you the best chance of realizing your big-thinking goal sooner rather than later.

Third, your own cognitive biases have the potential to sabotage your big thinking. Looking **inside** yourself and learning what these biases are is essential. Avoiding being trapped by your own biases is paramount to staying on your chosen trajectory.

Fourth, the cognitive biases of others can hinder and derail your progression. Looking to the **outside** world and identifying what these biases are, and learning how to navigate around them, will ensure that your best-laid plans aren't scuppered by other people.

Fifth, understanding how the physical **environment** that you spend your time in affects the possibility of you realizing your big-thinking goal is an essential component to moving forward. No matter what your working environment is like at the moment, insights from behavioural science will allow you to make small tweaks to your surroundings that will support your new endeavour.

Last, but certainly not least, in order to follow through and realize your big thinking, it is necessary to harness and hone **resilience**. Resilience, put simply, is not giving up on your big-thinking goal. Sounds good in principle, but how can you do it in practice? Understanding how your own reactions to interactions and circumstances affect how resilient you are will allow you to make minor changes in behaviour that can have large returns over the next few years.

These are the keys to changing gears in your life. To recap, they are:

- **Goal**
- **Time**
- **Inside**
- **Outside**
- **Environment**
- **Resilience**

These six topics define the content of the six chapters that make up the core of this book. Embedded within each of these chapters is a series of behavioural science insights. Each insight can improve the odds of you succeeding in realizing your big-thinking goal by taking regular small steps, starting today. However, what works for one person may not work for another. You will learn what works for you by trying the exercises, and using the tools that appeal most to your own experience. While you might choose to work through only some exercises, all the behavioural science insights listed in each chapter are worth considering. Understanding and remembering them will help you navigate your big-thinking journey that little bit more easily.

It might be that when you think big you discover two, three or four big ambitions that you want to shoot for. In order to work on these most effectively, I would recommend that you pick your top priority, and go through the book developing a plan for this one goal only. Then you might want to work through the book again, with your second and then your third big goal in mind. And while this book is focused primarily on the world of work, you can use these techniques to make your big thinking come to fruition in any area of your life. Perhaps you want to learn a language, write a novel or run a marathon – or all three! The processes detailed in the chapters that follow can help you get on track in any field.

Get this right once, and you can lean on the approach time and time again. It will become like a 'rinse, wash and repeat' for avoiding the biases and blind spots that *used* to hold you back.

So are you ready to think big, take small steps and build the career you want? Then let's get going . . .

Happy planning!

# CHAPTER 2

# GOAL

## IS THE STORY YOU TELL ABOUT YOURSELF TRUE?

When I was growing up in Ireland, I was terrified of needles. Really terrified. From convincing a friend that looked nothing like me to stand in for me, to passing out and requiring multiple stitches in my head, having blood drawn was always a dramatic event. My father likes to tell the story of him sitting in a doctor's waiting room chatting amiably to a nun while I was getting my blood taken. A nurse popped her head around the door and asked him to come inside. 'Your daughter is very distressed,' she said. 'Perhaps you should be with her when the needle goes in. I can see from her records that she has previously fainted.'

The nun looked at my father in disbelief and exclaimed, 'Shame on you! You should have been in there all this time. Poor little mite. A child needs their dad at times like this!'

My dad stood up slowly and responded, 'My daughter is twenty-five.'

My needle phobia continued to haunt me throughout the

rest of my twenties. It sounds hilarious in hindsight, but the cold sweats, shaking, nausea and fainting weren't funny to me at the time. So when I was told that I had type 1 diabetes in 2011, when I had just entered my thirties, it had a particularly sharp edge. I feel I took the news that I needed to inject myself with insulin five times a day for the rest of my life pretty calmly, given my severe phobia. I simply asked the consultant how long I was going to live without insulin because I had no intention of injecting. In my eyes, my quality of life would be zero, so what was the point?

This statement was taken so seriously that I was given a firm lecture about the possibility of being committed into an institution involuntarily. I was also told I would not be allowed to leave the hospital that night until I had injected successfully.

Today I inject five times a day, often in public without being noticed, and it's no big deal. While before I held tightly to the belief that I had an unshakeable fear of needles, my personal narrative has well and truly changed.

> The power of our own narratives to shape both our actions and inactions is tremendous.

Narratives cut across all aspects of our lives, including our ability to think big and make things happen in our careers.

## IS SOMETHING ALREADY BLOCKING YOUR PATH?

When we start to formulate any medium-term plan, the first thing we need to do is set a big-thinking goal. Otherwise you won't know when you've reached your destination. However, there is a crucial step that comes ahead of establishing your goal. Before you put pen to paper and conjure up images of what you will be doing in a few years, stop and think about the mental barriers that stand in the way of you visualizing the career of your dreams.

Have you ever thought about creating a podcast, only to push the thought out of your head because you have no experience of any of the stages of podcast creation? Have you ever considered learning how to fly a helicopter, only to file it away with all the other wishful-thinking projects? Have you ever wanted to go rambling around the world for months on end, only to smile and think it's just a pipe dream?

Do you have an idea of the person you want to be, but it seems so out of reach that you have already scaled back your ambition?

It is not too hard to formulate a plan that will enable you to achieve your big-thinking goal, once you have a final destination in your mind's eye. Later in this chapter, I will give you some behavioural science insights which, if followed, will help you on your big-thinking journey. These insights will ensure that you intentionally move towards ME+.

ME+ is the person you will be after you have realized your big-thinking. It is the person you will be when you finish your medium-term expedition. ME+ has the career that you visualize when you think big. Soon, you will do this visualization and create an image of ME+.

But before that, let's do the hard bit and uncover any personal narratives that may be holding you back . . .

What stories are you telling yourself that stand in the way of your success?

## WHAT NARRATIVES ARE HOLDING YOU BACK?

When I start something new, at some point close to initiation, I see a mountain but I cannot see the summit. So I procrastinate. I tell myself I don't have enough time to fit everything in. At my weakest moments – usually when I'm tired – I tell myself a story. This is a tale about how I'm doing too much already and I shouldn't continue. I don't carry out a time audit of the twenty-four hours available in my day – because that would reveal the many hours that I could put towards mastering my new task – and instead I let myself off the hook. I stop doing the activity.

I'm not talking here about the things that are a waste of my time, like pointless meetings and endless emailing. I'm talking about the big challenges that can really move the needle both in my work and beyond. My narrative – the story I tell myself – is that I am too busy.

There are many stories people tell themselves that prevent them from starting something. Perhaps, for you, it is, 'I'm not smart enough!' Or maybe, 'I'm good at enough things already.' Or perhaps, 'I don't take risks like that.' Another common narrative is: 'I will never be as good as those other people, so why even bother?'

You tell yourself you don't have control over what happens next. Maybe you tell yourself you don't want to start something that you can't give your whole self to. This tendency for perfectionism causes you to only initiate things that can be completed perfectly and successfully. The perfectionist narrative ensures your goals remain unfulfilled.

Stories like these serve a purpose. They insulate us from failure and keep us inside our comfort zone. They help us save face. Coming out of our comfort zone doesn't feel so good. It involves risk. It's scary. Narratives are a safety blanket that keep you wrapped up tight. But unless your big-thinking goal is to stay in your comfort zone, you're going to have to step outside it at some point.

## IDENTIFYING YOUR NARRATIVES

So you need to identify the narratives that are holding you back. This sounds easy to do, but it can be harder than you think. Take a moment now to ask yourself some questions. Do any of the narratives listed in the last section ring true for you? Are there others that come to mind? The narratives you tell yourself might be expressed aloud in the excuses you use when you are turning down an opportunity. They're the voices that creep into your head in the form of worries or doubts about whether you are up to the challenges that come your way. They may even keep you up at night.

Try to be as literal as possible about the narratives that apply to you. The more detailed you are, the more likely you are to identify them accurately – and also realize why they came about in the first place. For example, if you get an invitation to do some public speaking and the first thought that pops into your head is, 'I can't do that', ask yourself why. If the answer is that you are not good enough, probe your thoughts for the underlying reason. You may hear things such as, 'I'm not ready', 'I'm not a credible public speaker', 'I don't have that level of knowledge', 'I'll choke' or 'I'd be terrified'. Write these down. Chances are that these are stories that are not credible. After all, if they were true, why would you have been asked to speak in the first place?

The stories we tell ourselves are kept alive with the help of ***confirmation bias***.

Confirmation bias is a cognitive bias that causes people to favour information which confirms their previously existing beliefs, discounting examples that do not support the narrative that they hold on to. In other words, if you hold a narrative that you are not good enough to take a public-speaking gig, you will look for evidence to support that notion. You pay attention to the gaps in your expertise that you still have to fill, and ignore all the thoughtful and innovative contributions you have made in the subject you are being asked to speak on. Worse, you ignore the fact that external folk see you as enough of an expert to extend the invitation in the first place!

This is typical when it comes to confirmation bias. Disconfirming evidence is ignored, and instead we seek 'proof' that backs up our beliefs. Equally, if you hold a belief that you are doing enough already to move ahead in your career, and that your plateau is other people's fault, you look for evidence to support that notion. You focus on the added value that you gave in the meeting on Monday, and overlook the opportunity to network with senior colleagues that you chose to miss on Tuesday. And if you hold on to a narrative that you have no time to expand your business, then you will focus on how overwhelmed you feel about your current workload, and ignore the significant amount of time you spend on social media or watching TV. Worse, you might even load up your current schedule with meaningless tasks which do not add value.

If you want to change, you need to identify the false stories you have constructed about yourself. And then you need to do something to combat them.

Jot down the narratives that you think are holding you back in the first column of the table below. The second column is for the small steps that will help change these narratives – you will add these later.

| Narrative | Change |
|---|---|
| | |
| | |
| | |
| | |
| | |

## THE THEORY OF NARRATIVES

It may seem a bit unusual to be asked to reflect on whether your narratives are holding you back. After all, wouldn't you know already if this were the case? Well, not necessarily. Narratives are created unconsciously, and many of the most powerful ideas in psychology and personal development already recognize the power of such narratives. Let's take a whirlwind tour of some of the most important work that links to the stories we tell ourselves . . .

Cognitive behavioural therapy (CBT) has gained ground all over the world in treating anxiety and depression. Essentially, this talk therapy focuses on how your thoughts, beliefs and attitudes affect your feelings and behaviour. Negative thinking patterns can start in childhood. For example, if you didn't receive much attention from your parents, as an adult you may automatically think 'I'm just not good enough' when things don't go your way. But there will always be times when you 'lose' – whether it's a client, a promotion or a project. This narrative may make you feel so bad that you don't put yourself out there, and in the future you only seek situations where you feel comfortable. CBT forces you to challenge your interpretation of situations. Essentially, it helps you to change your narrative so you hear a different story.

In her insightful book, *Mindset: The New Psychology of Success*, Carol Dweck puts forward a theory which views people as one of two types. The first has a ***fixed mindset***. They assume that their abilities are innate and cannot be changed. A person with a fixed mindset might be heard saying, 'I'm just not good with numbers' or 'I can't speak in public'. A person with a fixed mindset hates to fail, so avoids situations where they might. If a person with a fixed mindset is forced to participate in an activity that they believe they are not good at, they view it through that lens. A fumbled sentence when speaking in public? That's evidence that they do not belong on a speaker's podium. They decline the request next time round. They lean on confirmation bias.

The second type of person has a ***growth mindset***. They believe that they can, at any time, acquire new skills. They thrive on challenges, and embrace their failures as learning opportunities. They believe that, with effort, anything is possible. The result is that people with growth mindsets are open to changing their narrative. They keep an open mind regarding the possibility that they can gain the necessary skills to become tomorrow's leaders, innovators and experts. We know that anyone can acquire new skills when they put their mind to it, so we should all try to develop a growth mindset by reminding ourselves of this.

Another powerful psychological theory is ***locus of control***. This is the extent to which a person feels that they have control over the events that influence their lives – or their career path. A person who believes that they have control over what happens is said to have an *internal* locus of control. A person who believes that they have no control over what happens has an *external* locus of control. For people with an external locus of control, regardless of what happens, there's no personal culpability and no lessons for them to learn. If their business fails, it was down to the economy. If they lose a client, that client is unreasonable. If their book gets rejected, it doesn't need revising.

In contrast, people with an internal locus of control take responsibility. They seek out opportunities. The narrative is always, 'I am responsible!' – whether the end result is good or bad. Luck has no role for a person with an external locus of control. They believe only in talent and effort, and claim you 'make your own luck'. Think about what that means for someone whose career faces a series of unexpected setbacks – for example, people who have lost their jobs because the economy has contracted. Lay-offs happen to talented people all the time. For those who are laid off and have an internal locus of control, internalizing the blame for this bad luck has a deteriorating effect on their well-being.

In *Happy Ever After: Escaping the Myth of the Perfect Life*, Paul Dolan highlights the power of narratives and documents how the stories we tell ourselves can really harm us in areas of life such as marriage, the pursuit of happiness, and income. He argues that we are addicted to doing what is expected of us. We internalize these expectations and a narrative emerges of what we 'ought to do' in life, which may not resemble what will bring us joy. This narrative becomes part of us, regardless of whether we are suited to it.

All of these psychological frameworks emphasize the importance of paying attention to personal narratives. You may have positive narratives in one aspect of your life and negative aspects in another. An 'I'm not worth it' narrative may have you stuck in a relationship that isn't good for you.

An 'I will never be as good as those people' narrative may be preventing you from starting Krav Maga, and keeping you binge-watching *Breaking Bad.*

> Narratives are pernicious – you often don't notice them because they're part of who you tell yourself you are.

But you can always change. And becoming aware of them is the first step.

## CHANGING YOUR NARRATIVE

When I made the decision to prioritize the self-care of my type 1 diabetes and start injecting, obviously I had little choice in the matter – it was literally life or death. But people all around us are choosing to change their narratives every day, by engaging in processes that ultimately fulfil a goal they seek to achieve. Smokers start vaping (new process) as a substitute for cigarettes, and so stop smoking cigarettes (ultimate goal). Social media addicts leave their phone by the door as they come into their home (process) to allow for quality family time (ultimate goal). To achieve any goal, you need to focus on the process. Over time, the narrative changes to 'I am a non-smoker' or 'I make space for family'.

Even if you cannot identify clearly what the narratives stopping you advancing towards ME+ are, by identifying a process that leads to a goal you want to achieve, you will cause a new narrative to be internalized. Every time you engage in the process, you are writing a new line in your narrative. At some point, you will have written a whole new character into your story. You will continue writing the story, but the effort it takes will be much lower once the character has been defined because you already know what they're going to do in a given situation. It may not be easy, but efforts to change personal narratives that are not serving you are well spent.

Think back, and try to remember a time where you changed your own narrative. What were the processes that enabled this change? If you had a bad spell in your relationship, how did you emerge from it? Maybe you committed to a date night? Perhaps you went to counselling? Or did you find a shared hobby? If you went from zero to decent at chess, how did it come about? Did you practise at a weekly club? Or online? If you learned a new language as an adult, how did you do it? Did you go to a class? Or teach yourself with an app? These are the processes that caused the emergence of a new narrative. You engage in these processes, and if you do them often enough, at some point you notice that the narrative has changed.

Below are some examples of negative narratives, and the processes that could be employed to disrupt them. Look back at the narratives you wrote down earlier (see p. 28), and identify one that is holding back ME+. Next, think of a process that can help you emerge from this negative narrative, and write that in the 'Change' column. What is the new narrative that engaging in this process leads to?[1]

Make a commitment to set some time aside each week, perhaps on a Sunday evening, to reflect on how successful you have been in your chosen process the previous week, and plan ahead for the next week.

Examples of narratives, processes to change them, and the new narratives that follow:

1 **Narrative:** I eat junk food daily.
**Process:** Make a conscious effort to prepare and freeze my lunches for the week every Sunday night.
**New narrative:** I am a healthy eater. I eat healthily most days, and have far more energy and fewer energy slumps.

2 **Narrative:** I am unproductive. I was unproductive every day last week and my to-do list constantly overwhelms me.
**Process:** Only check/answer emails and surf the web between 3 p.m. and 5 p.m.
**New narrative:** I am productive. My mornings are more productive and free from distraction. I get to clock off earlier each evening.

3 **Narrative:** I am not good enough. Everyone around me at work is doing better than me, and they are achieving their goals at a much faster pace.
**Process:** Benchmark my progress against myself, and don't devote time to comparing myself to others. Instead, track my own accomplishments and advancements once a week in a journal.
**New narrative:** I am proud of myself, as I am moving forward. My self-esteem has risen and I am happier at work.

Notice that, in the examples above, the process never relies on other people. This is a necessary condition when choosing the process. Engaging in such a process repeatedly allows a new narrative to emerge that replaces the older, negative narrative.

Have you ever heard that boys are innately better at maths? Have you also heard that girls are better at verbal skills? These claims are really just based on a straw man. Sadly, most children are aware of the stereotypes and end up actively internalizing them – little Jenny knows she is expected to be bad at maths and lives down to that expectation. This causes girls to do worse at maths – and, likewise, makes boys worse at verbal skills.[2] It is a self-fulfilling prophecy.

Self-fulfilling prophecies cause poorer performance. Once I believe something about myself it becomes a personal narrative, and personal narratives have tremendous power in determining the actions I take. If I tell myself I am bad at maths, I will approach every study session with a negative lens and each hour of study feels longer and more difficult. On the other hand, if I tell myself I love maths and that I'm a naturally brilliant mathematician, it isn't such a struggle.

In 2015 I met Jennifer, who had just given up on creating a new fitness app. Jennifer had all the ingredients for her new business down pat – a great team, a solid business plan and a great product. However, Jennifer also held a belief that she had poor interpersonal skills, and was bad at selling herself and her product. Because of this belief, the first time she met a funder she was nervous, fluffed her lines and did not inspire confidence. She did not get backed.

Jennifer internalized this behaviour. She gave herself a good mental kicking and labelled herself a failure. When she tried a second time, the same thing happened. And the third. And the fourth. And the fifth. Jennifer told herself a story regarding her strengths and difficulties which became a self-fulfilling prophecy. Of course, there is no reason why self-fulfilling prophecies need to have negative outcomes.

Rather than viewing your strengths and difficulties as fixed traits, it is much more useful to think of them as an external part of who you are, caused by your behaviour. Think of strengths and difficulties as being the result of a process that you engage in.

Too many people think of strengths and difficulties as an inherent part of who they are. It is true that there is a genetic component to many important human traits and life outcomes. For many of us, the three most precious things we will nurture throughout our life-course are health, happiness and intelligence. Do you think that these are fixed when you're born? Do you think that these parts of us are fully determined by our genetics? The answer – thankfully – is no.

When disentangling a genetic component as a determinant of a particular outcome, researchers often study twins. Such studies analyse what happens in the lives of identical and non-identical sets of twins reared in the same household. These studies exploit the fact that identical twins share all of the same genes, and non-identical twins share 50 per cent of them. Similarity in the outcomes observed in identical and non-identical sets of twins is thus taken as a genetic component, rather than attributed to the environment.

So what have these studies concluded about the genetic component of being happy and smart? The genetic component of intelligence is estimated by researchers to be somewhere between 20 and 60 per cent.[3] This leaves somewhere between 40 and 80 per cent of the variation in intelligence to be determined by your own deliberate small steps and daily circumstances.

Perhaps you care less about intelligence and only want to be happy? Research suggests that about 50 per cent of your happiness is determined by factors outside genetics.[4] The small actions you take every day really do shape your well-being.

So what should you take away from this discussion on genetics and heritability?

You can change your own life outcomes.

There is lots of wiggle room to go from suboptimal to awesome. A good starting point to get to awesomeness? Change the behaviour that you link to a particular narrative. Rather than labelling yourself as unproductive, take a small step (a process) to initiate change that aligns with your big thinking. How do you become a hill walker? You walk hills often enough and you get that label. How do you become a public speaker? You speak regularly enough to audiences on a topic you have expertise in, and you get to call yourself a public speaker.

Always focus on processes rather than outcomes because it is processes that are firmly within your control.

## BEHAVIOURAL SCIENCE INSIGHTS

Changing narratives that do not serve you well is hard but really worth the effort. To be crystal clear, I'm not asking you to change your authentic self. In fact, I'm asking you to do the opposite. I'm not trying to change introverts into extroverts. I'm not asking that those of you who shy away from competition become more competitive. Rather, I am asking you to have a vision of your ME+ that is free from mental blocks. Once you have that, you can set about identifying the skills that are required to get you there, recognizing the naysayer in your head as a constructed narrative that should be shushed when it tells you that you're not up to the challenge.

To help you think big and decide on a big-thinking goal for ME+, what follows are ten behavioural science insights. You should work through these insights one by one in the order they appear in the text. Your reward? You will end up with a medium-term plan complete with commitments to regular activities. These regular activities are the small steps you will take to ensure you realize your big-thinking ambition for ME+.

Are you ready?

### *INSIGHT 1: WHAT IS ME+ DOING DAILY?*

We all have the ability to think big regardless of where we are in our lives. The book you are (hopefully) engrossed in right now was conceived in November 2017, after I was discharged from being in intensive care. Having very successfully controlled my diabetes for many years, I took my eye off the ball in late 2017 and ended up with diabetic ketoacidosis, a life-threatening condition that occurs if type 1 diabetics don't control their sugars properly. I was discharged from hospital with strict instructions to improve the management of my chronic illness, a challenge I willingly accepted after being scared silly. On that day, I made a self-care plan, which – you guessed it – involved a lot of small steps to help me realize big health gains. But you want to know something else? I also made a plan to write a book that would bring behavioural science lessons to a wider audience than the students that I meet at the LSE. This plan included a list of the activities I would need to engage in to help me fulfil this ambition. These activities were the small steps that I incorporated into my daily schedule.

Back then, my ME+ goal was to write a book. Identifying

that big-thinking goal gave me clarity on the small steps I needed to take to get there. Wherever you are in life today, focusing on what ME+ will be doing in the future allows you to realize opportunities in a few years that seem far beyond the current horizon – and in a way that isn't all or nothing.

So how do you get started? You think big and visualize your ME+.

You must first set a big-thinking goal that can realistically be achieved with hard work. For instance, if you are holding out to be a professional rugby player but are not actively playing the sport, and are approaching forty, this is a fantasy. There is zero demand for rugby players of this age and experience. If you are approaching forty and hope to be a leader in business but do not have business acumen, there is a very long shot it can be your ME+. In this case, the obstacle is that you are very behind in experience compared to others aiming for the same goal, and the number of leadership positions is very small. But if you are approaching forty, have stagnated on the career rung just before middle management, and want to make it to a leadership role, this is a ME+ where major progress can be made over the medium term.

Thinking about your **future self** creates the space to consider how you really want to be earning your living. Don't focus on the lifestyle you want – it's no good thinking big about the holidays you're going to go on or the restaurants you want to eat in. Instead, concentrate on the activities you want to be engaged in that will pay for that lifestyle. Ideally, the thought of engaging in these activities will fill you with passion. You will be excited at the thought of getting out of bed every morning. These days, we work longer weeks and retire much later. Many of us spend the majority of our time either in work or thinking about work. So you want to get to a place where you are doing some of what you love. And your big thinking needs to reflect that.

When you are doing what you love, the cost of the effort in engaging in processes is near zero, and the odds of you delivering something special are high. Your work is not draining you. In fact, your work may even be life-enhancing.

Moving away from just wanting to earn a fat salary to identifying activities that you will enjoy (at least most of the time) is absolutely necessary if you want to create a plan for your journey that you will stick to, while also improving your quality of life. We are all programmed to want more money for doing less. (Although, if you are British, it is impossibly rude to say that out loud.) However, the evidence that links income to happiness is thin on the ground – once you pass a relatively modest level that allows you to have life's necessities with a small sprinkling of treats. If you only focus on money, you will lose the chance to find out what you love doing. You will also miss out on the opportunity to get paid for doing it.

> By thinking in terms of the activities that you really want to be doing, you can identify the small steps you need to take to realize ME+.

By thinking in terms of processes, you will develop a keen self-awareness of where you should be expending your efforts. And, most importantly, you will actively cultivate the narrative that you have control over who your ME+ turns out to be. The small steps become something you engage in regularly. They are the processes, and these processes get woven into your personal narrative.

I want you to visualize starting work on a morning a few years from now, as ME+. You could be getting dressed for a commute into anywhere from Palo Alto to the City of

London. Perhaps you're working from home, or sitting in a local café. You might be dressed in shorts, a suit or never get out of your pyjamas. But what will you actually be *doing* once your working day starts?

Now is the time to decide on the activities of the job ME+ will be doing. Do you want to coach and develop others? Do you want to make decisions on how resources should be spent in a company? Do you want to sell something – maybe your own invention, or a consultancy service? Do you want to write for a living? Do you want to care for others?

Take some time now to fill in the table below. If you already know what you want to do, it will be very easy for you to complete. There are separate questions for those of you who plan to stay on the same career trajectory but accelerate, and those who want to start on a new path – which may mean freelancing, starting a business or moving to an entirely new job.

If you are less certain on what ME+ will be doing, simply focus on identifying the activities you enjoy. Circle anything that you would like to be paid to do in the future, crossing through those that don't strike a chord with you. The activities that have no circle or cross-through represent those that you will do without complaint, but you wouldn't be upset if they were taken away.

If you still don't have a clear vision of what you want to do yet – fear not. Devote your attention to identifying a couple of activities that you would enjoy. Your approach can be something of a grid search. You will engage in any broad activities that you managed to identify, assess how much you enjoyed the experience, and define your tastes more clearly as you repeat the process and learn more about what you enjoy doing and the opportunities each activity opens up for you.

## WHAT ME+ WILL BE DOING

| | | | | |
|---|---|---|---|---|
| **Complete the following statements:** | | | | |
| The overall big-thinking goal for ME+ is . . . . . | | | | |
| ME+'s job title will be . . . . . | | | | |
| ME+ will be working in the . . . . . industry | | | | |
| The company ME+ will be working for is . . . . .<br>(If you are intending on starting your own company, note that here) | | | | |
| ME+ will be running (/working in) a company that has the following characteristics . . . . . | | | | |
| **Provide a list in response to one of the following statements:** | | | | |
| ME+ will be in a similar role, but my responsibilities will have expanded to include: | | | | |
| 1. | 2. | 3. | 4. | 5. |
| ME+ will be in an entirely new career, and ME+'s responsibilities will include: | | | | |
| 1. | 2. | 3. | 4. | 5. |

| **ME+ will be engaged in the following activities:**<br>**(These are essentially the processes that allow you to achieve your goal)** | | | | |
|---|---|---|---|---|
| Overseeing and allocating money to people or projects | Engaging in research | Monitoring processes | Supporting others in their work (as an administrator) | Disrupting how people think about things |
| Providing consultation and advice to others | Coaching and developing others | Managing other people | Staffing organizational units | Ensuring an organization or unit maintains a level of social responsibility |
| Project planning | Creating and designing new products or services | Developing policies | Engaging in physical activities | Handling and moving objects |
| Judging products or quality of service | Solving problems | Judging the ideas of other people | Updating and drawing on relevant knowledge | Assessing risk and return |
| Writing | Making strategic decisions | Thinking creatively | Running your own business's day-to-day activities | Developing high-level objectives and strategies |
| Analysing or evaluating data or information | Creating and selling art | Scheduling work and activities | Planning and prioritizing own work or work of others | Ensuring compliance with the law or other standards |
| Working with computers | Documenting/ recording information | Interpreting the meaning of information for others | Communicating with colleagues | Communicating with persons outside the organization |

| | | | | |
|---|---|---|---|---|
| Establishing interpersonal relationships | Assisting and caring for others | Selling | Influencing people | Resolving conflicts and negotiating |
| Performing for the public | Coordinating the work and activities of others | Working directly with the public | Developing and building teams | Training and teaching others |
| | | | | |

There is also a blank row at the end of the table. This is a space in which to write more specific activities. It will be most useful to those of you who have a clear vision of what ME+ will be doing. It allows you to move from the very broad activities listed in the table and narrow things down.

For example, building on 'Making strategic decisions' and 'Solving problems', you could have something like 'Deciding what capital structure will be for a pharmaceutical company, and offering solutions as to what debt-to-equity ratio should be maintained in the face of economic turbulence'. Instead of 'Coordinating the work and activities of others', you might have 'Coordinating the work and activities of others to ensure that orders are fulfilled and my customers are satisfied with my dog shampoo company'. Instead of 'Performing for the public', it might be more relevant to write 'Practising lines for my part in the latest Broadway musical'. And instead of 'Assisting and caring for others', you might write 'Bringing the children in my care to the park for a nature walk'.

You get the idea . . .

### *INSIGHT 2: WHAT SKILL SET DOES ME+ POSSESS?*

It is one thing to decide to be an author who will write a book to bring behavioural science insights to wider audiences. It is quite another to make this happen in a way that is actually a success story. Convincing both an agent and a publisher to support you – two necessary ingredients for success – in a world where scores of other people are trying to do the same, is a tricky business. During December 2017, I felt as if I had been slapped in the face with a wet fish when I realized that I lacked several of the core skills that would allow me to fulfil my dream of being a published author. While I may have been well-versed in the details of behavioural science research and an academic writing style by that point, I knew little about how to translate important messages in a manner that would entice people like you to read them on their commute, during their sacred vacation time, or before they turn off the lights at night. Writing in such a style was a skill I did not yet have. It was necessary for me to acknowledge this skill gap and address it.

What exactly is stopping you doing the activities you have identified? What are the new skills you need in order to be taken seriously as an expert?

It is time for you to identify the skills that ME+ will draw on, in order to make salient any gaps you need to address. The table below lists some common skills to help you do just that. You will notice a close resemblance between the activities in the last table and the skills listed here. That is because by doing the activity (for example, engaging in a negotiation process) you are taking a small step that hones a skill (allowing you to eventually become an expert in negotiations).

Can you pick out the skills in the table below that ME+ will need? Circle those that you will need the most. You

## THE SKILLS ME+ WILL HAVE

| **ME+ will be skilled at:** | | | | |
|---|---|---|---|---|
| Active learning | Active listening | Complex problem-solving | Critical thinking | Maintaining equipment |
| Instructing others | Judgement and decision-making | Learning strategies | Management of financial resources | Management of material resources |
| Managing personnel | Mathematics | Monitoring people | Monitoring processes | Negotiation |
| Persuasion | Programming | Statistical modelling | Quality control analysis | Reading comprehension |
| Systems analysis | Technology design | Systems evaluation | Sales | Time management |
| Trouble shooting | Writing | Active listening | Designing policies | Public speaking |
| Motivating teams | Problem-solving | Collating information | Comforting people | Being heard |
| Adaptability | Creativity | Communication | Lateral thinking | Mentoring |
| **I plan to be an expert in:** | | | | |
| | | | | |

should aim to circle at least three skills, and no more than five. Your journey to ME+ is a period of time where you will engage in small steps that develop these skills. The activities you identified in the last section will be some of these small steps, and the skills are the outcome.

I have left space at the end of the table for people who

already know the skills they need. The more detail you go into about these skills, the more focused your path to ME+ will be. Use this blank row to be as precise as you can possibly be.

If it is difficult for you to pinpoint the skills you need, another approach is to decide on the type of work you want ME+ to do and identify role models. Find three people already doing the kind of job you want who seem highly credible, and find out what skills they draw on daily. If you have direct access to the person, you can simply ask them what the most valuable skills they possess are. If you do not know the person, you can identify their skills by reading books that describe their journey to success, looking at their CV or LinkedIn profile, or googling them to find videos and articles about how they got to where they are.

### *INSIGHT 3: GETTING THE SKILLS ME+ NEEDS*

Rome wasn't built in a day, and I decided that 2018 would be the year for me to read a hundred or so books aimed at audiences like you. I would do this with intention, noting what I liked and didn't like about each, and paying attention to online reviews and critiques. My office at the LSE today is a graveyard for the books I studied, just in case I choose to resurrect them one day and reread the content or my musings in the margins.

I attended writing classes, creativity classes, and public events where newly published authors in popular non-fiction described their work and their personal journey. The worst part? I socialized at these events! I call this the worst part because I'm not a natural networker who usually enjoys chit-chatting with strangers. I'm actually quite an introvert.

Reading, studying and networking were the three activities

I did often in 2018 to cultivate the skill set that I knew would allow me to write this book. What activities will you do regularly to cultivate the skill set of your ME+?

In behavioural science, there is a lot of research to suggest saliency is essential if you want to provoke an action. Saliency means that something is made noticeable or prominent.

Now that you have identified the skills you need to develop, make an effort to keep them salient amid the hustle and bustle of daily life. How can you do that? I suggest writing them on Post-it notes and sticking them somewhere you look at every day. You need to start gearing your life towards these skills, and thinking about them as often as possible.

The next step to making your ME+ a reality involves incorporating the activities you identified in the first table in this chapter into your weekly routine. By doing these activites regularly, they organically become part of your narrative, and you hone the skills you have chosen.

Nobel Prize-winning economist Daniel Kahneman distinguishes between our brain's *System 1* and *System 2* thinking.[5] System 1 is the brain's automatic and quick responses: it is your fast brain. Your fast brain causes you to curse loudly when you stub your toe. It is why you find yourself driving to work rather than to the park on a Saturday morning. It's your brain on autopilot. Thanks to our fast brain, we plough through familiar tasks at work even when we are very tired. We also do not think twice about our habits or routines. Our narratives do not get time to chatter. It's all a bit robotic.

System 2 is slower, more deliberate. It allows you to solve a tricky maths problem. Our slow brain helps us figure out the terms and conditions of our mortgage. It is for heavy-lifting thinking and only used sparingly, when deep thought is required. Using our slow brain is tiring. This means that a lot of our actions are the result of decisions made by our fast brain.

You can change your career trajectory by making your engagement in activities (small steps) a regular event in your diary. By integrating specific repetitive actions into your schedule, you are reprogramming the fast brain or System 1. You are getting your fast brain to view yourself as a different type of person, with a new set of habits. Eventually, engaging in them will become part of your being.

Take Jerome. At twenty-four he decided he wanted to move from working as an analyst in banking into a job where he would get to write computer code for online games. What is really fantastic is that Jerome had a clear idea of what he wanted to do. The problem? He had never studied computer science, had never written a line of code in his life, and had no money in the bank to undertake a university degree.

Undeterred, Jerome researched online programming courses. Over the next two years he set about teaching himself to code in JavaScript and Python, using free online resources. He did this religiously from 8 p.m. to 10 p.m. every weekday, after he'd finished his dinner and gone on a two-mile jog. This was his process. This dedication to learning his new skill was difficult at first, but it soon became part of his new normal. Jerome is still on his journey – he hasn't quite secured his dream job yet, but he is freelancing and writing code for a variety of clients. By doing this, he is getting professional experience and also exposure to people who can recommend jobs and write references for him in the future. Crucially, Jerome is much happier than he was when he was working as a banking analyst.

So how can you cultivate the new skills you need for ME+? Simple. Begin by making a commitment to engage in one or more regular activities. These may be the activities you identified earlier this chapter (see pp. 42–3), or you may consider other activities which we will discuss shortly. The key to choosing activities is that they should be something that you have the resources (money and time) to do, and something that you can easily carry out at a regular time each day or week. Engaging in the activities should become part of your routine. You also want the activity to challenge you enough so you are outside your comfort zone, but not so much that you are overwhelmed. It should require you to be on your metaphorical tippy-toes but nothing further – so you are stretching but not stretched.[6]

Overall, there are three types of activities that I want you to consider engaging in:

1 *On the job.* Find opportunities for networking and training within your current job.
2 *Put yourself out there.* Get out and expand your current network to include people outside your immediate circle.
3 *Continuous learning.* Make time each week to advance your current skill set by engaging in continuous learning.

### INSIGHT 4: HONE ME+'S SKILLS ON THE JOB

Universities focus on the success of traditional peer-reviewed academic writing, look for quality over quantity, and aim to deliver excellent teaching to their students. Universities have many internal training opportunities, but none that would help me hone the skills I needed to write this book in 2018. At least, not at first glance.

One of the best things about working at the LSE is the regular series of free public events they run (worth checking out if you are ever in London – and you can listen to their podcasts if you are not), and sometimes I can get access to the people who are speaking at those events if I am tenacious. More and more, academics who have become known in a particular field are writing books that convey the messages of their learnings all in one place. By the time they were standing on the stage at an LSE event I was attending, some of them had successfully gone through the journey I was just embarking on. Surely this subset would have pearls of wisdom to share?

Whatever you do for work on a daily basis, take a moment to reflect on whether there are real opportunities on offer there that can move you forward. Like me, you may need to look more than once before you see what is on your own doorstep. For example, if you currently work for a big organization, there are likely to be internal training offerings. If the training offerings in your firm sound about as pleasant as a root canal and as useful as a chocolate fireguard, don't be put off. Ask human resources – or your manager directly – to organize a course that is in line with the skills you would like to develop.

If you want to pursue something far away from the job you have now, this is still a conversation worth having. More and more companies allow their employees to do developmental courses that don't have a direct link to their current role. You can also request funding from your firm to do courses externally (see Insight 6 below). In smaller or medium-sized firms, there is often cash set aside to allow employees to upgrade their skills – this is worth asking about, even if it is not advertised widely. And if you are the director of a company, freelancing or trying to scale your start-up, training courses are a legitimate business expense, making them more affordable.

Your current day-to-day work likely gives you plenty of opportunities to expose yourself to people who already do what you're interested in. These could be co-workers, clients, or people you collaborate with unofficially. There are two reasons why it is worth building relationships with these people. First, they can offer you valuable advice regarding your plans. Second, they may be able to give you – or point you towards – opportunities that are relevant for your ME+.

If you're not good at networking in groups (my hand is firmly raised here), commit to getting to know more people on a one-on-one basis. These meetings can be over coffee, lunch or a drink. Try to connect with people who have the skills you are trying to acquire, regardless of their level of experience. Do not solely look to those who are ahead of you; identify colleagues at any stage of their career who you see as being like ME+ in some regard. Aim to understand what they do, why they do it and how.

Start by identifying and reaching out to colleagues (or clients) who can give you experience or advice that will allow you to develop the skills ME+ needs. In general, none of us likes asking for help, out of a fear that we will be rejected (and possibly laughed at – later in the book I will introduce you to the saving face effect). The pain of potential rejection is caused by the uncertainty of whether the person will say yes, and our overestimation of the odds that they will say no.[7] It is the anticipatory pain of the response, rather than the actual pain experienced if we are told no, that prevents us from asking. But fear not! The probability of getting an encouraging response is high. We tend to underestimate how likely we are to get a positive response. This comes through clearly in a recent study of 14,000 people that illustrates that the tendency to say yes to requests is much higher than is expected by those doing the asking.[8] In general, we don't ask for help as often as we should.

We also overestimate the probability that other people will ask for our help when it is needed. One 2010 study, by Vanessa Bohns and Francis Flynn, asked peer advisors and teaching assistants at a university to predict the number of students who would ask them for help during the next semester. Overall, the advisors estimated that about 30 per cent more students would come forward than actually did!

As a fun self-experiment, when you are asking for help, write down whether you think a positive response is likely. Once you have ten or so requests in the bank, compare the actual outcomes to the predictions that you made. This allows for a fast check of the degree to which you personally underestimate your ability to get others to lend you a hand.

So now you've decided to ask for help in making ME+ a reality, how can you increase the likelihood of success in your request? In general, if you want a positive response, do it face-to-face.[9]

Behavioural science tip: put people on the spot when you need help, as the cost to them of saying no is high. Why? Like all of us, the person whose help you need will not like awkward conversations. They probably also worry that saying no may insinuate something about their feelings towards you.[10] And face-to-face requests are preferable to emailing. Yes, the time-cost of asking face-to-face is higher, but there is the reward of a much greater chance of success.[11]

More good news: behavioural science research shows that

once a person agrees to help, they are more likely be agreeable next time around. In fact, in behavioural science the ***Ben Franklin effect*** describes how people are more likely to do a favour for someone they have previously helped out than they are for someone who has helped them out. Why? We like to be consistent. If we think a person is deserving of our help the first time around (i.e. we said yes to their request), then it is logical that they will be deserving next time around (subject to them not behaving like a jerk in between).

Even better: if we ask someone for help and they say no, the second time around they are more likely to say yes (especially if you ask them face-to-face)! The cost of saying no and being viewed as socially uncooperative is even higher the second time at the rodeo!

How you frame your request when asking someone for help is important.

It should be clear to the recipient that it is mutually beneficial, or at least have a net benefit for them. Actually, I'll rephrase that: there should be an obvious benefit. Your newfound ambitions should not be taxing on your colleagues in terms of their personal time and effort. This sounds like a no-brainer, but you would be surprised at the number of people who think it's a good idea to email folk for support in a new endeavour with no thought as to how much the request eats into that person's time. Requests like these are easy to ignore – particularly if asked via email.

It has been shown time and time again that the ***framing*** of requests matters,[12] so ensure you emphasize the benefits of your request to the other person. In addition, always make it super easy for them to say yes. If you have to approach them via email first in order to meet them in person, provide a number of dates for the person so they can choose quickly what works for them. Otherwise, you will waste their time playing email ping-pong. Or worse, the time-costs of the ping-pong may be seen as too high, so they may not even bother responding. Finally, always keep emails short. Nobody needs an essay.

Overall, you should aim to reach out to one person a month on the job. This is a commitment that most of us can stick to very easily. It is also something you can commit to right now! In the space below, identify the people that you will reach out to over the next three months.

In the next three months, I will reach out to:

1) ______________________________

2) ______________________________

3) ______________________________

### *INSIGHT 5: HONE ME+'S SKILLS BY PUTTING YOURSELF OUT THERE*

It happened that my commitment to attending public events at the LSE in 2018 meant I was able to meet others who had written books for non-academic audiences pretty regularly. This allowed me to get some solid advice about the entire process that lay ahead of me in terms of writing this book. But for me, the most risky time – when I would truly be putting myself out there – would be when I sent my proposal to an agent, who could recommend my writing to a publisher or reject me in the blink of an eye.

So who should you meet? Like me, some of you will need to meet gatekeepers and other people who can make your journey towards ME+ possible. In addition, the responsibility for becoming known as a person with particular skills or abilities lies with you. No one else can do (or will do) this job for you. No one else *should.* Even if you are planning on staying within your current organization, there is a lot of added value in putting yourself out there and meeting new people. And if you are someone who is going to build a new business, work in the gig economy, switch industries or move to a new company, you absolutely need to be out there becoming known for the value that you add.

> You will progress much faster if you meet people outside your normal circles.

I am talking face-to-face discussions here, which can occur in person or virtually. One of the big lessons of the COVID-19 lockdown in 2020 has to be how the technology we have at our disposal allows us to build bridges in the absence of palm-pressing contact.

Decades of research in economics shows that larger social networks create more and better career opportunities.[13] If you are an entrepreneur, having a larger social network allows you to build your customer base more quickly. You'll have better access to talent that can enhance your business, too. Whether it's getting help with a one-off marketing initiative, hiring someone who can create an app, or providing evidence that your product actually works, you can use your network to find someone reliable to get the job done. Meanwhile, if you are working in the gig economy and looking for clients, having a wider network can help bring the clients to you, allowing you to focus on your core business: finishing projects and getting paid.

You should commit to paying deliberate attention to expanding your external network at least once a month. But how do you go about meeting these people in the first place?

First, loop back to the activities that you have identified your ME+ doing. Your external networking should give you opportunities to engage in these activities, or expose you to individuals who do them and are at the top of their game. Because you want to expand your network, any group event that you attend needs to have time to socialize before or after. This is a much easier task if you live in a big city, like London or New York, where there are endless low-cost or free events. In less densely populated areas, you may have to look a bit harder or be open to a commute. The important thing is that you broker at least one mutually beneficial relationship a month. This amounts to having a list of twelve new external contacts by the end of year one.

Remember that when you are putting yourself out there and attending talks and events, you will need to actually talk to people. If you are usually not able to bring yourself to approach people and introduce yourself, try arriving first so that you will have to speak to those who arrive second and third.

A seminal lesson from behavioural science is that **ego matters**. Ego is our conscious sense of our own self-importance. It causes us to behave in ways that make us feel good about ourselves. Ideally, you will speak with your new acquaintances in a way that makes them feel interested and good about themselves. It is worth creating an elevator pitch that can be drawn upon to help with these new interactions. Do ensure that the elevator pitch is interesting, and more specifically that the importance of your personal added value shines through. I have no idea how many times I have been asked for advice, followed by a question as to whether I think what the person is working on is important. This baffles me. If the person who is selling the idea needs to ask that question, the answer must be 'no', right?

I do sympathize with those who do not actively want to network. Having to talk to people when I am unsure of common ground can be draining. I also find superficial conversations pretty boring. Thankfully, there is a viable alternative. Identify people who are in a similar role to what you want to do, and email or message them and ask to meet. For me, this is much easier. The probability of rejection is larger (it is easier to ignore you virtually than face-to-face), but you are less likely to internalize this because email is less personal. As a rule of thumb, email is preferred for contacts that you do not know yet, or where there are multiple people who can answer your request for help.

When sending emails to new contacts, remember that the probability of getting a positive response increases with the number of people you email. So aim to email five people once a month, and resign yourself to the idea that one acceptance is an overall win.

Once you have your meeting in the bag, decide on what you want to cover. Ideally, this person will stay in your network, so understand that any pull on their time should also be beneficial to them. Go prepared, knowing the questions that you want to ask and any opportunities that you want to explore.

Pull your head out from this book and send five emails right now. There's no time like the present!

### *INSIGHT 6: HONE ME+'S SKILLS VIA CONTINUOUS LEARNING*

When preparing to write this book in 2018 I took to continuous learning with rigour. This was easy to schedule, as I relied on nobody but myself. In fact, I planned a continuous learning session for every working day. You know what? On at least one occasion per week, I failed to show up. Why? I am easily distracted, plagued by whatever and whoever is waving actively for my attention on any particular day. I stop-start more often than I would care to admit. But I never stop getting back on the horse when I fall off. On days when I noticed I had not done any continuous learning, I would set intentions and pull out material to work on so it was easily accessible the next day. While it would have been better if I had always honoured my commitment to show up, the simple act of recommitting for tomorrow was enough to get me to the finish line in the end.

What continuous learning activities will you commit to today? Some of the skills that you will have identified as necessary for ME+ will require you to complete additional training, whether it is formal or informal. As this is a medium-term expedition, I recommend avoiding signing on for expensive tertiary education programmes. You don't need a master's degree to get started. That can come later, once you are certain it is the right path for you.

In the beginning, you should spend some time becoming familiar with opportunities that are either free or low-cost. If your continuous learning costs a fortune, your own budget will ensure it can never be continuous.

Alternatively you can try short courses or summer schools. Most major institutions offer a wide variety of courses, ranging from regular evening offerings to a couple of intensive weeks. There are also heaps of excellent online options, allowing you to engage in continuous learning from the comfort of your own home. Luckily, advances in technology – making it cheap to record virtual offerings – mean this can often be done for free!

It is important to think about your learning as continuous, rather than simply looking to pass an exam that suggests you have acquired a certain skill. Continuous learning allows you to up your game and keep your skills current and in demand.

Of course, for certain people, getting a formal qualification will be necessary (say, if you have decided to become a heart surgeon or a lawyer), but for most of us, the routes to ME+ are diverse and the paths are numerous.

Making continuous learning a regular part of your week – by leaning on free or cheap resources – is a very scalable habit. For me, my morning routine involves reading sections of current newspapers and magazines that I enjoy (and some that I do not, so as to challenge my views and that dreaded confirmation bias). I do this over a leisurely breakfast, to set the right tone for the day. I do this even when I have a back-to-back day, too – I just get up an hour earlier. I have even been known to read on winter mornings, with a head torch and a muffin, during my ride on the way to the airport. Alongside my morning reading routine, I listen to podcasts of online courses on my commute or read non-fiction books.

Overall, your continuous learning should focus on advancing the expertise that you have identified ME+ as having. The time you set aside allows for a process (reading, viewing, listening or writing) which supports the goal you want to achieve (acquiring new skills). Engaging in this process will pay dividends if you practise it over the medium term. I recommend devoting 80 per cent of your continuous learning time to honing a key skill – with a view to becoming an expert – which allows some leftover time to investigate other interests. Exploring other areas of learning outside those that link directly to your future self will allow you to be unexpectedly inspired. It also gives you scope to discover further interests that you did not know you had.

But perhaps your responses to the ME+ activities and skills tables were a bit lacklustre. You know for sure that you want a different future self, but still do not know what you will be doing. How can you possibly engage in continuous learning that propels you forward? How can you know what to do? In this case, you need to cast a wider net, as you take some time to identify your interests and ultimately your passion. Keeping your options open allows you to discover new opportunities.

It is worth reflecting weekly on what you enjoyed about your continuous learning because engaging in this process will help you discover what your big-thinking goal is. Your objective should be to narrow your interests over time, so you are writing the CV of an expert in your future role, with your regular continuous learning becoming an established 'no pain' habit.

Make a commitment now that makes continuous learning an integral part of your week. Commit to engaging on specific days and specific times, setting reminders that nudge you to honour your new commitment.

Now, in the space below, write down one activity you're going to do *this week* to invest in your learning:

---

### *INSIGHT 7: LEARN BETTER BY ACHIEVING FLOW*

Like most days, Monday 1 April 2019 started with me being distracted. It feels like when I pick one thing to do, something else starts vying for my attention. At the LSE I am too often distracted by coffees, lunches and solo trips to the campus bookstore. So on that day I was working at home so I could get meaningful work done, as it was the very first day I would be working on this book as a commissioned author – I had just accepted an offer from Penguin to be my publisher. This made me beyond happy, but the downside was the happiness also brought a pressure which was now worming its way into my brain.

I had committed to what seemed like an absurd delivery date. Having spent sixteen months researching the book and writing a proposal, I would now need to complete a first draft of the project in a third of that time. It felt impossible, but on that first day of writing I did come prepared: I was surrounded by notebooks filled with ideas for the content of each chapter; my desk had been cleared to ensure minimal distractions; I had tea, water and various snacks to prevent me breaking my concentration to satisfy a basic urge.

But there was no concentration. The clock moved from 8 a.m. to 9 a.m., 9 a.m. to 10 a.m. . . . lunchtime came and went, and then at about 2.45 p.m. I finally achieved ***flow***.

Flow happens when you become immersed in what you are doing and are ultra-productive. Time seems to fly. As described by psychologist Mihaly Csikszentmihalyi, flow is a mental state that is experienced when you are engaged in continuous learning activities that are challenging enough to fully engross you. The good news is that if you achieve flow you will enjoy a feeling of great joy and satisfaction. The other states recognized by Csikszentmihalyi are anxiety, apathy, arousal, boredom, control, relaxation and worry. None of these states promotes optimal learning, but in my experience you have to go through at least one in a session to get to the flow state. With practice, a period of ninety minutes should allow for both the transition into flow and some productive work to be done. Of course, sometimes you may be more distracted than usual. On those days, it may not happen for you. Don't beat yourself up about it, just show up for yourself on another occasion as soon as you can.

In *Outliers*, Malcolm Gladwell emphasizes the ***10,000-Hour Rule***. To achieve a high level of expertise, a person must practise for around 10,000 hours. Of course, this is an average – some of us will require fewer hours and others more. The more important point is that the practice must be done the *right* way. And the right way is with flow.

This aligns with the messages from Anders Ericsson, a Swedish psychologist, who insists that practice is deliberate. You need to be in a zone where there are no distractions, so you can achieve flow. Ericsson also maintains that if you manage to get into the zone, you can expect to be tired afterwards. Why? Because you have been focusing so intensely it saps your energy. Therefore, ninety minutes is about all you can achieve in a session, regardless of how much free time you have.

We are all different in regards to when in the day it is easier to find flow. I am best first thing in the morning (7–10 a.m.) and later in the evening (after 10 p.m.). But I can only do one or the other in a given day. If you are flexible, it is worth experimenting with different times of the day for your ninety-minute session. This allows you to discover when the optimal time is for your own flow.

It is also worth setting aside a block of time for what I will call 'distracted learning'. This is continuous learning but with a lower level of focus, so you can multitask. Think listening to a podcast while on the treadmill or cooking, or reading while listening to music on your commute. Learning in this way has great benefits. It is how I managed to read 100+ books in 2018. You zone in on and remember items that interest you, and these can be saved for later if you wish to go deeper. It also helps build the narrative that you are a continuous learner. By engaging in distracted learning regularly, you are helping ingrain a new routine in your daily life.

If repeated enough times as a small step, it becomes a habit. A new status quo emerges.

### *INSIGHT 8: AUDIT PROGRESS TO ENSURE SUCCESS*

To have a first draft of this book written by the end of September, I wrote regularly and often. Over the summer I increased the intensity, and had a planned writing schedule for each day to ensure I would not be tardy. Guess what? I rarely made my own deadlines each day, but my progress was salient – in other words, clear and noticeable – and I could rejig my schedule so I kept to the same overall timeline. Getting in the habit of achieving flow as I immersed myself in the project meant I was always able to catch up. I managed to finish on time.

> It is essential to make your progress salient by auditing the activities you are doing and the milestones you are reaching.

To be effective in your journey and stay the course, you need to monitor your ongoing efforts. Set aside an hour a week to log what you have done over the last seven days. This is also a good time to set intentions for the week ahead. You should do this type of monitoring for your continuous learning, as well as your various networking efforts.

Monitoring ensures that you are fully engaged in the processes that will lead to ME+ being realized. It also serves as a reminder of the benefits you are accruing as you go. When I have had a particularly good week engaging in my processes, I feel a sort of smug satisfaction at my accomplishments. This feeling is likely driven by the fact that I have shown up for myself.

The following is a template for monitoring your activities, with some examples of how you might fill it in below:

*Last week I . . .*

*The activity I did last week helped me move towards my goal by . . .*

*When engaging in this activity, I felt . . .*

*Next week I will . . .*

*The activity I will do next week will help me . . .*

This template can be used to monitor continuous learning:

*Last week I . . .*
Completed session four of my online masterclass on Saturday.

*The activity I did last week helped me move towards my goal by . . .*
Helping me to understand balance sheets and income statements, a skill I need to be a responsible business owner.

*When engaging in this activity, I felt . . .*
Challenged, at times distracted, other times relieved when simple concepts became clearer to me.

*Next week I will . . .*
Complete session five of my online masterclass on Saturday.

*The activity I will do next week will help me . . .*
Understand cash flows and tax shields, a skill I need to be a responsible business owner.

This template can also be used to monitor networking attempts on the job and out and about:

*Last week I . . .*
Compiled a list of twenty people who are doing the job I will do soon(ish).

*The activity I did last week helped me move towards my goal by . . .*
Giving me a list of potential mentors who can advise me about the various pathways to my new role.

*When engaging in this activity, I felt . . .*
It was tedious, but after completing the task I felt organized and hopeful.

*Next week I will . . .*
Carve out two hours on Tuesday evening to send emails to my list of potential mentors.

*The activity I will do next week will help me . . .*
Secure one-on-one meetings with potential mentors. This will increase my network, and allow me to pick their brains about my new endeavour.

In the examples above, I am suggesting you reflect on the previous week's activities and explicitly recognize how these activities relate to your big-thinking goal. This serves to emphasize the benefits of each activity, and allows you to better visualize ME+. I want you to view ME+ as a real person who is worth your time, empathy and effort. By linking activities to your ME+, the point of the activities is made clear to you, helping you persevere even when life throws you a curveball.

The template also asks you to document how you *felt* when you engaged in each activity. Whether you are someone who is 100 per cent sure about who their future self is, or someone who needs to figure this out along the way, I strongly recommend you keep track of these feelings. This will allow you to more easily identify what you enjoy doing. It may sound like a redundant exercise, but as we've already seen, personal narratives are incredibly strong. They may convince you that you like an activity, even if it does not serve you well. Similarly, you may persuade yourself that you enjoy doing something beneficial that at first you hated.

It is worth noting here that 'liking' an activity is not binary. For example, in my day job as an academic, I love engaging with industry once a week. I always enjoy meeting non-academic colleagues, who often have a much faster approach to work than my fellow academics, and on this one day I can give my all to the occasion. Afterwards, I am on a high and am excited to move projects forward. However, if I do this more than once a week, I feel drained. The same goes for social events, and for speaking to academic audiences. For one day of the week I am able to be an extrovert, and absorb energy from the new people I meet and share ideas with. But on the remaining days I am an introvert, and do better on my own or engaging in meetings remotely. I need to recharge.

But I only realized all this by auditing how various activities were making me feel. Now I tailor the activities I choose to engage in to account for these preferences.

The monitoring template also gives you an opportunity to set intentions for the week ahead. By doing this, you are leveraging ***salience bias*** to your advantage.

Salience bias refers to the tendency of us mortals to give our attention to activities that are prominent and at the forefront of our minds.

By setting intentions – and linking those intentions to their added value in terms of your big-thinking goal – the activities that need to be done stay at the forefront of your mind. You are therefore more likely to complete them. The weekly ritual of setting intentions makes drawing attention to the activities of the week ahead a habit, and eventually this is done unconsciously as part of your routine.

Notice that the examples given above specify what the activity is (for example, 'session four in an online class', or 'sending five emails') and exactly when it will be carried out (the day of the week). This serves to put clear boundaries around an activity so that you know when to do it and when it is done. It is important not to pull the wool over your own eyes, which is easy to do if you set vague intentions to engage in 'reading' or 'online learning'. When there are no set end points or specific levels of commitment, it is too easy to persuade yourself that you've done something without actually having done it.

But please do not worry about non-compliance over the short term. If you miss a few weeks, just reflect on what sent you off track. Ask yourself if your old narratives are the culprit. Then continue with the process. The most important thing is that you persevere.

### *INSIGHT 9: MINIMUM NINETY-MINUTE WEEKLY COMMITMENT*

So what is the minimum commitment you should put in to get started on these activities? I suggest at least one session of ninety minutes per week.

The anecdotes describing my book-writing process may offer some reassurance for those of you who need convincing that a large project can be completed in a medium-term window once there is focus. However, for those of you who feel you have no work–life balance already, you may be feeling grumpy about my suggestion that you need to engage in activities regularly. You probably realize, quite rightly, that you cannot commit to the same level of intensity as I did in the summer of 2019.

You have no time. I get it. Chapter 3 is written entirely with your concerns at the forefront of my mind.

If you already feel overwhelmed, just stick with the commitment that you will set aside ninety minutes a week for ME+ related activities. If this is not possible during the working week, do it at the weekend. This is an investment in your own future – it is okay that it encroaches on some leisure time.

A ninety-minute commitment is small enough that it should not overwhelm you. But if you devote it to continuous learning it is also long enough for you to find flow and begin a virtuous cycle that moves you forward. And it is also sufficient time to attend a networking event, or spend some time with a colleague or a new acquaintance.

Committing to one time-block of ninety minutes ensures that you do something substantive each week, and allows you to see clear progress.

### *INSIGHT 10: MANAGE FLESH-AND-BLOOD OBSTACLES*

They say when you write a book there is a risk that the only people who will read it are your friends and family. Just in case this ends up being my future (success is a product of talent, effort and luck after all), it is probably best if I don't bash my core audience right now.

But one of the obstacles you may face is the reaction of friends, families and co-workers to the changes that you want to make. Perhaps some key people in your life engage in activities that are not aligned with your big-thinking goal. Maybe you have enjoyed engaging in activities with your loved ones that do not serve ME+. This might include drinking in the evenings, to the extent that it affects your next day's performance, or watching so much TV that it crowds out continuous learning, or eating so much sugary food you experience brain fog. All of these activities are fine once a month, or even once a week, but if done to excess they prevent investments in ME+.

Of course, they also give you instant gratification and are fun. For your companions, it may seem like you have ruined a very nice set-up when you announce that you are no longer partaking. In a sense, you have. But you are striving for a longer-term purpose, and some immediate benefits need to be sacrificed.

Managing the negative reactions of others is key. My advice is to give them certainty. If you plan on quitting the activity altogether, you need to let them know. If you plan to still engage, but on a less regular basis, give them definite dates. Keep your promises and show up on time with a smile on your face. If there are any reactionary guilt trips, do not internalize them.

Anti-role models are people who bring you down. When you leave an interaction with them, you feel lower than when it began. They may take every opportunity to point out that the odds are stacked against you. They may say things like, 'People like you (us) do not get ahead' or 'Opportunities are for people who are richer/smarter/look different' or 'You're certainly getting notions about yourself'. Of course, these messages are always most effective when they are delivered by those who are closest to you.

The result of these sorts of conversation is that your harmful personal narratives get fed. It is best to avoid conversing about your small steps and big thinking with negative people when at all possible. Stick to your path, and give as little detail as possible about what you have been up to. When it all works out you can let them know over a celebratory glass of champagne. (Cheers!)

To balance out the anti-role models who may be in your life it is important to search for role models specific to your journey.

Everyone needs support, including ME+.

Role models motivate. They give their time to help you find the best way forward when faced with an obstacle. There are no guilt trips. When you are with a positive role model, you can reveal your future self fully. You can be vulnerable.

Ideally, you will have at least one positive role model who understands what you are trying to achieve. If such a person is not already in your life, you should take the process of finding them seriously. This may be achieved through your commitments to 'on the job' or 'putting yourself out there'. I have seen great success when people approach the search for a positive role model as they would for a romantic partner. Reflecting on the attributes that you would like in this person can bear fruit. For example, will you need someone who listens and consoles you? Or should your role model push you to toughen up? Of course, the beauty of role models is that there is no need for monogamy. If you are lucky, you will have multiple people who offer a variety of perspectives for all seasons.

## READY, STEADY, GO

Your journey is going to take years. This is a long time. In this window it really is possible to transform your work set-up from lacklustre to spectacular – you just need commitment and perseverance. Some of you will only be aiming for moderate change, and that is okay, too. Having a purposeful plan will help you get there. If you stick to the recommendations in this chapter, the commitments you will make are not so significant that they will disrupt your life in the short term, but they will pay great dividends in the long run.

Let's take a moment and recap the behavioural science insights that will help you create your big-thinking goal and identify the small steps required to achieve it . . .

***INSIGHT 1: WHAT IS ME+ DOING DAILY?***

Start by identifying the things you enjoy doing currently, or things that you think you would enjoy doing, and allow these to shape your ideas as you think big.

***INSIGHT 2: WHAT SKILL SET DOES ME+ POSSESS?***

Define the skills that you need to acquire for ME+. Chances are you will need to advance your current skill set or hone new skills.

***INSIGHT 3: GETTING THE SKILLS ME+ NEEDS***

Make activities that relate to ME+'s overall goal a habit, so that you engage in them automatically.

***INSIGHT 4: HONE ME+'S SKILLS ON THE JOB***

Identify and commit to activities you can do on the job which will help move you forward. Make a commitment to engage in one or more of these activities in the coming month.

***INSIGHT 5: HONE ME+'S SKILLS BY PUTTING YOURSELF OUT THERE***

Progress faster by meeting people outside your normal circles. Make a commitment to engage in one or more activities that expand your network in the coming month.

***INSIGHT 6: HONE ME+'S SKILLS VIA CONTINUOUS LEARNING***

Identify continuous learning opportunities. Ensure that you set aside time weekly to embed continuous learning as part of your usual routine.

***INSIGHT 7: LEARN BETTER BY ACHIEVING FLOW***

When engaging in continuous learning, pay attention to the context and circumstances that allow you to achieve flow. Replicate these in future continuous learning sessions.

***INSIGHT 8: AUDIT PROGRESS TO ENSURE SUCCESS***

Set aside an hour each week to monitor your progress. Use this time to set intentions for the next week.

***INSIGHT 9: MINIMUM NINETY-MINUTE WEEKLY COMMITMENT***

Commit to, at minimum, a ninety-minute block of targeted activities.

***INSIGHT 10: MANAGE FLESH-AND-BLOOD OBSTACLES***

Guard your plans from family or friends who may not appreciate your efforts to change. Find positive role models.

The weekly commitments you have made while reading this chapter translate directly to the processes you need to engage in to reach your big-thinking goal. By auditing how you feel in each activity weekly, you will have information on how much happiness you got out of taking a particular small step. Because the commitments are small, your life is not disrupted. Your narratives should not be telling you to stop.

Happy goal-setting!

Before we move on, make sure that you:

- Identify the narratives that are holding back your ability to think big, and set in place processes to change them.
- Work through the behavioural science insights one by one.

## FIVE FAB BEHAVIOURAL SCIENCE CONCEPTS MENTIONED IN THIS CHAPTER

1. **Confirmation bias:** Refers to favouring information that confirms pre-existing beliefs.
2. **Future self:** A visualization of who you will be in the future. People often think about their future self in a way that evokes empathy and promotes investment in long-term gains.
3. **System 1 and System 2:** When we make System 1 decisions they are fast, instinctive and on autopilot; in contrast, System 2 is more deliberative.
4. **Ben Franklin effect:** When someone does a favour for another person, they are more likely to do another favour for them next time around, and this effect is stronger than if they had received a favour from that person.
5. **Framing:** How information or choices are presented with respect to their positive and negative aspects causes changes in their relative attractiveness.

# CHAPTER 3

# TIME

'It's pretty shocking, Gillian. They ended up with HIV from *the hospital* – the place that's supposed to make you well. I told you, there's *nothing* good that comes from needles,' I leaned across and whispered to my friend. We were wrapping up our mock (practice) Irish exam. It was 1997, and I was in my final year of secondary school in Ireland.

'What in God's name are you talking about the Hepatitis C and HIV tribunal for?' she replied. 'That was a hard exam. I still don't think I'll ever understand the *modh coinníollach*.'[1]

*Thump.* Mrs Buckley interrupted my thoughts, banging her hand on my desk. I rubbed my temple, lamenting the inevitable before it even happened. 'Grace Lordan! You cannot confer during an examination at this school. I am cancelling your right to results on your mock exams. Tell your mother that I want to see her.'

'My mother, Miss?' I questioned, despite Gillian's pleading eyes telling me to shut up. 'Why not my father? Isn't that a bit sexist? You know, I read recently that we tend to see mothers as both caregivers and disciplinarians due to a . . .'

As I rambled on, I could see Mrs Buckley's eyes bulging bigger and bigger. I would bet my morning coffee that she would have preferred to whack me upside the head in that moment, and she presumably only chose six weeks of Friday detention because flexing her ruler had been deemed socially unacceptable in Ireland by that time.

I can't recall why the Hepatitis C and HIV tribunal popped into my head that day, but that kind of random thought is common for those of us who are easily distracted or prone to procrastination.

Wandering thoughts aren't helpful when you are trying to accelerate your life. They don't just cause lapses of concentration at moments when you need your performance to be at its peak (like exams, important meetings, interviews, etc.); they can also cause you to get distracted by entirely different activities, like binge-watching TV or staying out too long socializing with friends – as your real priorities slip through your fingers.

Have you ever planned an ultra-productive day, only to finish it with nothing to show?

Time is your most precious resource. You cannot get it back, you cannot buy more, and in today's world there are oodles of things that grab at it indiscriminately. Fighting against distraction and procrastination is an ongoing commitment. You will lose battles, but with perseverance you can ultimately win the war.

I know this is hard from bitter experience. During my school years I was shouted at, pleaded with, told to sit at the back of the class and sent outside the class for being distracted, distracting others and distracting the teacher, and this happened too many times to count. No drugs, alcohol, sex, or smoking in the toilets for me. My crime was not being able to pay attention. Mrs Buckley was particularly grating for me. In the parent–teacher meeting right before my Leaving Certificate (the equivalent to A levels in the UK), she told my parents I was unlikely to get in to any tertiary education, let alone university. My mum was gutted. And yet I am now an associate professor at a prestigious international university. Was Mrs Buckley just a terrible judge of character?

Mrs Buckley was certainly a royal pain in my derrière. However, it needs to be emphasized that she had a valid perspective. My ability to study was poor because of the limits of my attention. Even though I wanted to go to university when I finished school, I was not on any kind of visible pathway towards doing so. It is easy to have ambitions. Figuring out how to make them a reality is the hard part. This involves hard work and a re-prioritization of how you spend your time.

So how did I end up scoring high enough in my Leaving Certificate to study computer science at my local university? All of it is owed to my doting mum, Rita. In the year running up to my exams, Mum quizzed me every morning on my daily study schedule. This schedule was written down the evening before, and stuck up over my desk in my bedroom study area. Timetables and check-ins served to make salient the activities that I was actually meant to be doing on a daily basis. This kept the activities in the forefront of my mind, and gave me the best chance of success. Back then, my mum did the hard work for me. She put simple structures in place that meant that I stuck to my plan, studied and ended up at university.

In the adult world, you need to do this for yourself. You need to create structures and systems that make sure you stay on track. Increasing the odds of succeeding is your responsibility.

## TIME IS FINITE

To stick to the plan you have imagined for yourself, it is pretty obvious that you need *time*. But time is a finite resource. I can't think of one person I know who doesn't always feel busy. Chances are you would say the same if we ever met over a cup of coffee. And I would probably have had to wait two weeks for you to make the time to meet me.

Why is everyone so time-poor? The majority of us simply feel busy because – from the moment we wake up – our time is gobbled up by useful and not-so-useful activities. This happens if you do not pay attention to time. The first step, then, is to identify where there is time in your current schedule that can be shifted from not-so-useful activities to your big-thinking plan.

Have you already figured out how you can make time to realize ME+? Don't pat yourself on the back just yet. That's the easy part. Sticking to the 'doing' part of it is what is hard.

Identifying where the time will come from to engage in your small steps each week is like a dieter identifying where in their daily food intake they will reduce calories. *Okay, that's easy, I won't eat all those jam doughnuts.*

What's the hard part? Not eating the jam doughnuts.

What's the really hard part? Not eating the doughnuts when you are tired, stressed – or, on the other hand, when you've had good news and fancy treating yourself.

It's the same thing for anybody who has ever decided to take up running. It is easy to write a plan to take you from couch to 5K. Run ten minutes, then walk for ten minutes on the first day; run fifteen minutes, walk five minutes on another day . . . It's only twenty minutes a day, you tell yourself, so how hard can it be? But fast-forward to run number five, and you're tired and a bit achy as you lace up your trainers that are *still wet* from yesterday's rain . . .

Would going back to bed for half an hour really be so bad?

Having the intention to take up running is easy. Putting a note in your diary of all the runs you're going to do before the big race is easy. Even doing the first run is usually pretty easy. There's a novelty to it. But not missing a single training session for three months is hard. Showing up regularly to execute a plan is where people fall down.

So let's do the easy bit first: figuring out where you will pull the time for your small steps. And after that we can get serious about using behavioural science to help you stay the distance. I'll highlight ten behavioural science insights you can draw on immediately, to develop the good habit of regularly committing time to your new journey.

## FINDING TIME IS EASY

Once a week, let's say every Sunday evening so that you can look ahead, you will set intentions for the next seven days. You'll allocate ninety minutes here or three hours there for the activities you've identified as important for your journey to ME+ (recall the activities you committed to in Chapter 2), just as you might list how you will devote your minutes of training in a couch-to-5K training plan.

Of course, you will need to find time in your already manic schedule to engage in these processes. We are all busy, but what is the biggest obstacle that stands in our way to find this time? ***Time-inconsistent preferences.***

What are time-inconsistent preferences? This is behavioural science speak for the fact that most of us don't do things that are in our long-term interests often enough because we lack self-control.

Self-control problems need tackling head-on when dealing with *intertemporal choices.* What is an intertemporal choice? It means you are choosing between immediate gratification and engaging in activities where the gains are a long way in the future, but the costs are felt today.

To put it simply: most of us are unlikely to choose to spend three hours writing our novel or learning Mandarin, when we could be spending that time in the pub with our friends, or watching TV.

If you are lucky, you will get instant gratification from the small steps you are taking to get you to your big-thinking goal. Maybe you love writing your novel or learning a new language, and every time you put effort into doing so you gain immediate satisfaction from achieving that immersive flow state. However, the major gains of these activities will still be reaped at some time in the future – your first royalty statement, say, or when you're chatting away to your new colleagues in Beijing at a level that goes beyond 'pass the salt'.

In contrast, there are many activities where the fun is delivered immediately and the costs come later. In behavioural science, these are called 'sins' or 'bads', but in this book I'm going to call them ***time-sinkers.*** Time-sinkers include binge-drinking, couch-potatoing, and endless engagement in online social networks. As well as being time-sinkers, these activities can have long-term costs in terms of your personal health.[2] Time-sinkers also include online shopping and gambling – as well as being time-sinkers, these activities will increase the cost of your next credit card bill. Even emailing, being in pointless meetings and dealing with office politics take away time now that you could have spent on more worthwhile activities.

> Your small steps shouldn't suck time from your health or your family or the things you do to relax.

The point of taking a medium-term horizon is to allow you to still go running, be a good friend, or get a Thai massage to loosen your knotted neck. Your small steps need to work around life-enhancing things you do day-to-day. Rather, this chapter is focused on reducing your time-sinkers.

## TIME AUDITS

Every year, the HMRC in the UK (or the IRS in the US) inspects people's income to ensure they are paying an appropriate amount of tax. A time audit is when you inspect how you spend the hours and minutes of a regular day. It allows you to see how your plans match what actually happened.

Commit to doing a time audit over the next seven days. I would suggest breaking each day into fifteen-minute intervals, to allow a level of detail that makes time-sinkers obvious.

A time-sinker is something that can (and should) be culled, avoided or cut down. Highlighting the time-sinkers with a neon marker in your audit can make it easier for you to see where you are unwisely sinking your time.

So what are your biggest time-sinkers? For me, they are pointless meetings, time spent checking and responding to unnecessary emails, and binge-watching box sets. I'm going to focus on each in turn and show you how much time I used to spend doing them, so that you can work out what your own time-sinkers are and how to combat them.

I committed to avoiding these time-sinkers partially by creating a structure that gave me the best possible chance of sticking to my plan.

**My time-sinkers**

**What:** Pointless meetings where I am clearly not needed and don't add value

- **Weekly time-cost:** 7 hours.
- **Commit to save:** 4 hours (don't want colleagues to think I am dead, so I should show up sometimes).
- **How:** Send polite apologies that give comments on the papers for the meeting, with the warmest of wishes. If no paper has been prepared for the meeting, just don't show up. If the organizers couldn't care less about the meeting, why would I?

**What:** Time spent checking and responding to unnecessary emails

- **Weekly time-cost:** Hard to estimate as checking emails is an automatic habit. I'm ashamed to say I am addicted, and sometimes the number of times I unconsciously check my email in an hour is in the double digits.
- **Commit to save:** 80 per cent of whatever the time-cost is.[3]
- **How:** Remove email from my desktop and phone, as this is where I tend to check the most absent-mindedly. Restrict emailing to my iPad. This will

cause my unconscious mind to no longer associate email-checking with my desktop and phone. Further, restrict my emailing to just after lunch and before I sign off for the evening. Remind myself I am not a heart surgeon and no one will die if I don't ping-pong a response to their email.[4]

**What:** Binge-watching boxsets, while also mindlessly surfing the internet on my phone

- **Weekly time-cost:** 1.5 hours each evening, plus about 5 hours in total across Saturday and Sunday.
- **Commit to save:** 6 hours in total.
- **How:** Okay, this was a hard one for me because it is also how I unwind. And for that reason, unlike endlessly checking emails or going to stupid meetings, I didn't want to totally get rid of my boxset addiction. However, by making the decision to cut down, I changed the habit from mindless watching to watching one full-length movie, or two episodes of a series per night. I also put all of my devices out of the room, so I no longer surf the internet while watching TV – meaning I watch TV with more focus and enjoy it more. Thanks to being able to easily cancel and restart contracts on Apple TV, Now TV, Netflix and Amazon (in behavioural science we call being able to cancel so easily 'low levels of sludge'), I now rotate the TV subscriptions so I have much more variation in what I watch. And this 'intentional watching' has had a very positive knock-on effect on my sleep quality.

Overall, changing the time I devoted to two of my time-sinkers gave me at least ten hours per week, plus a conservative ten hours (and I mean *really* conservative!) from changing up my emailing habits. Whoop! That's twenty hours a week to devote to progressing my big-thinking journey. People always say there aren't enough days in the week, but doing this practically gave me a whole extra day! With fifty-two weeks in a year, over one year, this is 1,040 hours! Over five years this would be 5,200 hours!!! Imagine how much better off I'll be from spending 5,200 more hours on fulfilling my ambitions over the next five years?

Identify your own three biggest time sinkers now . . .

**Time-sinker 1**
What:
Weekly time-cost:
Commit to save:
How?

**Time-sinker 2**
What:
Weekly time-cost:
Commit to save:
How?

**Time-sinker 3**
What:
Weekly time-cost:
Commit to save:
How?

## BEHAVIOURAL SCIENCE INSIGHTS

In Chapter 2, you set intentions for activities related to your medium-term journey. You have now identified time-sinkers via a time audit, which gives you time back to actually do the small steps that will allow you to realize your big-thinking goal.

So what else is standing in the way of your success? Getting distracted by things that are more fun or entertaining in the moment? Letting your mind wander from your core objectives because of intrusions in your mailbox, or random thoughts?

Managing to persevere when the small steps require tasks that are hard, or when external events dent your mojo – this is where the real work is. The truth is that sticking to your plans will be hard. Just showing up regularly for the small steps takes self-discipline. In fact, it requires a level of self-discipline that most of us do not have in plentiful supply.

There will be times when the work needed to attain your goal is tedious and boring. There will be times when you can't join your friend for that Aperol spritz, or go to a movie with your partner. But this is the path that you have chosen to get your desired life. Only you can make it happen. Don't let your time-sinkers drag you down.

But we are not necessarily destined to choose instant gratification every time. As I hope I've made clear, I am easily distracted and find it very hard to stay on track. But you're reading a book that took lots of time. It was very much a medium-term journey that required me initially to think big and later take very regular small steps to complete it.

Behavioural science has taught me that I can overcome distractions and stay on track by acknowledging the parts of me that cause me to become distracted, and by putting structures in place to safeguard me from myself. I outline these structures below – they are the very best insights that behavioural science has to offer to ensure you avoid your time-sinkers, take regular small steps and reach your desired goal. They are also easy to do, and either cheap or free to implement.

While each behavioural science insight will help some of you, they will not necessarily help every reader. You are all unique and special, and different things work for different people. I would still encourage you to try the insights, one by one. This allows you to consciously evaluate the success of each for you personally. If it works for you, keep doing it. If you see no benefits after one week, don't bother with it any more and move on to the next insight. You don't have to do them in order, either; go with what appeals most.

This is called ***trial-and-error learning***. You keep what works and discard the rest. I have carried out trial-and-error learning with great success. It has helped me manage my own attention span (or lack of) and therefore my time. I regularly treat myself like a behavioural science experiment. Okay, so it sounds a little odd, but the basic idea is that I take an insight from behavioural science and apply it to myself. I then sit down after seven days and assess if the change I made actually altered my behaviour in a direction I want. If it did, I continue with the change, monitoring how it affects my behaviour week to week, until it stops working. At this point I have adapted. The novelty has worn off. So I try something else.

If you keep an open mind, you may be surprised at what works for you. Personalizing the interventions gives you a far greater chance of success, and different things work for different people.[5] Trial-and-error learning means you simply stop doing the techniques that give you zero gains (or worse, distract you!) and stick with those that provide benefits.

There is an old saying that suggests we all end up becoming like our parents eventually. By regularly adopting behavioural science insights, I essentially became a version of my Irish mammy – intent on steering her wayward child safely to university. I intentionally steward my distracted self over the medium term to ensure that I fulfil meaningful medium-term goals, like completing this book. By the end of this chapter I want you to be in the same position: keeping yourself on the right track for success.

Out of the ten behavioural science insights I describe, I want you to pick the most appealing one now and integrate it into your life *tomorrow*. It is also worth journaling this entire process.

Learning what works for you is a journey of self-discovery in itself.

### INSIGHT 1: REBALANCING IMMEDIATE COSTS AND BENEFITS

The problem with having Mrs Buckley refuse to give me the grades of my mock examination meant that uncertainty around how I would actually perform loomed large over the next six months. Combined with the fact that all signs seemed to point to me being doomed to failure, my mum doubled down in her efforts to put me on the right track for success. Well aware of the fact that any gains her daughter might get from university were in the future, she set about ensuring that the costs and benefits of me devoting time to study in the present day were rebalanced to make me more likely to study.

There is a side look that only an Irish mammy can give that lets her child know she will not be won over. Worse still, a tirade of nagging will ensue if this look is not respected. I received that side look many times while studying for my Leaving Cert Examination. I was also subjected to plentiful nagging. These were palpable costs of bad behaviour, which in my case was not showing up for my daily study sessions.

With her side look, my mother was bringing the costs of not studying into the present. The very real and immediate cost of nagging outweighed the immediate benefit of watching TV or engaging in some equally frivolous activity. This is what a behavioural scientist would call a ***stick***. Like a real stick, it has the ability to poke you in a particular direction in a manner that is unpleasant.

But my mother wouldn't just nag, she would also coax and praise. 'I'm so proud of you, Grace,' she would say. 'I know it's a bit tedious but it'll be over soon. How about a cup of tea and some chocolate-covered marshmallows?' Along with the kind words, those yummy marshmallows served to give my study session a benefit NOW, which helped to keep me willingly sitting at my desk.

This tactic is what a behavioural scientist would call a ***carrot***. It's when you receive immediate gratification, thereby giving you an incentive to engage in a particular behaviour now that has the potential to also enhance your life in the future.

Mum provided plenty of variety in her carrot-giving: wholesome and comforting foods; good company during my breaks; movie rentals in the evenings to unwind; and a variety of study treats as rewards on my best-performance days (ranging from nice stationery to vouchers for my favourite shops).

Overall, Mum used a carrot (incentive) and stick (punishment) method. I needed Mum's help desperately at that time, as aside from my own tendency to chase dustballs with my brain, my school did not have the best record for students making it to university – so I didn't even have peer effects (the positive influence of my peers) helping me to get better grades.[6] The odds were against me, and I had to show up and study hard if I was going to tilt them back in my favour. I would later realize that there are great mammies all over the world who should be commended for the social mobility of their children against all odds. Many of these mammies instinctively leverage carrots and sticks to help their children fulfil their goals.

Today, when I am working towards something that has benefits that are uncertain and far in the future, but the costs to my leisure time are in the present and very obvious, I still rely on putting structures in place that alter the immediate benefits and costs.

> To begin creating your own carrots and sticks, ask yourself this one question: 'How can I lower the immediate costs and increase the immediate benefits of the small steps I need to take?'

You are essentially asking yourself how you can make the activities related to your big-thinking goal (which you identified in Chapter 2) more appealing *now*. A classic example relates to someone who wants to exercise in the mornings but always hits the snooze button on their alarm. How can they make it easier to engage in their planned behaviour?

They can put their alarm clock on the other side of the room, so they have to get up to turn it off. They could then leave their runners and workout gear next to their alarm, so they can get dressed quickly.

How does this help? Well, the alarm clock being further away serves to increase the cost of staying in bed (who wants to lie there with an alarm going off?) and simultaneously reduces the benefits of going back to bed once the person is up (that lovely dozy feeling has begun to wear off). Meanwhile, readily available exercise gear lowers the cost of getting ready.

Making small differences to the costs and benefits of the new habits (small steps) you are trying to adopt can have a disproportionately positive effect on the likelihood that you stay on track. For example:

- Distracted by email and social media while engaging in continuous learning? Try removing email and internet access from your immediate working environment, and giving yourself an offline space to work in. Increasing the effort needed to go online increases the cost of this activity NOW, and subsequently makes you much less likely to do it.
- Flaking on networking events because you're too tired? Give yourself an incentive to attend an event once a month by scheduling an indulgence the following evening. This could be a meal out with friends or a relaxing night in with a takeaway and a movie. This incentive serves to increase the benefits of attending the event in the immediate term, and may allow you to push through any fatigue barriers.

### *INSIGHT 2: CULTIVATE SELF-BELIEF*

'You can be anything you want, Grace. What that will be is entirely up to you. There are no limits once you regularly apply yourself. You're smart as a whip. I believe in you,' my mum said to me exactly three months before I sat my Leaving Cert.

I was very sceptical of this at the time. I can see myself sat at my desk on a rainy day in 1997, rolling my eyes to indicate that I had heard the message but it hadn't landed . . . yet. I saw myself as completely ordinary. Round about average. I certainly didn't think there were no limits to what I could be. For my teenage self, authentic self-belief was in very short supply. However, in the absence of self-belief, having someone else who believes in you can be invaluable.

Does it make a difference if someone believes if you are a high performer or a low performer academically? Harvard psychologist Robert Rosenthal and school principal Lenore Jacobson carried out a landmark study in 1968 that investigated how a teacher's belief in a student's ability would shape the child's entire future.

They administered a test to elementary school kids, who were attending school just south of San Francisco, that would identify late bloomers (children who would reveal themselves to be talented in the future). The test was said to allow Rosenthal and Jacobson to point to children who, despite not showing the usual signs of being excellent students, were expected to emerge as being innately brilliant soon-ish. The children the test identified as late bloomers were made known to their teachers.

What happened next? The teachers started to treat the children identified as late bloomers differently because of positive expectations. This became known as the ***Pygmalion effect***. What is more, at the end of the year, they tested the students' academic ability again, and the results showed a big difference between the gains of those earmarked for greatness and the rest of the students. So what did this mean? The assessment they'd administered had predicted the late bloomers perfectly? Well, not quite . . .

The students they had identified as late-blooming top performers had been randomly selected. Basically drawn from a hat. They were as likely to be top performers as low. The selection process had no relationship at all to academic chops or test-taking capabilities. Rather, the experiment emphasized that a teacher's belief in the ability of certain students was a self-fulfilling prophecy: the students rose to the teacher's expectations. It wasn't an innate ability that gave those children the edge. Rather, the teacher gave the students identified as late bloomers more attention because they believed in their potential. As they did so, the students' effort increased and this translated into better grades.

When embarking on any medium-term plan, cultivating self-belief pays dividends. Why? If you believe in yourself, you will also hold a belief that you can realize your big-thinking goal, and gain access to all the associated benefits. The certainty that you can do it could be the link you need NOW to ensure that you show up for your daily activities. You can generate your own self-fulfilling prophecy or Pygmalion effect.

So how can you cultivate self-belief?

Regularly remind yourself that you can change your own skills and other characteristics with sustained effort. These things *are* malleable. It sounds oversimplified perhaps, but the belief that you can actually change your abilities is one of the key ingredients in realizing change. At the LSE I taught econometrics for many years – a statistics-based economics subject that many students are fearful of. A stylized fact that I am happy to share with you is that the fear of the subject was very often the factor that stopped students doing well in it. As an instructor, stripping out that fear was incredibly helpful for my students – as it ensured that they didn't avoid studying simply because they perceived the subject as intimidating. The best thing I could do for them was to alter their self-belief for the better, so they stayed on the learning curve.

How did I know that reminding yourself that *you can do it* in the face of a hard task would pay dividends? There is extremely compelling evidence to show that positively changing self-belief improves all sorts of valuable life outcomes.

For example, a 2011 study of more than 15,000 children illustrated that those encouraged simply to believe that intelligence could be learned secured far higher scores in a difficult task, compared to a control group that did not hear these messages.[7] Letting people know that they possess the ability to improve their own intellectual capabilities has also been shown to improve the grades of students in a number of other contexts.[8] An awareness that you can realize your big-thinking goal helps you show up for the small steps that ultimately will get you there. There is also evidence that reaffirmations of this form of personal adequacy are worthwhile for goal attainment.[9]

Want to hear something truly encouraging? You can also develop soft skills at any point in your life,[10] meaning you are never too old to improve your behaviour, self-esteem, grittiness and resilience. Overall, behavioural science research tells us that simply believing you can improve in a wide variety of skills gives an immediate boost to performance in those areas.

Want to give yourself the best shot at succeeding on your big-thinking journey? Why not set aside a moment to reaffirm that you are more than up to the challenge of becoming ME+. Think about all the small steps that you have taken so far, as evidence that you are well on your way to your destination. The key to this working is repetition. Do it every week.

If you find yourself unable to do this for yourself in the beginning, can you identify a boast buddy? Someone who is in your corner? Someone who is aware that you are working towards ME+ and can help you move your own needle of self-belief on those occasions when you need a morale boost?

When you do wobble and suffer a blow to your self-belief, taking some time to remind yourself that the feelings of insecurity you are experiencing are transitory – rather than permanent – can help.

What's the evidence? One brilliant randomized control study emphasized gains of 0.3 on grade point average for college freshmen who read reports from a fictitious past pupil stating that feeling out of place was a temporary phenomenon when they started on their own journey at university – as compared to students who didn't hear this message of hope.[11] The simple act of being made aware that it was normal to feel overwhelmed at the beginning of a medium-term journey helped these students stay on course!

So if you are feeling out of place at networking events, or don't feel like you belong on your training course because you cannot keep up, or think you have nothing worthwhile to say in meetings, remind yourself that these are transitory feelings.

Keep showing up with this mantra in mind. Keep reminding yourself that the feeling of not belonging will soon pass. Why? If you stick around anywhere for long enough, you will eventually belong!

### *INSIGHT 3: GIVE YOURSELF EXTRA TIME*

There were ups and downs in the run-up to my Leaving Cert Examination. I entered one particular trough around mid-April 1997, when despite the best of intentions and a number of false starts, I couldn't quite get it together to prepare for an English revision class at school . . .

'I didn't think it would take so long, Miss . . . I didn't think it would be so mind-numbingly boring that I would have to restart the first ten pages over and over and over again.'

That's me trying to explain to Mrs Fitzgibbon, my English teacher, why I had no idea how the ending of *King Lear* qualified as tragedy. What kind of a question was that anyway? All teenage Grace knew for certain was: 1) the task of reading *King Lear* was tragic full stop; and 2) she had grossly underestimated how long it would take to read it, both in absolute time and taking into account her extreme levels of procrastination.

When making plans to undertake any activity, there are three parameters that we make estimates of, either consciously or unconsciously. First, how long it will take. Second, how much it will cost. Third, the risk involved with the activity. My *King Lear* planning had no costs other than boredom, but I had grossly underestimated how long the reading would take. Worse, I had underestimated the risk of my own procrastination and ability to avoid reading this play. But I'm not alone in being a bad planner, both as a child and now as an adult. Even people who plan professionally get things spectacularly wrong.

In the last few decades, nothing divides the opportunities of children born in Ireland more than whether they fell on the good or the bad side of the 'Celtic Tiger', a colourful nickname for a period (mid-1990s to late 2000s) that was notable for its rapid economic growth and better incomes for most. Over that time, the country initiated – and overran in terms of costs and time – lots of big projects. One of these was the locally infamous Dublin Port Tunnel, which in early talks carried a price tag of €100 million. The tunnel opened in 2006, two years late, and cost €600 million more than was planned. Even worse than that, innovation had already made the tunnel obsolete for some drivers by the time it opened. Why? It had been built with too low a roof to allow the latest lorries to pass through it.

The Irish are not alone in spectacularly bad planning. Down under, in Australia, the Sydney Opera House underwent a detailed planning phase which resulted in estimates of a four-year build and $7 million budget. How did those plans stack up to the eventual reality? Ten years too short and $95 million shy. Meanwhile, in Canada, a planned coliseum with a retractable roof for the 1976 Summer Olympics came with an estimated cost of $120 million. Guess what? It wasn't fully finished until 1989, and the roof alone carried the original price tag. The Channel Tunnel between the UK and France? Same thing! Late, and with a budget blown to pieces.

Are you starting a new business? This is the type of medium-term plan that frequently overestimates the probability of success by underestimating costs and time. Thirty per cent of managers estimate their probability of failing as zero (which is statistically impossible in a world of economic uncertainty!), and 80 per cent of them view their odds of succeeding as being 70 per cent or more.[12]

What is the underlying cause of all of these planning failures? The ***planning fallacy*** – the recognition of which is owed to work by Daniel Kahneman and Amos Tversky from 1979.

The planning fallacy is the tendency of people to consistently underestimate the time that it will take them to do any activity, even if they have knowledge that similar activities have taken them longer than their estimates in the past. We are just too bloody optimistic about our productivity, and this spills over into how easy we think an activity is to complete. Consequently, the time we allocate to various activities is too low to allow us to complete them.

When we plan to do something, we assume that things will run smoothly. We assume that we will experience a best-case scenario, even when this has not transpired in the past. We assume zero procrastination, fatigue, distraction or interruption. And this optimism has a knock-on effect on our time allocation.

Strictly speaking, the planning fallacy refers to our ability to badly underestimate both the amount of time and money needed to achieve any goal. However, the evidence is clear that for individual-level decisions, money estimates can be pretty spot on. Either way, people – over and over again – underestimate the time it will take to achieve a goal. To put it bluntly, we completely suck at estimating the time it will take us to get things done. We struggle with time management. We struggle with sitting down and getting through the boring stuff, which would leave us free to stay on track and meet our milestones and deadlines.

I'm pretty sure that the plans you made in Chapter 2 will suffer from the planning fallacy. I would take that bet as a dead cert. And not allowing for the planning fallacy means you set yourself up for failure. Imagine sitting down later this week to complete an activity that you assigned a three-hour window to. What will it mean if you only get 50 per cent done? Many of us would be disappointed that we did not perform as expected. Others might view it as evidence that they are simply not up to the challenge of realizing ME+ and allow the setback to derail their progress. If you repeatedly fall victim to the planning fallacy, you're increasingly likely to feel like it's all too much and give up.

So how do you overcome the planning fallacy?

A good starting point is holding a mirror up to yourself and confirming that you are a victim of this particular cognitive bias. How? Audit all of your *planned* projects over the last year. Essentially, you want to come up with a list of any projects you planned in the last twelve months, regardless of whether you completed them.

List each of them in the table below, under the heading 'A plan I made'. These projects might include things like painting the shed, running a 10K or helping your sprog catch up on their maths homework, alongside the usual work goals like getting promoted, securing ten new clients, or finishing a book in time for the crazy deadline you committed to. The list can also include more mundane plans like books you planned to read or dental check-ups and other health screenings.

In the second column, make a note of which life domain each plan is associated with, using the following categories:

*Work* (this is your 'think big' classification)
*Finances*
*Friends and family*
*Health*
*Me-time* (i.e. time for self-care)
*Personal growth* (which may come from sticking to your big-thinking journey)
*Romantic relationships*
*Self-image*
*Society* (giving back to the world at large, including fundraising and community work)
*Spirituality*

For each plan that you have listed, tick one of the final three boxes depending on whether you 'crushed it' (meaning that you achieved the plan within the expected timeframe), 'missed it' (meaning that you did achieve the plan but it took longer than expected) or 'never did it' (meaning the plan never got done).

| A plan I made | Life domain | Crushed it | Missed it | Never did it |
|---|---|---|---|---|
| | | | | |
| | | | | |
| | | | | |
| | | | | |
| | | | | |
| | | | | |
| | | | | |
| | | | | |
| | | | | |
| | | | | |
| | | | | |
| | | | | |
| | | | | |
| | | | | |
| | | | | |
| | | | | |
| | | | | |

Take some time to reflect on what you've written in the table above. If you ended up with an entire column of 'crushed it', you are probably not being honest with yourself about the things that you planned to do in the last year. Or maybe you could do more, and stretch yourself further?

Most of us will notice that we tend to crush it in specific life domains, but in other areas balls get dropped much more regularly. Perhaps there are life domains missing altogether, and this explains your lack of 'never did it'. It is worth considering if you have neglected one area of your life intentionally, or whether it was because of poor life planning.

Often the people I meet in business who are crushing it in terms of profit or client generation are dropping the family or health ball without intending to. This can be detrimental to their own well-being, and it is very different from intentionally not making plans in a particular life domain.

Everyone has different priorities, of course. I have friends who couldn't care less about having a life partner or going on dates, however I would be lost without my (much) better half. At the same time, I couldn't care less about my self-image, and I am very unlikely to devote time to following fashion trends. These days my self-image is low-maintenance, and I do not count it as a life domain worth planning for.

When filling in the table above, you may also have found that certain plans contribute to two or more associated life domains. For example, I get personal growth from writing this book as well as it contributing to my work domain. At the same time, I often focus on some life domains more intensely than others at different points in time. To advance certain work projects, I like to dive into periods of solitary work. This means I see much less of friends and family as I hole up and work hard. How do I square this with my loved ones? Everyone is aware of what I am up to, and we always have quality time scheduled for the near future. This type of time trade-off is intentional, and the distinction is important. The ball isn't dropped, but it's not in active play.

Now reflect on your 'never did it' plans. Why did you sink those projects? Did you have something more appealing to pursue? Or was there a worthwhile reason? Let's imagine that you enrol in an online course, and by the fourth lesson you are certain that the content does not interest you. Perhaps you expected something different, or you're simply not engaged. So you ask yourself whether the course is the only pathway to get to where you need to be within the allocated time. The answer is 'no'. You then attend the fifth lesson and are miserable the entire time. Should you take the time you have already spent on the course into account when weighing up the costs and benefits of continuing? The answer is 'no'. If you did, you would be like someone in a restaurant who insists on finishing a meal even when their belly is full, just so they can 'get their money's worth'. Or someone who has paid for a movie ticket and insists on staying, despite being bored to tears and having better things to do with their time. You would be falling victim to the ***sunk cost fallacy***.

It is okay to quit if there is an intention to do something much more worthwhile.

But what if you quit without intention? This happens a lot to people like me. Like my intention to run a weekly 5K in the beautiful Richmond Park. The time it takes to complete the training gets nobbled by other plans (or just my procrastination), and it's a big tick in my 'never done it' column.

Meanwhile, even though you're reading it now, writing

this chapter was a tick in the 'missed it' column – because the planning fallacy was lurking in the shadows when I set out. I imagined it would take roughly forty hours, and I could allocate forty hours to a one-week period. But life got in the way, I got distracted and ran over.

What causes me to run late with my writing deadlines? A myriad of things! On this occasion, part of the reason is that I spent twenty minutes zoned out and chewing on my shiny new pencil (no judgement please). How could I have predicted that would happen? Nobody starts their day with pencil-chewing scheduled as one of their activities. You don't usually plan for distraction.

Auditing all of your planned projects over the last year should convince you that we consistently overestimate what we can achieve in our daily lives – and very often the best-laid plans are discarded for no reason. It should also illustrate that poor planning crowds out good intentions. By not leaving enough time for writing this chapter, I missed the endorphin rush of exercising alongside the deer, butterflies and bunnies in Richmond Park.

Your audit in the table above likely makes it crystal clear that you also regularly succumb to the planning fallacy, which will negatively affect the execution of your plans across several life domains. Just knowing about this bias may help you to drop your planning fallacy habit. However, heightened saliency may not be enough.

To be more proactive, it is worth scaling up the time you predict your activities will take by a significant factor – say, by 1.5. So for each hour you have committed to activities related to ME+, you should now allow an hour and a half.

Next, commit to refining this scaling factor to reflect the areas you struggle with most in terms of the planning fallacy.

Each week, assess what proportion of the activities you planned to do was achieved within the allocated time window. Take care to account for any days you worked later than planned. As the weeks go by and you repeat this process over and over again, you will begin to more accurately predict the time it takes to complete tasks – and also the number you need to personally scale by to offset your optimism, and beat the planning fallacy. You may even need different multipliers for different activities, which will allow you to refine your scheduling further. But a rule of thumb of 1.5 is a great place to start.

### INSIGHT 4: RECOMMIT REGULARLY TO YOUR BIG-THINKING GOAL

'I can't imagine myself enjoying any of these, Mum,' I said, exasperated, as my finger scrolled through the university catalogue, bypassing law, business and dentistry. But at the same time, I could imagine I might enjoy all of them. 'How am I supposed to know right now what I want to do for the rest of my life? I haven't a clue what it would be like to work in any of these fields. I haven't any idea what my passion is. Can we flip a coin to decide?'

Only one month away from my final exams, I was finding it hard to figure out what I wanted to do at university. This would all be okay, but by not connecting my long study days to a good outcome, I was also making it harder to show up for my planned study blocks, both physically and mentally. I was making it harder on myself unwittingly – until, that is, my finger paused at a BSc in Computer Science, and images of how cool it would be to create video games, movie graphics and online shopping experiences appeared vividly in my mind's eye. Now these were careers worth getting excited about! These were careers where *King Lear* could be a distant memory.

And with that, I declared loudly, 'I'm going to be a computer scientist!'

Having a clear big-thinking goal in your own mind's eye will motivate you to show up week after week for the activities you chose in Chapter 2. Without this, it will be harder to muster up the motivation to complete the necessary small steps because you don't know what you are aiming for.

I should note here that I am still not a computer scientist. While the goal you set should allow you to move forward, it doesn't need to be so inflexible that it defines your ultimate destination forever. The key is to keep learning and honing skills that will be useful to ME+, and keep revising your vision of ME+ as new opportunities open up.

The benefits of setting a goal are readily verified by behavioural science research.[13] But what is the mechanism through which goal-setting operates? Well, in essence, by visualizing ME+ you are bringing your future self forward. By visualizing your big-thinking goal, you keep in mind the bigger picture of what you are aiming for. This, in turn, reminds you of the future benefits your medium-term journey will bring once you reach your destination. Simply acknowledging these future benefits, and reminding yourself of your vision for ME+, can help you stay on course.

Set aside some time each month to review and recommit to your big-thinking goal.

This can be done alongside one of your more regular weekly planning sessions. Imagine what it will feel like once you have realized ME+. This serves to actively keep your goal salient in your mind. The more clearly you tie your small steps in the present to ME+, the more purpose you will find in doing them.

While having a specific goal makes you far more likely to achieve it, you also want to avoid being so focused and closed-minded that you miss out on other appealing opportunities. Do take care to avoid being a victim of ***inattentional blindness***, a phenomenon explored by Daniel Simons and Christopher Chabris in a well-known 1999 study. To illustrate the fact that when we focus on only one thing we block out the rest of the world, the researchers got a group of adults to observe two teams passing a ball to each other on a makeshift basketball court. Their task was simple. They were to count the passes made by the team wearing white shirts, and actively ignore the passes made by those in black shirts. The participants took to their task with gusto, diligently counting away. However, their super-narrow focus meant that they did not see the person dressed as a gorilla who came on to the playing court beating their chest. Yes, you read that correctly! They did not see the gorilla! The participants' intense concentration meant they missed this fantastic spectacle.

To avoid missing gorilla-shaped opportunities that come your way because of inattentional blindness, take some time during your monthly recommitment to your goal to assess new opportunities that are opening up to you that may pivot your plans or give you new experiences.

### INSIGHT 5: MEANING IS A MOTIVATOR

'I'm going to study computer science.' Once I had made up my mind, I was pretty defiant about what I would be studying at university. My family, friends and even strangers whose ears I would bend were surprised, and couldn't quite see the logic in this decision-making. At that time, I knew little about how there would be only five women for every ninety-five men studying my chosen degree. I knew less still about the exact jobs that a computer science degree might open up. To be honest, I didn't even know that Java wasn't a foreign language when I sent off the application forms that would seal the fate of my next four years.

But I finally had a goal. And despite my lack of knowledge of the ins and outs of studying computer science, my goal did have overall meaning. I was aware of how technology was shaping the world, through creating products that were useful in society. I wanted to be involved in building technologies that would make the world a better place. Technologies that would allow people to live their best lives. Technologies that would give easy access education.

In Chapter 2, you chose activities to engage in as small steps towards realizing your big-thinking goal. Because taking these small steps will allow you to become ME+, you have already identified their meaning. This innately gives the small steps purpose.

But does your goal serve a higher purpose? Are you pursuing a big-thinking goal that aligns with your own core values? What will the work you plan to do bring to the world in terms of added value?

Identifying this added value connects the dots as to the overall meaning of what you are trying to achieve, and this can keep you motivated when your energy wanes. You can start to view the small steps, and the time they take, as a production process – and the result of this production process is a meaningful end product. It is worth reminding yourself of this when you get disillusioned.

Why does identifying the meaning of your goal tend to keep you on track? There is ample evidence that when a goal is identified as meaningful, individuals put much more effort into fulfilling it,[14] and viewing your ME+ – your big-thinking goal – as meaningful will dramatically increase the likelihood that you fulfil your plan.[15] It can be a morale boost that keeps you showing up. Another nice side effect is that finding meaning in one's daily activities (your small steps) has been linked to increased happiness and higher levels of motivation,[16] as well as lower levels of stress and cynicism.

So how can you identify the *meaning* behind your big-thinking goal? Start by drawing attention to things about the work you want ME+ to do.[17] Ask yourself whether you think your future career will:

- Cause you to feel happy, fulfilled and/or proud.
- Create positive ripple effects that go beyond the immediate benefits generated by you – such as benefits to the community or even humanity.

The first of these categories is about the meaning that the work of ME+ brings to you personally. What makes us happy, fulfilled or proud might include growth opportunities, respect, connection to others, altruism, prosperity, the ability to create, and status. In contrast, the second category is about the external meaning of your work. For example, ME+ may empower, empathize, bring safety to, make life better for, create jobs for, care for or teach others.

Take a moment to identify the meaning behind the work you have chosen for ME+ in terms of these two categories. Armed with this information, think of a skill that you have now, or a skill you are cultivating for ME+, that would allow you to do this meaningful work well. This exercise allows you to tap into authenticity and self-efficacy as mechanisms to increase the meaning of the work you intend ME+ to do. You gain authenticity by realizing that the skills you possess, or those you are working towards, allow you to carry out this meaningful work, which benefits you and/or others directly. Self-efficacy improves by increasing your self-awareness of what it means to have these skills.

I recommend that you repeat this exercise regularly, perhaps at a set time each day, so the meaning of what you are trying to achieve stays salient throughout your medium-term journey.

Linking yourself – and your unique skill set – to the meaning of your work enhances your intrinsic motivation to stick to your planned small steps.

Committing to doing this simple mental exercise can even harness motivation for jobs that are not particularly pleasant to do on a day-to-day basis.

I provided evidence that finding meaning in one's work can improve productivity, even for the most boring tasks, in a 2019 field experiment conducted with Alberto Salamone at a manufacturing firm in the US. The workers we studied were employed in jobs that involved very repetitive tasks. These jobs, to most people (including the workers themselves), would be described as 'boring'.

We put posters on their production floor on a random day, which made salient to these workers the meaning and importance of the job they were doing. There were three parts to each poster. The first was designed to recognize the workers' own skill sets. The second was designed to emphasize the wider purpose of the product they were making – in this instance, we were reminding the workers that they manufactured the lights that keep people safe when they cross train tracks or drive on the road. The third component personalized the benefits of the product they made. We showed them the faces of the people they were helping to keep safe.

Overall, our study showed that making the meaning of work salient through this three-step process hugely increased the intrinsic motivation of these workers, causing them to work longer hours and miss fewer days. At times of low motivation, it is worth visualizing the people who will gain from your future work – whether that is children you will teach, consumers who will be better off with the service you provide, colleagues who will gain from your fantastic leadership, or your family who will gain from you having a better work–life balance. If you want to go all out, you could even design a poster and put it in a prominent place!

### *INSIGHT 6: WHAT GETS MEASURED GETS DONE*

At the end of every study day in April 1997, I unpinned my timetable from the wall and crossed off my achievements so it represented what I had actually done on that particular day. With fewer than five weeks to go until my first exam, I noticed that my planning had markedly improved. Back then I didn't know anything about the planning fallacy – least of all its name – but this simple self-assessment made the symptoms of this cognitive trap so clear that I found myself automatically giving myself extra time for certain subjects in order to get through the allocated material.

ME+ is a construct of thinking big. The activities you have chosen need to become routine processes that you engage in regularly, otherwise you will not fulfil your ambitions. To give yourself the best shot at regularly engaging in these small steps, planning them ahead of time is crucial. More than that, engaging in a post-mortem that maps what you actually did against what you planned to do will help you plan better for the future. It also ensures you hold yourself to account.

So how can you incorporate a post-mortem into your planning? You will already be writing commitments to carry out activities at the start of each week. This makes clear your intentions. You could also add to this list what you hope to achieve in each session. For example, if you are writing a proposal that you expect to be 10,000 words long, you may set intentions for Monday to write 2,000 words over a three-hour period between 8 p.m. and 11 p.m. When you have finished your writing period, a post-mortem would then note how many hours you actually wrote for, alongside the word count you delivered.

Notice I counted words as an output along with time taken. Why? Word count better represents visible progress towards a big-thinking goal. It also ensures that the real progress that is being made is clear because seeing progress improves performance.[18] If you've written 5,000 words of a 10,000-word paper, you know you're halfway.

Monitoring in this way works well for all kinds of things. For instance:

- Securing new clients for your food delivery business? Count the number of emails and telephone calls you make and follow up on. Compare this to the number that you intended to do.
- Doing small-business-related administration tasks such as tax returns, filing expenses and payroll? When setting intentions, make a list of all of these tasks and commit to doing a specific number per session, marking them off as you go.

You get the idea . . .

Overall, by embracing a philosophy that **what gets measured gets done**, your progress will not slide too far without you knowing.

And for those of us who also need carrots to show up for

ourselves, you can easily embed incentives into a post-mortem. How? Reward yourself on the occasions that your output exceeds your plans by a significant margin. For example, if in a week of writing you find yourself 2,000 words in credit, you can give yourself the evening off to indulge in whatever gives you instant gratification, relaxed in knowing that you are right on track.

### *INSIGHT 7: LUCK VERSUS EFFORT*

The main event had arrived and one exam went spectacularly badly: an English paper.

'It's not my fault, Mum. How was I to know that so much of the exam would be on *King Lear*? It was just bad luck,' I exclaimed.

Of course, it wasn't bad luck. Everyone knew it was definitely coming up. I was simply ill-prepared. To add insult to injury, the question on the exam had asked whether the ending of *King Lear* could be seen as tragic . . .

Over the course of your medium-term journey, there will be some major milestones to overcome, like interviews, public speaking events, pitching opportunities to investors, and assessments of the work you put out into the world. Some of these occasions will go well. Other occasions will not go so well. Disentangling whether the outcome – be it good or bad – is owed largely to luck or effort allows you to continuously improve and learn from the milestones you have passed.

In the last section, I suggested you commit to a post-mortem of your regular daily commitments – being honest about whether you had showed up for yourself. Now I am suggesting you carry out a post-mortem for major milestones, with a realistic assessment of whether your efforts are the true cause of you getting ahead (or falling over).

Committing to engaging in post-mortems to answer why you ended up failing a particular milestone – or why you didn't put yourself forward for an opportunity – can provide a clear perspective as long as you simultaneously commit to being brutally honest with yourself. Back at school I was failing on the honesty component. I knew the importance of *King Lear* in my exam, and the preparation question given to me at school bore an unquestionably canny resemblance to what had actually come up in the real thing. If I had done an honest post-mortem, I would have concluded that my performance was hampered by a lack of effort, rather than bad luck. This would have allowed me to prepare better for my next time at the test-taking rodeo.

Remember that any outcome in our lives is a product of both effort and luck.

In variable ratios, luck and effort determine your marital status, the number of children you have, the amount of money you earn, and the work you do for a living right now. Luck is random and very much outside your own control. It is being in the right place at the right time. I do like to distinguish fair luck (for example, winning the lottery) from luck that is determined by privilege (being born into a wealthy family). However, for the case of a post-mortem, you can combine luck and privilege because, just like luck, you did not choose your privilege.

You should undertake a major-milestone post-mortem when you have had a big win, experienced a failure or an unexpected opportunity has arisen. This type of major post-mortem should be approached with the knowledge that it is possible you have experienced a good outcome simply because luck dominated, and equally you may have experienced failure because bad luck dominated. View this major post-mortem as a time to reflect on the decisions and efforts that you made, and how they got you to where you are on that day. View it as a time to learn, rather than a time to lament or be too self-congratulatory.

The template below can be used for your milestone post-mortem:

| **Major Milestone:**<br>**Outcome:** | | |
|---|---|---|
| **What decision was made?** | **What went right?** | **What went wrong?** |
| 1. | | |
| 2. | | |
| 3. | | |
| 4. | | |
| 5. | | |

Think about the last major milestone that impacted you. This could be anything from taking an examination at school or university, to unveiling a product that you have been working on, to attending an interview. It can even be something outside the world of work if you prefer.

Make a note of the milestone that you are thinking about, along with its final outcome, at the top of the table. Before your day of reckoning came, there would have been a series of decisions you made which partially determined how successful you were in terms of that milestone. List them in the spaces above. Notice that I have left space for five decisions. This is to encourage you to reflect on *all* the decisions that got you to that point. People often try to distil the success or failure of major milestones down to one or two key decisions, but this rarely reflects reality. Try to stretch yourself and identify at least five decisions. Now take the opportunity to write out what went right and what went wrong for each decision.

Why is this useful?

It is important that you judge your progress by the quality of your decision-making, as opposed to the quality of your outcomes.

After all, outcomes conflate luck with effort. You will no doubt notice in your 'What went right?' and 'What went wrong?' columns that you encountered luck. Perhaps you made a decision to study only a subset of questions, and they came up in your examination. Was this an informed decision guided by the teacher or did you take a risk in order to reduce the effort you would have to make? Or maybe you only tested your product on a millennial audience prior to unveiling. Was this strategic? Or did you exclude a large proportion of your customer base?

A major post-mortem also allows you to ask yourself if the

outcome encountered in the milestone – good or bad – came about because of intentional actions. If the reason you're flying high right now is because of a lucky break, you can't guarantee that you're going to keep getting lucky breaks. By all means ride the wave, but don't expect it to have any bearing on future outcomes. For example, if you put yourself forward for a freelance project and get the gig, it is worth assessing the level of effort that you put into the bid, and where possible find out what your new client liked about your pitch. This might teach you more about how much preparation time you need to give yourself to ensure the best chance of success. It also allows you to identify which attributes of your product or services are doing the heavy lifting in securing new clients, and which are not being noticed. It is possible that, during this process, you recognize that your pitch was lacking in some ways, even though it succeeded. Perhaps you notice that you were affected by the planning fallacy when writing it, and had some sleepless nights trying to get it finished on time. Perhaps you recognize that your bid had blind spots. Maybe you excluded some people from the service you were offering without meaning to. Or maybe you realize that this kind of pitch is going to take an extraordinary amount of time, and while it provides a pay cheque right now, it doesn't serve your longer-term purposes very well.

On occasions when you didn't get the gig, the major post-mortem keeps the same format. You reflect on whether or not you truly gave the pitch your best shot in terms of preparation time, and where possible find out from the client that turned you down about why your pitch wasn't successful. Even if you cannot access such feedback, you can actively ask yourself whether the bid represents your best work by rereading it. Or maybe there was some other aspect of the bid that clearly negatively affected the outcome – were you asking for too much money, perhaps?

It can happen that when you reread your pitch, you still view it as excellent. On this occasion, maybe you just got unlucky. It's important when you don't succeed to not always blame the world for being unfair, particularly if you encounter the same problem again and again. Rather than blaming others for your failures, try to salvage the positives from the experience. Glean as much information as you can from any failed process. Proactively make a list, using the template above, of all the things that you did to make it go well, and also where you let your efforts slip. This is a process that will stop you judging yourself only by successful outcomes – which are, in part, driven by luck. Learning provides a silver lining in the face of failure, helping you persevere.

There will be many situations in your journey when you intentionally put yourself forward for something that requires time and effort up front. It could be anything – job interviews, public speaking, article-writing, pitches to potential investors, an oral examination in a foreign language, leading a meeting, or even elections for office. A major milestone post-mortem using the template above is always beneficial.

You can help the post-mortem process along by defining what a good outcome looks like to you before you even put your hat in the ring. This is pretty clear when you are bidding for a freelance gig, but what about when you are public speaking or leading a meeting? How will you define success? Having a clear idea of what a good outcome is will help you when it comes to doing your post-mortem after the event. You will know for sure what 'good' looks like.

### *INSIGHT 8: MIND YOUR EMOTIONS*

'Maybe I should dump the idea of going to university altogether. I've had enough. I hate maths,' I complained during my maths revision. It happened that my mum was folding the laundry in the next room. Aware of the crash and burn in English Paper 1, and not wanting this failure to cause an emotional reaction that would affect my long-term future unnecessarily, Mum was quick to offer me a break from berating myself.

'Why don't you take the rest of the evening off, Grace? You've been working really hard. You should have a well-deserved break and watch a movie.'

Throughout your journey, you will make a few big decisions and many small decisions. The small decisions you will make are things like deciding to show up for your activities on a daily basis. The big decisions are things like deciding what those activities actually are, and the big-thinking goal to aim for. Together, these big and small decisions will determine whether you succeed.

As a teenager, the negative experience I was having during my study periods for my Leaving Certificate exam (my activity) was threatening to have a knock-on negative effect on a bigger, high-stakes goal (going to university – after all, a computer science degree needed a good grade in maths!). Aware of the role of emotions in poor decision-making, my mum leapt in to separate the big decision of not going to university from the emotional reaction related to expecting to do badly on Maths Paper 1. Mum also avoided drawing attention to the fact that the frustration I was feeling was transitory. It would probably pass by tomorrow.

Whatever the size of the decision you are making, it is worth remembering that emotions play a large role in determining what you do.

This is particularly relevant when you are about to either quit or start something that will have a big impact on your big-thinking goal. It is also useful when there is a trend of you not showing up for your regular activities. You should consciously probe the emotion behind your decision. Are you not showing up because you fear failure? Or is it that the learning curve is so steep you are trying to avoid feeling frustrated?

Your big-thinking plan is ambitious, and on some occasions you're going to feel out of your depth. This is natural. If it were easy, everyone would be achieving the goals they set for themselves. Accepting that whatever you are feeling – a fear of failure, a frustration at your lack of progress – is transitory can help you persevere.

In 2007, Paul Slovic and colleagues showed that emotional reactions feed into our performance and the decisions that we make. There are two categories of emotions that can disrupt us. First are those emotions that are integral to the task at hand. For example, the fear you legitimately feel before an interview, an important pitch or a public speaking event can cause an emotional reaction that impacts your performance. Second are so-called incidental emotions, caused by the other things that are going on in your life – like dealing with toxic co-workers, caring for an ill relative, or worries about personal debt – that also impact your performance.[19] Both types of emotional response are more readily handled by individuals with higher levels of emotional intelligence, a skill that is learnable and worth developing. (We will talk more about building resilience and handling emotional reactions in Chapter 7.)

The bottom line for now? Beware of your emotions when making decisions, and do not make big decisions in haste.

In behavioural science, when emotions impact on actions it is called the ***affect heuristic***. This interplay between heart and mind means that, when assessing options for ME+, you may have a tendency to view some through rose-coloured glasses simply because you have positive feelings towards them, and conversely you may overlook options for which you have negative feelings. When any opportunity arises, question the direction of your response, and probe if it is being driven by emotion. Maybe it is your gut reaction to turn down opportunities when asked by people you do not yet know or have built a rapport with. Or perhaps you are spending your precious time doing tasks that do not stretch you with people whose company you enjoy.

You may also make errors in judgement because of your emotions when you are deciding how to allocate time among the small steps for your big-thinking journey. All the steps are necessary, but engaging in them gives you different levels of pleasure. If two skills are necessary for ME+, you may find yourself overinvesting in small steps that hone the skill you find the easiest. Behind this decision is likely an emotional reaction. No one feels good about themselves when they are engaging in an activity they do not find easy or enjoyable.

What can you do about this? Remind yourself that the emotions you have towards that particular activity are transitory, and will pass as soon as you have reached a certain level of mastery. Make the promise to turn up ten times and engage in the activity you find difficult. After you have done this, reassess to see if the unpleasant emotions have disappeared with the time.

When making any key life decision, it should be done with a cool head.

In practice, this means asking for time to let thoughts settle when you are put on the spot by other people. For some, this time can be used to make a list of the costs, benefits and risks associated with the various pathways that are available to you. This process can allow you to more closely mimic rational decision-making, in which you account as much as possible for the upside, downside and risk of each option. For others, the simple fact of having some time is enough to prevent knee-jerk reactions and allow you to feel certain about your choice. Although it is possibly not the most romantic tactic if someone proposes marriage, this approach should help you feel more satisfied with your decision-making come post-mortem time in your big-thinking journey!

***TOP TIP: JOURNALING CAN HELP WITH DECISION-MAKING***

Being more mindful of the role emotions play in determining whether you show up for your activities – and how you react to big opportunities over the course of your journey – can be helped by journaling frequently. Keep in mind that you should never make a decision that will impact ME+ when you are angry, aroused, hungry, upset, disgusted, fearful, exhilarated, or feeling any other intense emotion. By all means discuss options with others in an emotional state, but put some time between that moment and when the decision needs to be made.

This is also a good rule of thumb for when someone irritates you – don't immediately react in person, via email or on the phone. Give yourself some time to put emotional reactions behind you, and respond when you are more measured and calm. In the meantime, don't let anyone poke the bear!

### INSIGHT 9: IT'S NOT ALL OR NOTHING

Back in Ireland in 1997, the Leaving Certificate exams took place over about a one-month period in June. In the beginning, exam days come thick and fast, but towards the end the gaps between them are as much as a week apart. I had a gap of eight days, with the primary goal being swotting up on my final subject. However, I soon found myself growing frustrated, suffering from concentration lapses and unrelenting procrastination. My nails and pencils were thoroughly chewed as I stared despondently at my lack of progress on the third of those eight days.

'Everything doesn't always have to be all or nothing, Grace. Maybe some days you should be happy when you show up and make progress, even if it's half of what you had planned,' Mum counselled, in response to my expressed frustration that I had only made it halfway through my planned chemistry revision session.

Some of you will fail to launch. You will set intentions for small-step activities and not manage to complete them in their entirety, despite trying week after week. There are two main reasons why this happens . . .

First, you may be overcommitting yourself and falling victim to the planning fallacy: you think you can do too much within an allocated time window. You might want to check your scaling factor.

Second, you may not yet have the mojo needed to create a rhythm and execute the activities (notice that I said *yet*!) when the allotted time arrives. You daydream, make tea and WhatsApp your friends. At networking events you stand and chat with the person you have known for years. Anything but do the one thing that you intended to do.

So how can you change this?

Why not check if the ***compromise effect*** can work for you?[20] When planning activities, the typical approach is to commit to doing one specific thing fully, and then crossing it off once completed. However, rather than framing it as all or nothing, how about setting different workloads that are low, medium and high? You can then allow yourself to choose which to complete depending on how you feel on the day. If the compromise effect works on you, you will find yourself hitting the medium workload much more often than not.

***TOP TIP: INTEGRATING THE COMPROMISE EFFECT INTO YOUR DAILY ROUTINE***

What does the compromise effect look like for a daily activity in practice? Let's imagine once again that you are trying to write that pesky 10,000-word proposal. You might set intentions for workloads on Monday as follows:

1. HIGH – write 2,000 words over a three-hour period between 8 p.m. and 11 p.m.
2. MEDIUM – write 1,000 words over a two-hour period between 8.30 p.m. and 10.30 p.m.
3. LOW – write 500 words over a one-hour period between 9.30 p.m. and 10.30 p.m.

If you are exhausted on Monday, you may choose the low or medium option. But once you get going, perhaps you hit flow and manage the high workload after all.

### *INSIGHT 10: ADD A STICK TO YOUR WEEKLY PLANNING*

'I'm so glad that I came through this time, Mum. I would have been gutted if I'd had to hand over my Féile tickets to Gillian. The threat of losing out on that has been enough to keep me on track and smash all of my study goals. Thank God the bet is over and I can stop worrying about losing those tickets.'

Teenage Grace kicked off her shoes and settled in smugly to watch her favourite sitcom. Since the tickets to that year's most awesome concert were safely in my hands, and the Leaving Cert was over, my younger self felt relaxed and was waiting for her grades to be announced . . .

Every week you may set intentions for activities for the week ahead. However, I would hazard a guess that there won't be any huge consequences if you don't get the job done, aside from a bit of self-berating. If you are good at post-rationalization (telling yourself a convincing story as to why it is okay not to show up for yourself daily), self-berating won't get you back on the horse. It will also make you feel bad, and encourage a narrative that you have failed. If you know what I am talking about here, it might be time you add a stick into your weekly planning as a ***commitment device***.

> Incorporating a stick into your weekly planning means that if you don't meet your intended targets, you have to give up something of tangible worth.

Incorporating 'punishments' that involve the loss of hard-earned cash – or giving up something you were looking forward to – is a great way to make sure you follow through on your planned activities. It brings the costs associated with not completing an activity into the present day. You lose cash now versus only losing out on a goal that won't be realized for five more years anyway.

The pain involved in the commitment device is immediate. It puts 'skin in the game'. There is a lot of hard evidence that suggests that commitment devices modify hard-to-change behaviours.[21] Just anticipating the loss keeps the goal fresh in your mind.

***TOP TIP: PUTTING A COMMITMENT DEVICE INTO PRACTICE***

**How:** Commit to handing over cold hard cash or something else of value in the event that you do not complete an activity.

**Who:** Make the commitment to yourself, a friend, a family member, co-worker or online.

**What happens if you fail:** You lose the cash or item of value you have committed. In practice, it can go to a charity, or you can even pledge to give to a cause that you really disagree with. For example, those who are anti-guns could promise to give money to the National Rifle Association, and those who are anti-hunting could pledge to donate to a hunting club. This may be more effective than promises of charitable giving. Why? Because to give money to a cause that you hate would mean you are acting in a way that is out of line with how you see yourself. Your ego helps ensure that you avoid doing this because if you did there would be an unpalatable psychological cost.

**Online resource:** If you are interested in commitment devices, it is worth checking out stickK.com, which allows you to create a commitment contract online to ensure you follow through with your intentions. At the time of writing, almost 500,000 commitments have been created on the site, and almost 50 million dollars have been pledged. You can customize the goal you want to work towards (whether it's finding a new career or running a marathon) and then decide on how much money you will lose if you don't follow through on your plans. If you do need a stick to be automatically administered when you miss your commitments, then stickK.com may work for you.

## REACHING YOUR GOAL

Rebalancing costs and benefits so that they occur now rather than in the future is the key to ensuring you carry out your planned activities and realize your big-thinking goal. Always remember that time-sinkers drag you down. They may be fun in the moment, but they will cost you dearly by stealing time that could be invested in realizing ME+.

In this chapter, we've explored and identified where you will find the time to invest in activities that move you towards ME+. Reflect on the ten behavioural science insights, and think about which one you'd like to work on first. These insights can help you stay the course, and should be referred to at times when you are struggling to keep motivated.

Let's recap . . .

***INSIGHT 1: REBALANCING IMMEDIATE COSTS AND BENEFITS***

The time you will devote to your small steps has a cost now, and the benefits are far in the future. Setting yourself carrots and sticks for achieving tasks can help you see these long-term costs and benefits in the present.

***INSIGHT 2: CULTIVATE SELF-BELIEF***

Take time to cultivate self-belief, safe in the knowledge that it is malleable. When starting difficult tasks, remind yourself that the uncertainty you may feel about your abilities is transitory, and will disappear if you keep taking small steps towards your big-thinking goal.

### *INSIGHT 3: GIVE YOURSELF EXTRA TIME*

Scale up the timings you have suggested for individual tasks by 1.5, to allow yourself more time than you think you need.

### *INSIGHT 4: RECOMMIT REGULARLY TO YOUR BIG-THINKING GOAL*

Set aside time regularly to bring your big-thinking goal into clear focus. Making salient the benefits of the time you are devoting to your new journey will mean it is more likely that you keep showing up.

### *INSIGHT 5: MEANING IS A MOTIVATOR*

Identify the meaning of the work ME+ will do, and bring it to mind regularly to help you stay motivated.

### *INSIGHT 6: WHAT GETS MEASURED GETS DONE*

Do regular post-mortems of the activities you have committed to, as this will help you assess and identify the obstacles that are holding you back.

### *INSIGHT 7: LUCK VERSUS EFFORT*

When reflecting on how tasks have gone and whether you succeeded or failed, consider whether the outcome was shaped more by luck or effort. This allows you to see more clearly the occasions when your decision-making caused the outcome, versus factors outside your control.

### *INSIGHT 8: MIND YOUR EMOTIONS*

When making decisions that will significantly affect your big-thinking journey, always do so with a cool head. This will give you the best opportunity of accurately assessing the long-term costs, benefits and risks, rather than acting on fleeting emotions.

***INSIGHT 9: IT'S NOT ALL OR NOTHING***

Consider creating high, medium and low workload aims for the activities you plan to do, so that when it comes to doing the task, you can complete the version that best matches your energy that day. Small progress is better than no progress.

***INSIGHT 10: ADD A STICK TO YOUR WEEKLY PLANNING***

If smaller carrots and sticks do not work to keep you on track, consider commitment devices, with a harder punishment like the loss of hard-earned cash or something else that is valuable.

To help you on your journey experimenting with these ten behavioural science insights, begin by choosing one that sounds easy and appealing. Pay attention to the benefits that this insight brings in terms of accomplishing your planned activities on time. If you see no benefit after one week, stop doing it and choose another insight. If it does work, keep doing it, and add a second insight to your regime. These insights are not mutually exclusive, and by taking a trial-and-error approach, you can build up an arsenal of tools to help you work better and keep you on the path to success.

I know for sure that if you commit to this strategy, you'll be far more likely to take regular small steps and realize your big-thinking goal. Not only are there oodles of behavioural science research papers that convince me that's the case, but I also have my own lived and learned experience.

As a teenager, my mum was there to motivate me, and she unknowingly drew on many lessons of behavioural science to help me stay on the path to university. Mum made accomplishing great things so much easier, despite my tendency to favour happiness today over contentment tomorrow.

My preference for choosing fun today over a big-thinking goal of tomorrow is still a knee-jerk reaction. How do I address this limitation in my psychology? In the same ways I have pointed you towards in this chapter. I took the general learnings from the behavioural sciences literature and applied them to myself, one by one. After a week, I assessed if the change I had made had made a positive difference in my behaviour. If it did, I continued with it. If not, I tried something else. Simple!

I am here – as a living and breathing experiment – to tell you that it's worked for me. And if it worked for me, it can work for you too!

Happy intervening!

Before we move on, make sure that you:

- Do a time audit and identify time-sinkers that you can free yourself from.
- Select one behavioural science insight that you will incorporate into your daily life from tomorrow.

## FIVE FAB BEHAVIOURAL SCIENCE CONCEPTS MENTIONED IN THIS CHAPTER

1 **Carrots and sticks:** Rewards and punishments that are used to induce behavioural change.

2 **Planning fallacy:** The tendency for people to underestimate the time that it will take them to do any activity, even if they know that similar activities have taken them longer than their estimates in the past.

3 **Affect heuristic:** A mental shortcut that causes people to take actions or make decisions quickly while influenced by their current emotions.

4 **Compromise effect:** The tendency to avoid extreme choices when making decisions.

5 **Commitment device:** A pledge that an individual makes now which alters the costs and benefits of choices made in the future.

# CHAPTER 4

# INSIDE

It was September 1997, and I had managed to get into university to study computer science. There was a lot of fuss made in my family, particularly by my mum. She oscillated between mega proud and mega sad, celebrating and lamenting the loss of her youngest child in equal measure.

Because I had attended a school where few girls went to university, nobody had bothered to tell me that girls normally don't pursue science, technology or engineering at university. This was a stereotype that I was never presented with, and so I never internalized it. In fact, I had never really thought about what a computer scientist should look like, and I hadn't noticed that all of my role models over in Silicon Valley were male. It should, then, have been quite the surprise to attend my first Java coding lecture on a wet Monday morning at 9 a.m. only to find that, of the 150+ students on my course, fewer than ten were female. I say *should* have been, but again I didn't really notice.

My lack of awareness of the stereotypes was to my benefit. These kinds of social stereotypes usually form expectations about what sort of life we should lead. But social stereotypes have next to nothing to do with our skills, abilities or hard preferences. Or, to put it another way, girls are told so often that they don't like computer science and they are no good at it, that eventually they start to believe it – even though there is no evidence to suggest that girls are any less suited to computer science than boys are.

*Sigh.*

We have explored how the human need for immediate gratification can stop you fulfilling your big-thinking goal. Now we will look at how a number of cognitive biases have the potential to make you veer off course, too.

> Cognitive biases are errors in our thinking that occur because of our brains' attempts to simplify the world and make decisions quickly.

Some of these biases are caused by remembering past events inaccurately, and others are down to the limits of our attention, meaning we pay attention to only a selection of what is happening in the world around us.

Cognitive biases can affect your ME+ journey by holding you back and preventing you from taking the small steps needed for progress. Whether we like to admit it or not, we all have biases: how we view the world has been shaped by our experiences up to this point. When I was growing up, many girls avoided science, technology and engineering because of ***stereotype bias***. Cognitive biases will have shaped key aspects of the big-thinking planning you conducted in Chapter 2. These biases are worth discussing. Remember, your cognitive biases are *yours*. They are different from biases that are held by other people which can hinder your progress. We'll get to those in the next chapter, but for now we're going to focus on *your* biases.

If you are rolling your eyes at the idea that cognitive biases are holding you back and you're thinking, 'I don't have any biases, I see the world for what it is,' I am afraid you're wrong. And that eye-rolling is probably caused by the ***bias blind spot***![1]

The bias blind spot is our tendency to see ourselves as less affected by biases in comparison with other people. For those afflicted, cognitive biases are other people's problem, and they themselves are above them. What's more, if this book has whetted your appetite for all things behavioural science, you may be more likely to fall victim to this particular blind spot. As you learn more about the litany of biases that affect people's daily decision-making, it's easy to fool yourself into thinking that they don't apply to you. Try not to fall into this trap!

But if it's easy to spot biases, why is it so hard to stop them from slowing down your progress? Many of these biases are engaged by System 1, your fast brain, at an unconscious level. So while it's easy to understand that we all have biases, it's not easy to stop ourselves from having them.

The good news is that while it is difficult to rewire our brains to avoid bias, it is not impossible. Extra effort to spot these biases popping up should be made when we are making big decisions or approaching major milestones. Behavioural science has taught me that I can overcome cognitive biases at key moments by acknowledging their existence, slowing right down and making a conscious effort to avoid them. In this chapter, along with drawing attention to the areas of your big-thinking plan that may be most affected by cognitive biases, I will provide behavioural science insights on how they can be mitigated. You can choose to embrace all of the insights, or select a few that you view as the most relevant for your own journey. All I ask is that, once you have selected the insights you would like to action, you pay attention to whether they have benefits for your big-thinking journey.

### *INSIGHT 1: BIASES IN YOUR NETWORKS AND INFLUENCERS*

Back in 1998, as a dedicated student of computer science, I took to assignments in my Java programming course with gusto. Each one would begin with a project idea, given to us by a professor, that we would have to turn into a real-life object. I built simple games, designed automatic lighting, and more. To learn what we needed to know we had regular two-hour coding labs. I often devoted many hours to ensuring I had got my projects right. It was on one of those occasions, about midway through my first term, that I collared my professor at the end of class for extra help – something wasn't working but I had no idea what was going wrong. We had been together for more than an hour, with him still not having helped me find a resolution, when, in an attempt to break the silence, I asked a seemingly innocent question.

'Do you think there is an issue with there being so few women in computer science, as this is the field that determines the types of technologies that will be created in the future . . .?' I trailed off as I saw my professor grimace. At that precise moment, the computer spat out another error.

In Chapter 2, I offered suggestions for how to get out into the world and get to know some new people that can guide you and give you access to new opportunities. You came up with the names of three people that you would meet over the next three months (see p. 54).

Take a look back at that list now. Write next to each name the following information about each person: gender, age, race, country of birth and where they were educated. If you do not know, give it your best guess. Do they all share a lot of similar characteristics? If so, you may have been bitten by stereotype bias. You may have a certain (false) belief about who can help you move ahead in your journey, and it is causing you to seek out interactions that align with this stereotype of what a 'good' person looks like. Some common stereotypes link entrepreneurship to masculine traits, technological savviness to youth, and occupations involving care to women.

The people on your list may also have an awful lot of similarities to you. Write down any observable characteristics about you that you view as major parts of your identity, and compare them to those of the people on your list. I did this thought experiment with Erica, a friend of mine. Erica is an ambitious thirty-something climbing the management ranks in retail. Her list ended up being a cast of females around her own age in retail, who were all flat-lining in middle management. While education and race varied a bit, each woman had children. Actually, each woman had exactly two children. And guess what? Erica also has two children.

Behind Erica's choices was the need to have her sentiments confirmed that being a working mother is hard – too hard, in fact, to pursue her ME+ with gusto. And yes, to some extent, Erica is right. It is hard to juggle work and children, and it's even harder as a woman. However, pursuing this strategy would not have allowed Erica to expand her network as she had intended it to. Rather, it would have given her a healthy dose of confirmation bias and ended up as a time-sinker. I am not saying that each of these women would not have had something valuable to say to Erica. But there would have been considerable overlap in what they had to tell her. Swapping in some more diverse choices would therefore be worthwhile.

Say hello to ***similarity bias***. This is our tendency to surround ourselves with people just like ourselves. We like our own company very much, and want to replicate it over and over again. These folk tend to have similar viewpoints to us, making it much easier for us to confirm our ideas as brilliant – in other words, to be affected by confirmation bias. While a group of similar people may challenge you, they will all challenge you in roughly the same way. This may work out well if your group has power and can hire you for the activities you want to be doing. However, assuming the journey you want to take is about personal growth, I encourage you to think again about who you spend your time with or seek advice from.

One of the easiest ways to grow quickly is to get feedback from people with diverse backgrounds and life experiences.

Why? Different types of thinkers give you different types of advice. If you are setting up a business, do you want only one type of customer? If you are designing a product, have you thought about how women's needs are different from men's? If you are writing an article, do you want it to be read only by people in their twenties – or older people, too? If you are advancing in your firm, do you want to be supported by only one type of colleague? Whatever you are doing, your mind should be as open as possible to all opportunities.

There is an intuitive reason why diverse teams are better problem-solvers, better at predicting the future, and more innovative.[2] Their members have lived different lives, pursued different skill sets, and each of them has a different stock of knowledge. They do not all think the same way. They do not all repeat the same ideas. As a result, they can get to the front much quicker than teams with only one type of background, skill set or knowledge base. Combat similarity and confirmation biases by reassessing the people that you have chosen as your potential influencers. If need be, make some changes so that the viewpoints you hear are different from your own – and from each other – giving you a higher probability of success.

The best managers I have observed are always willing to hire people that are better than themselves. There are two reasons why this is a great idea. First, the average productivity of the team is mechanically raised. Second, having a colleague that performs better than you raises your own game. However, lots of managers would not make this call. Why? Ego causes them to want to be around people who have similar or lower levels of performance to themselves. When choosing your new network, do not fall into the ego trap. Remember that you are on a learning curve, and to acquire the expertise that you need it can be helpful to be around people who have far greater knowledge and perform much better than you do.

There is a lot of evidence to suggest that who we surround ourselves with determines how we perform. In their 2009 study of cashiers in a US supermarket chain, Alexandre Mas and Enrico Moretti provide clear evidence that people change their level of effort depending on who they are working with. The researchers found that having an above-average worker starting their shift increased the effort of the other workers by 1 per cent. They also found that the high-productivity worker coming on to the floor only increased the productivity for the co-workers who could see them. Productivity here was defined as the number of items scanned per second.

Think about the role models and peers you expose yourself to.

There are two reasons why it is important to do this.

First, the people you surround yourself with will hopefully be sharing their knowledge with you, so it is important that you seek out those of a higher ability or who know different things than you do. Don't worry too much about being the smartest person in the room. If you are, it probably means you're not advancing much.

Second, you are likely to mimic the behaviour of those around you without realizing it. The people you surround yourself with will expose you to new norms, and this can cause you to develop new habits.[3]

One explanation offered by Mas and Moretti for the rise in productivity observed in the cashiers is social pressure. Social pressure can change behaviour, as it sets a new normal. There is a reason why children in school do better if put into classrooms with children who perform better than them. It's the same reason why people are more likely to regularly exercise if they are part of a group. And it's why we end up working later when we look around and see that our colleagues aren't rushing to go home.

We like to follow in the footsteps of those around us. But most of the time we are not aware that we are following others – instead we think we are doing things for ourselves.

Identifying the helpful – but also the *unhelpful* – social norms you surround yourself with is a useful exercise. What social norms are in place among the people you spend most of your leisure time with? Do you engage in activities together that encourage personal growth? Or do you spend the majority of your time lolling around in front of the TV or on bar stools? Are you supportive of one another's ambitions? Or is there jealousy and mean-spirited competition?

The people we expose ourselves to can change our behaviour and skills without us even realizing.

We are the product of those who we surround ourselves with. We mimic our networks and ingrain new habits as a result. Remember this when reassessing the list of people you plan to contact and connect with over the next three months.

### *INSIGHT 2: DID YOU PICK THE RIGHT BIG-THINKING GOAL?*

During my first year at university, I worked in a women's fashion retail store. I loved that job because of my fantastic colleagues. It totally eclipsed all the other part-time jobs I had held previously: butcher's assistant, waitress, grocery-store till operator, and personal assistant. I moved my hours to full-time in the summer after my first year, covering week-end and evening shifts that nobody else wanted to do, while the rest of my university friends headed off to travel around the world. I spent a lot of time merchandising that summer, making the shop look great for its customers, which although it required concentration of sorts, gave me a meditation-style sense of calm.

On one of the days when I was helping rearrange the stock on the shop floor, I had an epiphany. I realized I was not enjoying my computer science degree at all. There are very few moments in my life, either before or after, that brought greater clarity. All of a sudden, I knew that I was on the wrong path!

At this point you may be questioning the big-thinking goal you have identified. If you are, I am sending you a virtual fist bump because these doubts are worth speaking about. After all, if cognitive biases crept in and influenced your choice of mentors – what's to say your goal isn't a victim of the same biases? The truth is, it probably is.

The good news? If you pursue your chosen goal anyway, you will look back later in life and label it a good choice. This is ***choice-supportive bias***.

When we look back on our choices, we tend to think that they were the right ones.

We don't know the reason why people exhibit choice-supportive bias; however, my gut instinct tells me that it was born out of the need for us to sleep at night without regret – with a clear conscience about our actions. Post-choice rationalization allows us to cleanse our minds of our many transgressions. If you are happy with your goal, you may as well try for it.

However, for those who want to reflect on their big-thinking goal a little bit longer, consider the following biases and how they may have affected your goal choice.

First up, the ***ambiguity effect***. It is worth thinking again about why you have chosen your specific big-thinking goal. Might you be looking at options that have a very clear path of progression, rather than exploring paths which may be less certain? Do you lack information about the options that are available to you? The ambiguity effect causes people to select a ME+ option where there is a known likelihood of success, rather than potentially better options for which the probability of success is less certain.

Or are you simply following in the footsteps of those you surround yourself with? Are you doing this because you truly want to be doing the same thing with your life as they are? Or are you succumbing to the ***bandwagon effect***, which is causing you to jump on your personal social circle's bandwagon and choose a similar occupation? It is not an accident that children often follow their parents into occupations, or choose jobs more regularly that involve similar tasks to those carried out by their parents.[4] But knowing someone who does a job and enjoys it doesn't mean that you will too if you follow in their footsteps.

It's worth reflecting on the mechanics of your chosen goal. What's the day-to-day grind like? Will you really enjoy engaging in the activities required to get the job done? I have met many an undergraduate at the LSE who hated studying economics. They are doing it solely because their parents or teachers have told them they will 'get a good job afterwards'. In this case, *good job* means 'loads of cash' or 'safe' – rather than 'loads of happiness'. In a world where our working lives are longer than ever before, finding a job that you get some joy out of is important.

On the other hand, there is ***reactance bias***. When I look back with a critical eye over my own work-life choices, I see its effects all over my CV. For those of us who don't like to conform just for the sake of it, the bandwagon effect can be replaced by reactance bias. For me, it comes into play when I have an idea that I think is wonderful, and then some kind-hearted soul tells me it is not the best use of my time at that point in my career. What happens? I double down in reaction to the do-gooder's attempt to constrain my freedom of choice. It is one to watch for: reactance bias causes a strengthening of resolve for an alternative view, regardless of its relative advantages. Reactance bias explains why 124,109 people – the highest number by a large margin – voted for a UK polar research ship to be called *Boaty McBoatface* in 2016. For our purposes, it might cause you to choose a goal that proves a point rather than one that fulfils a passion.

> ***TOP TIP: HOW TO RECTIFY A TENDENCY FOR BIASED GOAL-SETTING***
>
> Consider the big-thinking goal you set in Chapter 2. Recall the activities that you will be engaged in if you realize that goal. Will you enjoy doing them day after day until you are ready to retire?
>
> If you answered 'yes', this is fantastic.
>
> If you answered 'no', you should revisit Chapter 2 and the goal-setting process.

#### *INSIGHT 3: LOSS AVERSION*

Although I realized in the summer of 1998 that I was on the wrong path pursuing computer science, it was quite some time until I finally got around to telling my mum of my intention to find a new path. The delay in this communication was driven by classic ***loss aversion***.

> Loss aversion – and more specifically how we imagine we will experience losses – has the potential to delay conversations that would accelerate our journey.

For example, if your goal is to get promoted, and you imagined a timeline of five years – why is five the magic number? Why not four years? Or three years? Can you reassess the factors that drove you to establish this timeline?

For most of us, the promotion criteria we face at work are what an economist would call 'noisy'. That means it is hard to say exactly what needs to be done to get promoted. It is hard to know when you have ticked the right boxes. The noisier the criteria are, the more often you will see people getting promoted earlier than expected – and others much later than expected. Why? Well, to get promoted you need to put yourself forward. And whether you put yourself forward strongly depends on your level of ***risk aversion***.

For most jobs in the day-to-day, your level of risk aversion does not affect your performance (save for folk defending our streets against crime, our houses against fire, or betting recklessly on securities on a trading floor). It is therefore less than ideal that it disrupts people's career progression. It is also not ideal that women are typically less risk-averse than men; highly educated folk are not as risk-averse as less-educated folk; ethnic minorities are more risk-averse than white individuals in the US; and the wealthy are less risk-averse than the poor.[5] To put it another way, the door is wide open for rich, white, university-educated males to create an attainment gap, simply because on average they roll the dice more often and take a punt as compared to others. It has nothing to do with skills or ability – it boils down to how comfortable the person feels with risk.

Risk aversion can also affect the type of job a person is likely to apply for. With any job advert, there is usually a lengthy job criteria list. The truth? It is really hard for the evaluators to determine whether or not a person that applies meets the criteria. So how can someone know when they have made the cut?

Throwing my hat in the ring says more about my levels of confidence and risk aversion than anything about my ability to do the job. And do you want to hear something interesting? The correlation between competence and confidence is super low. Combining more than 150 correlations which reported on self-rated intelligence (i.e. how confident someone is in their own ability) and actual intelligence, Alexander Freund and Nadine Kasten's 2012 study estimates the commonality of these two variables to be just 10 per cent.

But are more confident and risk-loving people wrong to put themselves forward? Ultimately, the answer is 'no'. This may irritate you, but they are acting in their own best interests, given the costs and benefits that they face. The probability of success is positive – because in any process where the criteria for success are noisy, there is a positive chance (or probability) of success when you put yourself forward. It may be tiny, but it is positive. And for those who aren't hampered by the anticipatory fear of rejection, they can roll with the punches that come with failure. They may even get a rush out of trying to frame their expertise in a way that meets the criteria. The only cost for this group is the time associated with throwing their hat in the ring. If this cost is low enough, they will put themselves forward. They are the kind of person who keeps their CV up to date, after all.

So why don't more people embrace a positive probability of success? The answer is that risk aversion is partially driven by loss aversion. Most people feel losses more than gains. Furthermore, risk aversion is driven by ***anticipatory loss aversion***, which is about how painful you *expect* being turned down to make you feel.

> Anticipating failure is a negative life experience in itself. It is so powerful that the mere thought of failing can stop people even trying in the first place.

Risk aversion, loss aversion and low confidence are a dangerous combination that can stop people moving forward. Women tend to be more loss-averse than men.[6] While the reason for this is unknown, I have a theory as to why men might be less loss-averse – and it has to do with dating. Traditionally, when teens begin dating, the majority of the time it is the boys that have the knee-wobbling job of asking a girl on a date. Very early on in their development, boys get used to dealing with rejection – and they come to realize it is not as bad as they expected it to be. This is a fantastic lesson that will result in some amazing benefits all the way through life.

Risk-loving, confident people are not going to stop putting their hat in the ring too early and often. Some organizations try and circumvent this by having regular feedback sessions, but the sheer number of overly confident extroverts at the top of those same organizations signals that this system is less than perfect.[7] Of course, if you are freelancing or setting up a company, there isn't the luxury of safeguarding by a human resources department. So if you are an introvert with a caring demeanour, you really need to do everything that you can to restack the odds in your favour.

**_TOP TIP: RESTACKING THE ODDS IN YOUR FAVOUR_**

1 Reframe putting yourself forward when there is an uncertain outcome. Remind yourself that the probability of success is positive. It may be low, but it is always positive.
2 Never focus on the outcome. Focus on your decision-making process. It is only your decision-making that you can control.
3 Remember that anticipating failure feels worse than failure itself. You will always learn something from the process, even if you fail.
4 Remind yourself that continued exposure to loss aversion will make you realize that losing isn't as painful as you expected it to be. In other words, it will get easier!

### INSIGHT 4: KNOW YOUR VALUE

When trying to make a high-stakes decision such as deciding whether or not to quit your chosen university degree, taking your mind off it can sometimes help you make a better decision. Although not an activity I would recommend today to decompress, while pondering my dilemma in 1998 the activity I found myself doing a bit too often was shopping.

Long before I was aware of behavioural science, I became aware of ***anchoring*** while browsing my favourite department store in my home city of Cork. It was there that I saw the most beautiful black leather bag. I thought about how it would placate me if I did decide to return to my boring computer science degree. My thoughts see-sawed back and forth during that summer – one minute I wanted to do something totally different, the next I wanted to continue at university. And this bag could carry all the books I needed for uni if I stayed, along with the notebooks I insisted on carting around. However, this same beautiful leather handbag carried a price tag of £500 (Ireland was still some months away from adopting the euro). Then one day I glimpsed a sign which told me that it was 50 per cent off all handbags. Do you think that the '50 per cent off' sign caused me to view the bag as a bargain? Do you think that I would have viewed the bag in exactly the same way if it had been priced £250 in the first place?

These questions link to the well-established behavioural science concept of anchoring, in which people over-rely on pre-existing information when making decisions. So (to use the example of my shopping experience) a bag priced at £500 with 50 per cent off is perceived to be a better bargain than a bag originally tagged £250. It also explains why many of us jump online for those regular flash sales they have these days.

Take a moment to reflect on what drives how much you get paid right now. Are you being paid your worth? Is anchoring determining how much you are taking home?

> How much we have been paid in the past is a major mental reference point when we make decisions about how much we are worth today.

Let's imagine that Justin is accepting a new job and he's been asked to state his salary expectations. Justin is going to give this a lot of thought. He will take into account the knowledge he has about the firm and the standard of living he's hoping to achieve, and he may even get advice from friends and family. But despite this, his current pay will be one of the main factors that drives what he asks for. He may end up asking for 10, 20 or even 30 per cent over this number, but it is still the primary reference point in his negotiations.

Our current salary is such a powerful anchor that it may even stop us leaving our current job. This is certainly the case for my friend Cara. Cara is so obsessed with securing a salary that is better than her current financial package that she has turned down many opportunities that would help her get to where she wants to go more quickly. Fair enough, I suppose. Nobody wants to take a pay cut. But do you want to hear something funny? Cara *hates* her job. She barely sleeps or sees her friends, and she doesn't enjoy the work she has to do at all. Cara's anchor is keeping her stuck and unhappy.

The superpowers of anchoring also imply that it is possible you are being underpaid. You may be selling your innovative product too cheaply. The rates you are charging for consultancy work might be too low. And you may not ask for enough of a raise during your annual review simply because you are anchored to your current salary.

How can you tackle this? You need to reset your anchors. In some cases, for example if you are selling a physical product, this will be very easy to do, as the prices of your competitors are known. For freelancers offering a service, rates are often not published and they are agreed upon when you connect with a new client. This means that with each new client there is an opportunity to reset your anchor. Why not let them suggest the rate, and see if it is higher than you have previously been charging? Or why not increase your rate by 5 per cent and monitor the reaction?

If you are working in a large firm, very often the distribution of pay across job types is published, allowing you to easily compare your salary to that of your peers. If the pay distribution is not available, this is information that you can gather from your network and (if you are brave enough) by pursuing an outside offer. How we are rated within our own firm is affected by other people's cognitive biases. The fastest way to blast a fuzzy or negative perception of you away is to get an outside offer for a job that is clearly better than your current role. After that? You are due a conversation with your boss!

### INSIGHT 5: WHY DON'T WE ASK FOR WHAT WE NEED MORE OFTEN?

In the end, I didn't have to speak to Mum about wanting to drop out of computer science. Why? I spoke to one of my professors, who was nicknamed Java James.

The start of my second year was only a few days away, but it was still tumbleweeds in the corridors of my university. Only Java James's door was ajar on the departmental corridor. With stubbornness embedded in my DNA I sidled up to his office, confident that I was going to quit for sure. Then

I knocked and entered Java James's office without being called in. No point wasting any more time . . . I had the rest of my life to get on with.

'Ah, Grace,' he greeted me. 'How has summer treated you?'

'It's been good, Java James – so good that I've decided not to return to university. I didn't miss computer science while I was away, and I don't want to spend time studying something I don't love.'

'Love?' he chuckled, at my announcement. 'Anything worth learning is going to be difficult, Grace. You aren't supposed to love every second of it. I doubt any of your peers missed class either. We have a hiatus over summer for precisely that reason: the course is meant to be intense. But perhaps you're just not cut out for it.'

I've already mentioned that my choices in life have been frequently shaped by reactance bias – a tendency to show up for something simply because someone says you should not do it. Perhaps that kicked in. Whatever it was, Java James's response grated pretty hard on me given that I had walked through his door ready to walk off the computer science course.

'Of course I'm cut out for it!' I bristled. 'It's just so boring, and I suppose it is pretty hard to boot. I can't see myself thriving over the next three years.'

'Hmmm, well it doesn't have to be all or nothing, you know. What do you want to do instead?'

'I want to . . . I don't know. Can you help?'

Java James talked me through my options and I ended up studying economics alongside computer science for the rest of my degree. Simply by asking for help, I got what I needed: a university path that was more suited to the interests I had at the time.

We don't ask for help often enough, even when we really need it.

From getting advice on how to think big to asking for the conditions that we deserve in the workplace, we often baulk at the idea of that level of intimacy in a professional conversation. We dislike feeling vulnerable. We fear the uncertainty of what the response may be, and put it off for too long.

Is the thought of having a conversation with your boss about promotion filling you with dread? Is the thought of asking for help in accelerating your goal making you want to cancel the meeting with your mentor? Maybe broaching the subject of salary anchoring with human resources gives you goosebumps? Some of us fear that asking will make us look too greedy or too needy.

Take conversations about increased income. I have heard so many people relay how much they love their work and how wrong it seems to ask for more pay. And many owners of small- and medium-sized enterprises avoid having this conversation with their clients in case they look money-grabbing. But this is a very upside-down way of looking at the world. When we go to work each day and produce something of value, we deserve to be paid at a rate that reflects the value added. Our work is a transaction that should be mutually beneficial. Leaving money on the floor with your employer or client is not the right way to think about avoiding greed. Accept getting paid your worth, and quell any fears that you are being greedy by paying your taxes and giving to charity.

Or perhaps it is not a fear of greed that is holding you back. Perhaps you have faith that your boss will let you know when the time is right for any advancement or pay rise. That they are watching you closely and will ensure that you get your just deserts. Is this realistic? Not always. It might be that you are affected by the ***curse of knowledge***. Try and be cognizant of the fact that when you know something is true, it can be difficult for you to imagine not knowing it. You think that your boss has the same insights as you do regarding how good you are. You sit at work all day long and assume that your manager sees how productive you are, and tailors their advice appropriately.

The curse of knowledge can also lead to something called the ***tiara syndrome***. This is the expectation that if you work hard every day, a time will come when you are rewarded and someone will effectively put a tiara on your head. But the people who you are relying on to give you this reward are navigating their own paths in work. They are busy. Perhaps they themselves are beginning to think big. So it is up to you to draw attention to your value and your desire to move forward. It is always your responsibility to ask for what you need in terms of advice and guidance.

> It is up to you to join the dots and highlight your progress, to ensure you are adequately rewarded.

Showing others the progress you are making and where you want to go will bring more opportunities your way. Better yet, identify opportunities yourself that are mutually beneficial: remember that it is always best to understand the perspective of others when making requests for help.

#### *INSIGHT 6: TWO-WAY CONVERSATION*

Out of a class of 150+ students, getting individual feedback on my work during my undergraduate degree wasn't something that came easily. The conversation I had with Java James in the summer of 1998 was an outlier, born out of needing a resolution to my see-sawing (combined with escalating credit card bills from all the retail therapy I couldn't afford). By the second year of my undergraduate degree, we were about sixty students – a lot had failed and/or dropped out – so it was much easier to get feedback. Still, it wasn't necessarily forthcoming. I had to actively seek it out once I had recommitted to studying computer science.

Back then, just like now, I had little time for people telling me what I did correctly at length. I preferred critical feedback. I once sought feedback from a rather nervous teaching assistant on an assessment that had me design an elevator user interface that could operationalize an elevator in a department store. He must have talked for twenty minutes about the aspects of the assessment I had carried out correctly. I don't recall the exact words he said, but it was so sweet and light that I tuned out and played circus music in my head to pass the time. He eventually realized I wasn't listening, and asked if there were specific things about the assessment that I wanted to discuss. He seemed baffled when I responded, 'Yes, tell me what the awful parts were!' with a level of enthusiasm people normally reserve for getting good news. He rose to the challenge and we spent a much more interesting twenty minutes tearing apart my assignment.

In Chapter 3, I emphasized the importance of giving yourself regular feedback as a way to combat a variety of cognitive biases. It is also valuable to seek feedback from others for the very same reason. Today, I view feedback as the best mechanism by which to improve, as it allows you to discover strengths and difficulties in your skills and abilities that you didn't know you had – and also how to play to your comparative advantages. I still prefer to devote more time to critical feedback, but over time I have recognized the benefits of learning what I am doing right through a fresh pair of eyes. After all, how else will you know what your comparative advantages actually are? If I got to choose, I would split feedback time 80:20 in favour of criticism.

The value of seeking feedback from others in terms of promoting learning and enhancing performance has long been discussed in the behavioural science literature.[8] If you recognize that you are suffering from anchoring, the curse of knowledge or tiara syndrome, or if you are hamstrung by loss aversion, actively seeking feedback can be your friend. Someone who refuses to pursue or listen to feedback offered in a manner that is non-threatening is someone who should never hold a role where they interact with or lead people.

If you are serious about progressing over the medium term, seeking feedback gives you the best chance of achieving your goal. Why? If you ask the right people for feedback, they can make salient the actions that you need to take to get ahead quicker, and hold up a mirror to your current blind spots. This is invaluable.

> It is your own responsibility to seek feedback regularly and with a specific agenda.

Who the best people are to seek feedback from depends on what your specific big-thinking goal is. If you are staying in a similar role but plan to accelerate your career, feedback from managers and executives within your firm is relevant. If you plan to improve the product you are offering in your business, your current customers and potential new customers are relevant. If you are changing jobs entirely, people who are currently in a role like the one you want are worth talking to.

The best feedback that you can get involves a critical aspect, and highlights the areas in which you need to improve. Don't expect the person offering this type of feedback to give you a solution to every problem they have identified. If they do, that is a bonus, but their job is not to solve the problems they raise for you. Try not to view critical feedback emotionally. Depending on the personalities involved, emotions can render the feedback process redundant. There is a reason why meta-analysis suggests that over one-third of feedback causes performance decreases.[9] So if somebody says you do something poorly, don't become overly focused on the fact that you do something poorly – concentrate instead on what steps you need to take to improve. Remember that the affect heuristic (when the emotions you are experiencing at the time influence your decision-making) may determine how you hear feedback. So if you feel emotional during the process, take notes and reflect on what was said when you have a cooler head. Assume that the person giving the feedback had good intentions, and try to see things from their point of view.

Always approach feedback with an open mind and a thick skin, regardless of how clumsy the person advising you happens to be with their words. People who aren't well versed in the politics of how to deliver feedback are often the folk who have the most astute comments to make. It is also important to disentangle content from fluff. Regardless of how the conversation goes – clumsy or otherwise – every person you meet is still only one data point. Any criticism raised should be verified by additional feedback sources or objective data before you go and upend your entire goal and big-thinking plan.

If you recognize a problem identified in your feedback session as accurate, make sure to remind yourself that it can be addressed. A problem in your performance is not a fixed trait, and it can be modified by adjusting behaviour and actions. Whatever it is, it can be changed with effort.

Do watch out for ***attentional bias*** in any feedback session. This is when your perception of the feedback you are receiving is skewed by whatever is dominating your mind at that time. In the same way that we are more sensitive to the smell of bread when we are hungry, you may pay more attention to any criticism that aligns with your existing view of where your weaknesses are. Note-taking can help here, as can giving your mentor a chance to speak freely at the beginning of the session without interruption, rather than immediately guiding their commentary. Pay attention to whether their attention is drawn to areas that you don't necessarily focus on yourself. Of course, there is no reason to believe that the mentor isn't also a victim of attentional bias, but assuming you rely on more than one person for feedback, this should not pose a major problem.

Feedback from your diverse external network is a golden opportunity for you to identify elements of your plan that are not working out, and which need to be refined or sunk. You must avoid the sunk cost fallacy – when you continue with a plan simply because you have already invested time in trying to execute it. Academics succumb to the sunk cost fallacy when they continue to write a paper even after they notice that something nearly identical has been published elsewhere. Inventors are victims of the sunk cost fallacy when they continue to invest money in a product, even after becoming aware that an identical product has already been launched. Freelancers commit the sunk cost fallacy when they keep chasing a client who asks for endless meetings but is yet to commission them for any paid work.

If you receive feedback that causes you to believe that an element of what you are doing isn't working, it's time to reflect on how you can pivot to what does work. For the academic in the above example, they need to determine how they can add value compared to the paper that beat them to the punch. For the inventor, they need to go back to the drawing board and consider how they will differentiate their product. For the freelancer, they need to devote their time to approaching and nurturing new client relationships.

Remember, if you receive feedback that an element of your planning is futile, it should be verified elsewhere. After all, one person's opinion does not a trend make. You also need to remember that these pivots will take time, and that bad luck happens. But make sure you don't fall victim to the ***ostrich effect*** – that is, sticking your head in the sand and avoiding negative information that can ultimately help you.

### *TOP TIP: HOW TO SEEK FEEDBACK*

Start any session by allowing the person giving you feedback a chance to speak freely without interruption. This could be in response to a document you sent, or to a short elevator pitch of what you are trying to accomplish.

Next, ask for very specific feedback on what you are doing right, and what you should work on – noting that you are particularly interested in critical feedback. Great feedback allows you to translate the points raised into workable objectives. An objective is workable if you will easily know when you have achieved it. For instance, 'Get better at time management' is hard to track. Whereas 'Deliver project ***x*** by such-and-such a date' is very easy.

With positive feedback, a workable objective will allow you to identify which small steps you should be doing more of. If you are freelancing and receive positive feedback more than once on a specific product, you may want to consider doubling down and making this your speciality. If you are seeking to be a leader in your organization and receive positive feedback on the way you ran a meeting, you may want to self-reflect on what went right so you can make it your individual style. If you are seeking a career change and your feedback sessions repeatedly identify the same strengths, you may want to devote some time to identifying formal ways that you can signal to a new employer that you have these strengths on the CV that you submit. Signals of this kind might be formal qualifications or recognizable work experience.

For negative feedback, a workable objective will allow you to identify the small steps you need to focus on to address gaps or deficiencies in your CV or product. It is also an opportunity to identify any small steps that you should stop taking, in order to focus on those that are more likely to get you to where you need.

Along with approaching feedback with an open mind and a thick skin, it is worth encouraging the person giving the feedback to move away from vague statements towards relaying things in a straightforward manner. It is also helpful to pursue feedback in a timely fashion – when you pass key milestones like suffering a failure or experiencing a success. Feedback that is current has been shown to be more effective and more likely to be acted upon.[10]

When choosing who to elicit feedback from, the best choices are people who will encourage your ambition and genuinely help you rise above any difficulties you might have.

The selection process can involve some trial and error, but if you find yourself getting feedback that is ill-thought-out, cruel or patronizing, you can repay the feedback 'favour' by not returning for round two. After all, time is your most precious resource, so it makes sense not to schedule time-sinkers that will waste it.

### *INSIGHT 7: SAVING FACE*

I finished my computer science and economics degree with excellent grades. Mum and Dad stood proudly in the auditorium, clapping with vigour as I graduated. After the event, I was invited to my aunt's, great-aunt's, neighbour's and even a few random strangers' houses to celebrate my achievements.

But the celebrations could have been very short-lived, as I had no immediate job prospects.

Why? The first reason was that the dot-com bubble had burst, meaning that jobs in computer science were haemorrhaging rather than being created. It was hard to stand out in that market with a degree from my local university in Ireland, and I fully failed to do so.

The second reason was that I had forgotten to apply for all the 'good' jobs everyone had told me about, which my economics degree would have helped me with. These included the civil service, as well as graduate schemes in major accountancy and banking firms. Here 'good' meant pensionable, with a decent income and a shot at permanency (the golden trio for many an Irish parent).

The truth is, the application process for jobs like these happens long before graduating, and I dropped the ball way before I found myself on that graduation stage. (In fact, I realized that I should have applied only a couple of days after the closing date for most of them.) I loved economics deeply. But like friendships that come naturally or an established long-term romantic relationship, it didn't scream for attention as it all felt intuitive to me. I wasn't paying attention to the career options it opened up. And so I had missed all the key deadlines.

My need to save face in front of other people – and not admit to failing as a fully functioning adult who takes responsibility for themselves – meant that I never willingly asked for help. I sat with knots in my stomach for ten long weeks, wondering what to do. At that time, I had a job as a temporary assistant to the vice president at my university in Cork. It sounds important, but in reality I just worked Fridays to cover one of the other employees who was working flexibly. As bosses go, he was a good one. He was intelligent, enjoyed a joke and was keen to expand my network at the university. Through him, I would get to know the head of the economics department, who in the middle of my self-pity parade made the mistake of reminding me how adding economics to my undergraduate degree insulated me from market fluctuations in technology. My reaction? I broke down and confessed to having missed all of the deadlines associated with this career insurance policy. Unruffled, he suggested I apply for a master's in economics with a scholarship, as the application process was still open.

My need to save face had held me back for a while, but then this impromptu meeting with an unexpected mentor opened things up. Without this lucky meeting, I probably would have continued to save face and been stressed and idle . . . but instead I stood on the graduation stage able to reciprocate my parents' enthusiasm. I didn't have a job, but I felt pretty good about my decision to read for a master's degree in economics. Of course, we cannot rely on luck to give us mentors when we need them. It is always safer to rely on our own efforts and find them for ourselves!

More often than not, the ***saving face effect*** will cause us to slow down our personal development. Saving face is tangled up with anticipated loss aversion, but I like to disentangle them.

Anticipated loss aversion refers to the fear you expect to feel from a loss. For example, how you expect to feel personally if you do not get a promotion. Meanwhile, the saving face effect refers to the judgement you expect to get from *others* when you experience a loss. It's about what you expect other people to think about you when you do not get a promotion.

We often hold ourselves back simply because we are concerned about what other people will think and say about us.

Consider Nora, who is an extraordinarily talented creative who works in product development. Her job is to generate ideas that innovate and push the frontiers of what her firm offers their customers. And you know what? She is great at her job. But she works in an industry where the fast pace means that nobody is going to take her by the hand and walk her through the promotion process. You want to know something else? Nora is chronically under-confident. Again, the pace of her industry means that people are not telling her how wonderful she is all the time. If you stopped her colleagues in the corridor and asked them, you would hear a near-unanimous agreement that she is worth her weight in gold. Yet if you talk to Nora about her inertia, the reason she identifies is not wanting to face her colleagues in the café if (she would say 'when') she fails. I kid you not!

For all of us, a public rejection – meaning a rejection in front of colleagues, friends or family – hurts many more times than one experienced in private. Why is that? Why do people worry about what their neighbours will think if their marriage breaks down? Why do we find it hard to face our colleagues if we didn't get promoted as planned? For those of us who want to lose a few pounds, why is the idea of other people seeing us exercising in our gym gear enough to keep us at home?

It took me a long time to figure out that telling someone who cares about you that you got turned down for something that was important to you is pretty comforting. I think I was scarred from years in a school where if you didn't get something right the teachers did their best to draw attention to your agony. These days, I have a circle of confidants who make me feel better when I fail. Folk who make you feel bad about the failures you experience don't deserve to hear about them. Seriously, **** them. Anyone who makes you feel bad about putting yourself out there, rocking the boat or taking a shot at something is not going to genuinely cheer you on.

To manage these people, who unfortunately are sometimes unavoidable, where possible you should fail silently. Let them know about the promotion only when you get it. Put your hat in the ring for a job where the criteria are just out of reach, and don't tell them. Let trusted confidants only into your plans, and reduce the saving face effect by reducing the number of people who know what you are up to.

But sometimes we cannot fail silently. You may need to pitch for investors in front of a crowd, or run for election, or take part in an open tournament. Or perhaps an activity you really need to nail is public speaking. You can't very well do this by talking into a hairbrush alone in your bedroom. So what then?

First, take some comfort in knowing that people do not pay as much attention to you as you may think – we stand out in our own minds, so we often have a mistaken belief that we also hold the attention of others far more intensely and much more often than we actually do.

This is called the ***spotlight effect***, a term coined by behavioural scientist Thomas Gilovich. He and his colleagues demonstrated that, even if you are feeling embarrassed and are filled with certainty that everyone notices your anxiety, the reality is very different. People are self-involved and too caught up with their own needs to pay you much attention.[11]

You are not in the spotlight as often as you think.

Don't be disappointed by this. It is very freeing to realize that your mistakes and failures are noticed less often than you fear. And it's time you made some more.

Embrace the reality of the spotlight effect and don't let the image of how you want to be seen in public stop you doing things that can advance your plans. If you have messed up, like I did by not applying for jobs in university, seek advice from those you trust and brainstorm a solution to help you move forward.

### *INSIGHT 8: REMAINING OPEN TO NEW OPPORTUNITIES*

Today at the LSE I am surrounded by people who have tales that describe their calling to academia. I read applications from people yearning to come and read for a PhD on our famous London campus. I always admire people who have a clear idea of what their career path will be. But my path to academia was slightly different.

After graduating from my MSc in economics, I received a job offer for a research fellow role at Trinity College Dublin. The job itself was appealing for a number of reasons – I would get to work with large data sets to hone my data modelling skills, the hours were flexible, and I would have extraordinarily high levels of autonomy. It was located slap bang in the middle of Dublin (a decidedly cosmopolitan city which is small enough to get to know but large enough to retain a degree of anonymity), and I would travel to London a lot to spend time at a collaborating university. The problem? The salary was poor, and rents in Dublin were high. In August 2005, I had to make a hard phone call to Professor Normand, who had offered me the job.

'Professor Normand, many thanks for letting me know that I had a successful interview,' I began. 'I've been thinking about the offer over the last few days, but the salary is way too low to allow me to live and work in Dublin given the current rents. I was wondering, is there any room to adjust the income north a little way?'

'Grace. I didn't lie when I said that there is no room to manoeuvre your salary,' he replied. 'I would if I could. But I do think this job is a great opportunity for you. It's too good to miss, really. So while I can't increase your earnings, I can allow you to do a PhD in economics, fees paid, while you're here. Would that help get us to where we need to be?'

I had never thought about doing a PhD until that moment.

How should you approach opportunities that arise out of the blue? You can start by being aware of how ***omission bias*** and ***action bias*** affect your decision-making process on these occasions.

Omission bias and action bias work in opposite ways.[12] Omission bias causes us to judge activities that do us harm as much dumber than inactivity that harms us just as much. Not taking action does not usually give us sleepless nights, as we have not taken any risks and have maintained the status quo. It is a form of psychological inertia. Standing still is preferred. In contrast, action bias can be summed up as 'nothing ventured, nothing gained' – we simply take action, whether or not it is the right decision.

The behavioural science evidence convinces me that whether we encounter omission bias or action bias in our decision-making is down to both the context and the individual. The behavioural science literature on regret also distinguishes between how people think about action and how they think about inaction. Looking backwards on their life, someone is much more likely to regret not doing something, as opposed to taking action.[13] This evidence relates to a wide variety of populations and contexts, suggesting that your ME+ will worry more about you suffering from omission bias than action bias. Or, to put it another way, you can expect to worry less about what you do than about what you don't do. Why is that, when they can both harm you equally?

According to psychologists Shai Davidai and Thomas Gilovich,[14] when people do something that they regret they have an opportunity to react, which probably reduces the intensity of the regret they feel when they look back on it. There is nothing to react to if you stand still and the opportunities that come up over the course of your life simply slip away. Of course, you can't say yes to everything either. By all means be discerning when considering the options available. Just remember that opportunities that come up out of the blue are best mulled over with a cool head.

Want to know something wonderful? When you do take advantage of unexpected opportunities, the odds are stacked in your favour that you will end up satisfied with the decision in the future. We are pretty damn good at finding ways to justify our actions, no matter how badly we fail – processing them in a way that allows us to sleep soundly at night. We find the silver linings in failures.

But there's no silver lining in doing nothing and standing still. So more often than not, you may as well do it, as you're likely to figure out a way not to regret it in the future.

This is why you should pay particular attention to omission bias when opportunities arise out of the blue. Particularly if they show promise of accelerating your journey, or even of putting you on a previously unimagined trajectory. And omission bias is also relevant elsewhere. Many of us have friends who hate their job but never quit.

Many of us know someone who would make a convincing entrepreneur but will not pursue their dream for fear of failure. Every day, people avoid having hard conversations, they don't ask for help, and they baulk at sticking their neck out to advance their own careers, for no other reason than a preference not to act.

You don't have to take risks all the time to succeed, but you do have to commit to regular small steps. And you can now add to that a resolve to seriously consider any new opportunities that come along.

### *INSIGHT 9: TAKE RESPONSIBILITY AND GROW*

There's a lot more to a PhD than most potential students realize. Including me. You have to find an academic voice, and contribute ideas that are creative enough to get published in international journals that are highly regarded. You need to communicate your ideas at public speaking events with large (often scathing) academic audiences. Depending on what you are studying, you may have to hone skills in data science, maths, deductive reasoning, interviewing, writing, communicating, teaching . . . the list goes on.

This is how, in the summer of 2007, I found myself in a large auditorium at New York University, discussing one of my PhD papers in front of more than a dozen esteemed professors of econometrics. I take creative licence in using the word 'discussing' because on that day I choked. I stumbled over my words, stuttering, sweating, forgetting what I had to say . . .

I had thrown my hat in the ring. I had taken a risk. But I had failed.

It was important that I recognized my own part in this failure. I had never invested any real time in developing my presentation skills.

It happens. We don't always nail it the first time. Sometimes we mess up. But when we do, it's essential that we don't succumb to ***self-serving bias***, which is the tendency to take kudos for positive outcomes and lay the blame for failures at someone else's door. Don't point to bad luck or even skulduggery for failure. Remind yourself that any moment of failure is a good time for self-reflection. Were you responsible?

But is self-serving bias always a bad thing? Possibly not on occasions when you need to rally quickly. It is certainly a way we can post-rationalize our choices to ensure we get an appropriate amount of sleep at night. It is also, at its core, an act of self-preservation. It helps avoid paralysis in the future when we need to put ourselves out there again.

However, the problem with self-serving bias on occasions like my horror-show presentation is that we miss an opportunity to self-reflect when a genuine failure occurs. It may also cause us not to develop the new skills we require to move on. I needed to work on my presentation skills – I couldn't blame that on circumstance. If we do not self-reflect, how can we know what to improve for next time around?

Self-serving bias may have influenced the skills and traits that you committed to developing in Chapter 2. Did you pick the skills that you already have as the ones that you need to develop? Were you puffing up your ego by emphasizing the value of qualities you already have, and neglecting to notice skills you don't have but really need?

A study by Jeffrey Cucina and colleagues from 2005 illustrates this nicely. They asked participants to identify the personality traits that are necessary to ensure academic success. And what did they find? A significant overlap between the student's own personality and the personality dimensions they chose as important. Another study by Rory McElwee and colleagues from 2001 came to a similar conclusion. In their work, they led participants to falsely believe that they were talented at either maths or verbal skills. (Scientists can be deceptive!) Then they showed them a bunch of college applications and asked them to rank each applicant in terms of suitability for college. What did they find? That the study's subjects were far from objective – showing strong preferences for applicants they believed were most like themselves (remember, they were falsely led to believe they were skilled in specific subjects) rather than choosing the legitimately best candidates.

So do you think you are overemphasizing the skills you are already strong in as those to cultivate for your big-thinking journey? Are you unsure? It is a question you could ask your new network. Specifically, ask them what the most important traits would be for ME+ to cultivate. Compare their responses to the traits that you decided to develop, and swallow your pride if revisions need to be made.

Don't let ego stand in the way of your progression.

Get out there and hone the skills ME+ actually needs. You may have some bad experiences on your new learning curve, like me choking at NYU, but it is all part of the journey!

### *INSIGHT 10: DON'T FORGET TO BREATHE OUT*

I completed my PhD successfully in September 2009. I did my viva (an oral examination) on a Thursday, and left to go backpacking around South-East Asia the following Sunday. Prior to this I had also secured a tenured lecturing job in Australia, which would start in October. In the run-up to that period, I had been on fire in terms of my research productivity. I had everything figured out.

Well, sort of.

I had used up all of my willpower to finish my PhD early so I could make it to Australia and honour the tight start date I had agreed. As I sat drinking the complimentary prosecco on my Qantas Airways flight, eagerly anticipating a new adventure in Thailand, I was wearing elasticated tracksuit bottoms. But this wasn't to ensure a comfortable long-haul flight. Rather, I had gained two stone in the final two months of my PhD. It had been too hard to muster the willpower to be healthy after consistently slogging away for fourteen hours a day for more than six months, and my body and my energy levels had taken a hit.

Remember that your journey to ME+ is a marathon, and not a sprint. It can happen that you fall into a sustained level of intensity on the course of your journey that doesn't allow for other things in your life, and this throws your balance off. Take notice of where you are using up your energy and willpower, as these things are not infinite in supply.

Behavioural scientists call the phenomenon of sacrificing willpower in one area of life for another ***ego depletion***. The literature also provides evidence that it can be offset with morale-boosting treats or activities.[15] If you don't pay attention to ego depletion, good behaviour in one area of life (like taking small steps towards your big-thinking goal) can cause bad behaviour in other areas (like eating healthily), as you don't have the energy to do both.

Think of willpower as a muscle that needs to be exerted. Through exertion, willpower weakens. It can be replenished, but it takes time. The lesson here? Identify some treats and activities that will give you a boost when you are feeling depleted. These might include a massage, walks in the park, a timeout to meditate, a freshly brewed cup of an exotic herbal tea, or an episode of your favourite TV show alongside (in moderation) chocolate, booze or whatever else tickles your fancy. Having an arsenal of treats at your disposal is better than relying on just one thing.

If you see yourself sliding into bad behaviour in another area of your life because you are intensely working on your big-thinking goal, it is worth taking the small step to schedule one of these treats to help avoid ego depletion.

So let's recap the ten behavioural science insights covered in this chapter . . .

***INSIGHT 1: BIASES IN YOUR NETWORKS AND INFLUENCERS***

Go back to the list of three people you came up with to expand your network in Chapter 2 (see p. 54), and ensure that they are sufficiently diverse.

***INSIGHT 2: DID YOU PICK THE RIGHT BIG-THINKING GOAL?***

Can you say for sure that the activities that you love doing define your ultimate stated goal?

***INSIGHT 3: LOSS AVERSION***

Don't let the way you think about failure stop you from putting your hat in the ring. Remind yourself that there is always a positive probability of success.

***INSIGHT 4: KNOW YOUR VALUE***

Research how much other people that are doing jobs like you are earning (your market rate), to help deal with anchoring on rates that are too low and ensure you're getting paid what you are worth.

***INSIGHT 5: WHY DON'T WE ASK FOR WHAT WE NEED MORE OFTEN?***

Don't assume that the people around you are noticing your progress. They are busy. Join the dots for them and highlight your development to ensure you are adequately rewarded.

***INSIGHT 6: TWO-WAY CONVERSATION***

Approach feedback opportunities strategically. Develop a thick skin and be open to critical feedback. When you receive feedback you don't agree with, remind yourself it is one data point, and take the time to verify it with other sources.

***INSIGHT 7: SAVING FACE***

Avoid the saving face effect by recognizing that, regardless of whether you fail or succeed at something, very few people will notice, and if they do it will be short-lived.

***INSIGHT 8: REMAINING OPEN TO NEW OPPORTUNITIES***

Take opportunities that come out of the blue seriously. Remind yourself that people always regret inaction more than action.

***INSIGHT 9: TAKE RESPONSIBILITY AND GROW***

Don't blame others or cosmic injustice for any failures that may occur. Take the time to reflect honestly on whether a lack of effort on your part or perhaps poor decision-making led to the bad outcome.

***INSIGHT 10: DON'T FORGET TO BREATHE OUT***

This is a marathon, not a sprint. Make efforts to avoid ego depletion by scheduling well-being enhancing treats after intense periods of concentration or dedication.

Don't be discouraged when you realize just how many biases you need to watch out for. Remember that while a lot of these biases operate unconsciously, they are not fixed. Using the behavioural science insights highlighted in this chapter can limit the influences of your cognitive biases on your big-thinking journey and stop you holding yourself back.

Happy de-biasing!

Before we move on, make sure that you:

- Slow down and recognize that most of the decisions you make are affected by cognitive biases and blind spots.
- Read through the ten behavioural science insights and adopt some of these tips and tricks, in order to reduce the impact of biases and blind spots on your big-thinking journey.

### FIVE FAB BEHAVIOURAL SCIENCE CONCEPTS MENTIONED IN THIS CHAPTER:

1. **Bias blind spot:** The tendency to see ourselves as less affected by biases than other people are.
2. **Choice-supportive bias:** When we look back on our choices, we tend to think that they were the right ones.
3. **Anticipatory loss aversion:** This relates to how painful you *expect* being turned down to make you feel.
4. **Ostrich effect:** Sticking your head in the sand and avoiding negative information that can ultimately help you.
5. **Self-serving bias:** The tendency to take kudos for positive outcomes, and lay the blame for failures at someone else's door.

# CHAPTER 5

# OUTSIDE

I met Alex after a public talk in 2018. Rather than asking me loads of questions on biases and other behavioural-science-related matters that linked to my talk, Alex jumped right in and started describing a new product idea.

Alex was an extraordinarily enthusiastic individual, filled with entrepreneurial spirit. Alex also talked at me rapidly, blissfully unaware that I was zoning out. I captured some soundbites that told me Alex was certain that this product was mass-market. These included, 'Every person needs it!' and, 'Parents will love it!' Something was also said about weight loss, and something else about bulking up. In a nutshell, Alex was seeking world domination.

But then Alex kept talking. It was now getting to the time in the evening where I should be making my exit, but despite scanning the room repeatedly I couldn't see my coat. It was getting harder and harder to concentrate on this uninvited monologue. That's until one sentence snagged in my brain – 'I'll show them all, they're wrong!' – to which my knee-jerk response was: 'What people exactly?'

Alex's story turned out, in the end, to be pretty interesting.

But I only realized this once I turned my attention more fully to what was being said, and turned (or rather forced) it into a conversation rather than a speech.

Alex had been pitching a new product idea to syndicates of angel investors all over London. Something was working because Alex had secured meetings with more than twenty groups of very busy people. Despite being turned down repeatedly, Alex still had enough energy left to keep pushing. That in itself was very admirable. The problem? Alex wasn't listening to feedback.

The feedback received at these meetings was remarkably similar across all of the groups. So what was it? Well, they'd all said that while the product idea was creative, Alex was too disorganized to pull it off. I could have had an hour of my life back if I'd been told this to start with.

I looked at my watch. 'Alex, we've been speaking for almost an hour after you declared that you're going to show everyone just how wrong they are. I can hear your enthusiasm about your business idea, but how will you prove to them that you aren't disorganized?'

This totally stumped Alex. I took the brief silence to say my goodbyes, and made my exit.

I have already used the old adage, 'If everyone says you are dead, lie down.' It is one of my favourites, and it definitely applied to Alex. Alex was ignoring really valuable feedback on being disorganized from more than twenty different groups of people, and being held back by a blind spot. But the blind spot didn't belong to other people. It belonged to Alex.

The key factor here is that Alex had elicited feedback from (far) more than one person or group, and they were independent of each other. In other words, it wasn't just a case of a few people taking a dislike to Alex and going to town.

The really sad part? Alex had wasted so many valuable opportunities in front of credible future funders by not taking feedback seriously and addressing it. You'd think by the fifth, or even the tenth presentation, the penny would have dropped.

And as a critique, being called disorganized isn't even all that bad. It can be easily fixed. The solution can also be outsourced. A more organized partner can be brought to the table, or Alex could have employed a personal assistant. Maybe it was Alex's ego that was getting in the way. Even in our short tête-à-tête, it was obvious that Alex needed to listen more. Or maybe Alex was truly too disorganized to take in the feedback. Either way, Alex was being blocked by an inability to address the only thing that made Alex a bad investment choice. Alex was self-sabotaging. Alex clearly needed Chapter 4!

All of us at one time or another won't get out of our own way. We are held back by our biases and blind spots. I see cases of useable feedback being ignored time and time again! An executive assistant who is repeatedly given feedback that their communication skills need some work, insists that all the naysayers are against them. They stagnate. A junior manager working in retail whose staff give them feedback that there is a better way to do the rota, with no negative effect on customers, refuses to listen and leaves their staff's morale in the gutter. A leader is told every year that they intimidate their colleagues; they tell their colleagues to grow up. A school-leaver being offered advice on their university choices declines to listen. Yes – all around the world, great advice gets cast aside by people who keep doing the same thing and somehow expect a different outcome.

However, it is not just your own cognitive biases and blind spots standing in your way.

How people see you may not reflect your abilities, skills and talent at any one moment in time.

Others may hold a different narrative about your suitability for jobs, leading projects or heading up a company, and this narrative may relate to factors that have nothing to do with your capability to do the task at hand. Even if *you* have developed a keen self-awareness of what you can offer, do not expect this to match the belief that others hold about you. Other people see you differently from how you see yourself, and their own cognitive biases and blind spots tint their view.

So why does this matter?

At any one time, you know many people in the world. How each of those people views you differs. How do I know? It is easy to demonstrate, when you think about people in the public domain. Take Donald Trump. His presidency in the US has been plagued by contradictory narratives. Some people view him as a superhero, here to bring American jobs back to the US from far-flung shores. The ultimate warrior against globalization and the establishment. For others, Trump is an incompetent bully, crossing boundaries at every given opportunity and setting America back decades. These narratives, although totally contradictory, are held at the very same point in time by different people. They co-exist, and are espoused by the two sides as if they are facts. These narratives cause fights around dinner tables. These narratives divide nations.

Try it yourself. Think of someone in the public domain who you think is perfect in each and every way.[1] Now google 'I hate [insert name here]', and you will see plenty of evidence that other people hold the exact opposite narrative to you. The fact that you are seeing so many webpages with negative comments tells you that people are even willing to pay a cost – time – to vent their frustrations. As I emphasized earlier, time is our most precious resource. Those people have spent their most precious resource telling the world how much they hate this person you like.

So should you care if people differ in their opinion of you? As a flippant response, it is very easy to say 'no', you shouldn't. Sod them! Why should you care about the sentiment of someone else when you have big thinking and small steps to be getting on with? You know who you are – and if they don't see it, stuff them!

But what if the person – or persons – with the biases and blind spots can influence your progress? What if they can derail your planning altogether? This can happen if the people who will review your work do not accurately see your skills, abilities and talents. It can happen if the people who will determine whether you get investment, a gig or a stretch assignment do not accurately assess your capabilities, potential, or the value you can add.

This chapter will help you identify big moments when the behavioural biases and blind spots of others are likely to get in your way. If I met you and you were the manager, leader or owner of an organization, we would have a conversation about how you should change structures and processes in your place of work, so that such biases do not disrupt the progression of talent. If you were an investor, we would discuss structures and processes that would allow you to navigate the same types of biases and blind spots in others, to ensure your investment choices give you the highest return. But in this case, I am going to take the behaviour of the other person as a given, and provide you with advice for navigating it. This is not satisfactory for those of us who want to live in a more socially responsible and equitable world, and once you make some real progress on your journey you will be in a better place to challenge and change structures that you do not like or that are unfair, thereby ensuring that those coming up behind you have to worry less. But for now, the behavioural science insights I outline in this chapter will focus on tools that allow you to circumvent the biases and blind spots of others and give yourself the best shot of realizing your big thinking sooner rather than later.

But before we get to these insights, it is worth spending a little bit of time trying to understand how the behavioural biases of others manifest in the first place. Like many unhelpful phenomena, there is not one single cause, and nor are the causes mutually exclusive. Let's take a moment and explore the three main causes . . .

## UNCONSCIOUS BIAS

There are many people who deny they see the world with biases and blind spots. If I am speaking to a group of a manageable size, I often try an experiment to illustrate this. I managed to do this pretty successfully about a year ago, with a group of around forty people who worked in IT. Each person in attendance sat at a table of two. Seating was randomly assigned, based on a list of names I received before the event. I let the group know that their task was to prove their skills of negotiation and that there was £100 at stake.[2]

Within each pair, roles were assigned. One person was the proposer. Their job was to write on a piece of paper how much they were willing to give their partner out of the £100. At the same time, their partner – the responder – wrote down the minimum offer they would accept. In this situation the proposer wants to get as close as possible to the minimum acceptable offer, to prove they are master negotiators. Too low and there is no deal – and neither the proposer nor responder receive anything. Too high, and the proposer is giving away money unnecessarily.

However, I was being ever so slightly sneaky. In reality, I didn't care who was a master negotiator. I was trying to find out if people would be treated differently by some observable characteristic like gender, age or whether they were wearing a suit. Would the proposers consistently offer less to certain groups of people?

Within this group of IT professionals, ***unconscious bias*** was clearly revealed. On average, male responders were offered more. (It should be noted that both male and female proposers offered more to men.) Older responders also garnered more generous offers. This held true no matter the age of the proposer. And yes, those who were wearing smart clothes also received more generous offers.

Why?

> You might not think you judge on looks, but you do. The fact that you don't think you do is why it's unconscious bias.

There are many published academic studies that draw the same conclusions with sample sizes that allow for credible statistical analysis. One study focused on gender, and had two distinct scenarios.[3] In the first scenario, the proposer and responder cannot see or hear each other. Therefore gender is invisible. In the second scenario, the responder and proposer sit opposite each other, as in my exercise with the IT professionals, so they are aware of one another's gender and the pair get to exchange pleasantries.

The findings? Regardless of the scenario, the average proposer offer did not depend on the responder's gender. Fantastic!

The second result was more troubling, and consistent with my own findings. The responder was usually offered more when they were male. The third headline result? Male responders often got the best offers from female proposers.

This is a pretty neat way to illustrate the potential for individuals to be treated differently because of visible aspects of themselves (for example, gender, race, age or presentation) that do not correlate with the things that actually matter: skills, ability and talent.

'So what?' you may be asking. 'This is all low-stakes stuff, right? No one is getting hired or fired. No life-changing opportunities are forgone.'

Not true. There is enough evidence from high-stakes field experiments to convince me that this is something which could, for instance, seriously disrupt your big-thinking journey. Other people's unconscious bias is something to take seriously.

Consider the stock of knowledge that has come from CV experiments. Here, the basic idea is to send CVs in response to real job adverts, randomly varying the name that appears on the top. For example, by gender to test whether males are more likely to get picked than females. Choosing names with a particular ethnic origin demonstrates whether screeners have an unconscious preference for candidates with a particular ethnicity.

One of the most influential CV studies was carried out by Marianne Bertrand and Sendhil Mullainathan. In 2004, they sent out 5,000 CVs in response to 1,300 job adverts in Boston and Chicago. They randomly assigned African-American- or white-sounding names to these CVs, to test whether ethnicity mattered for callbacks. What did they find? The fictitious white CVs received 50 per cent more calls for face-to-face interviews.

What's more, this stark favouritism for the candidates with white-sounding names was found across all occupations, industries and firm sizes.

Experiments based on fictitious CVs have also provided convincing evidence that people are discriminated against for being too old, being a woman, and being a woman of child-bearing age.[4]

But surely, you cry, things have moved on in the last fifteen years? I'm not wholly convinced they have. Meaningful gaps are still being found in more recent work, too. A study in the UK, published in 2019 and conducted by the Centre for Social Investigation at Nuffield College, Oxford, highlights this dismal fact. The study included candidates from thirty-three different minority ethnic groups who were randomly assigned to different job vacancies. The findings? White applicants received one call for interview for every four applications sent. For other ethnicities, the number dropped to one in seven.

Still don't believe me? There is even more evidence that people may be treated differently for reasons that have nothing to do with ability, skills and talent. Combining twenty-four labour market experimental studies in a meta-analysis in 2017, Lincoln Quillan and colleagues illustrated that since 1989 there has been no decrease in the discrimination against African Americans in the United States. A very well-known study by Claudia Goldin and Cecilia Rouse illustrated that the adoption of 'blind' auditioning by US orchestras in the 1970s and '80s increased the probability that a woman advanced to selection rounds by 50 per cent. In a study that I carried out with David Johnston in 2016, we presented evidence strongly suggesting that, in times of recession, non-white workers are losing their jobs more than white workers because of racially prejudiced employers and managers.

In times of scarcity all workers are more likely to rely on creating in-groups (an exclusive group of co-workers that share information, opportunities and comradeship) to keep them safe from losing their job. Quite often, in-groups are created around characteristics that have nothing to do with skills, ability or talent, so they are bad news for organizations. What is more, the creation of in-groups is often unconscious.

## REPRESENTATIVENESS HEURISTIC

In the opening paragraphs of this chapter I introduced you to Alex, the wannabe start-up rock star who was refusing to listen to feedback. The person who cornered me to tell me how great their new product idea was. The person who had blown twenty pitches for funding . . . (If you are not with me, take a moment now to flick back a few pages.)

Got it? Did you come up with an image of Alex in your mind when you read that story? Pause. Notice the gender, age and any other attributes you conjured up for this person?

Now take a moment to reflect on your choices.

Was your image of Alex a man? If it looks like a duck and walks like a duck . . .

Guess what? Alex is a woman!

When we judge the probability that a person belongs in a particular job simply by looking at the degree to which that person resembles the majority of people already in that job, we are employing the ***representativeness heuristic***. In this case 'resembles' might mean a shared gender, age, ethnicity, or any other attribute that can be inferred upon first meeting a person: their levels of extroversion, for instance, or how organized they are.

Consider the following: Jess is a movie buff who enjoys

attending film festivals around the world. Growing up, he enjoyed putting on one-man plays and entertaining his family members and friends.

Which of the following statements is most likely? 'Jess is a film critic for a major newspaper' OR 'Jess works in banking.'

In the same way that many readers will have assumed that Alex is a man, a large share of readers will naturally assume that Jess is a film critic.

Why? Because Jess's description matches the stereotypes many of us hold about film critics far more than the stereotypes we hold about bankers. In reality, Jess is most likely working in banking because employment in banking makes up a far larger share of jobs in the world and in any country in which you happen to be reading this. There just aren't that many film critics, and plenty of bankers are movie buffs on the sly.

And why will many of you assume that Alex is a man? Because entrepreneurs are more often male.[5] I didn't tell you Alex's gender, so you likely made an assumption based on the representativeness heuristic. We all use mental shortcuts to make judgements and inferences. In this case the mental shortcut relies on you having a stereotypical image in mind of what an entrepreneur should look like. You rely on your image of what an entrepreneur is from your past encounters with entrepreneurs, or how they are represented on TV. This is not problematic here, as Alex is blissfully unaware and, so far as I know, you cannot hurt her future prospects. However, the representativeness heuristic is problematic in high-stakes decision-making, and can affect your big-thinking journey by causing people to judge your suitability – whether you have a particular ability, talent or skill – on unrelated characteristics that you possess.

# STATISTICAL DISCRIMINATION

I met Julie at a lunchtime roundtable that discussed the behavioural science lessons for honing resilience. Julie had emailed me ahead of time and asked that we get a coffee afterwards. What keeps the memory of Julie in my mind is that she suggested a walk-and-talk coffee so we could get some fresh air and I could make my way to my next destination (in other words, she made it easier for me). Julie ended up walking me the two miles to the LSE campus. On the way, we took in some London sights and she told me about coming back to the office seven weeks ago, after two months' maternity leave. Yes – not a typo! – two months. Julie had been working on the day she went into labour and delivered Jack at a healthy 7 lbs 2 oz. She had planned to take only four weeks, which turned out to be a classic planning fallacy, and delayed her return by a few weeks to allow herself to recover and get into a regular breastfeeding routine. At that point, Jack was being taken care of by Julie's mum, and Julie returned to her job ready to throw herself back into serving clients and generating money for her firm.

But Julie's clients had been reallocated while she was away, and there was a reluctance from her colleagues to give them back. This wasn't totally unexpected. Julie had seen it happen before. She could also see why. Her colleagues were rewarded based on how much income they brought in, so pinching lucrative clients could bring them benefits.

Julie had been prepared to have a strongly worded conversation with her manager to get her client assignments back, but she was not expecting the soft-toned approach she got instead. Julie's manager Helen reminded her that most women in their company took six months' maternity leave, and while it was great that she was back, she was not expected to perform to the same level given her new commitments at home. Helen recommended that Julie slow down and take on a supporting role to her colleagues.

Julie had become a victim of ***statistical discrimination***. Helen had assumed that the preferences of a group (other new mothers in the same firm) would apply to Julie. But Julie wasn't like the other mothers at her firm.

If I asked you to tell me five things that describe somebody you just met, you would likely describe their age, gender and ethnicity, plus a couple of things about their appearance (scruffy or dapper, hair colour, facial hair, etc.).

> Statistical discrimination implies that at the very same time that you're registering hair colour and sartorial choices, you are making unconscious assumptions about a person's character based on the things that you see.

For example, it is a stylized fact that women take more time out of the labour force than men because they rely on maternity leave when they have children and also take on more responsibilities in the home environment. So people may then assume that Jane is likely to do the same. In the UK, on average, black people receive a lower level of education than white people, so people may incorrectly assume that Frank has a relatively low education level.

Why does this matter? It matters to Jane if an interview panel makes these assumptions. The job may go to John, who they expect to take less time off. It matters to Frank if people at a networking event make these assumptions because they may not invest their time in talking to him.

When I teach at the LSE I like to differentiate occasions

of statistical discrimination from stereotype discrimination. Jane and Frank are being unfairly held back because of what Arlie Hochschild called the 'second shift' in her 1989 book of the same name and because of inequality in the British education system, respectively. These averages are then being applied to them without pause for thought.

The evidence of these inequalities can be seen in data. However, it is also possible for false stereotypes to affect groups as well. A false stereotype is one that is applied to a group with no data to back it up. For example, unfounded beliefs about ability differences in maths between the genders undoubtedly affect career outcomes. Boys are considered to be better than girls at maths. Are these differences supported in the data? Definitely not!

Biases are formed based on stereotypes and statistics. These biases feed into the representativeness heuristic. An image is painted of the type of person who suits a particular role, even if intuitively these images do not make any sense. We are faced with these biases throughout our lives, and many of you will experience them as you work towards your big-thinking goal.

So is there anything you can do about it?

Of course there is!!!!!

### INSIGHT 1: HALTING UNCONSCIOUS BIAS, THE REPRESENTATIVENESS HEURISTIC AND STATISTICAL DISCRIMINATION

We have just discussed unconscious bias, the representativeness heuristic and statistical discrimination. These three concepts can be separated theoretically. However, when you are faced with one of them, it can be hard to pinpoint the origin of what is happening. You will simply recognize that you are being judged on an attribute that does not relate to your ability, skills or talent. The concepts are not mutually exclusive, and it may even be said that statistical discrimination and the representativeness heuristic are two underlying causes of unconscious bias.

The good news? While you might not be able to distinguish between these concepts easily, the things you can do to circumvent all three are quite similar.

First, never let the images driven by stereotypes and heuristics sway you when you think big. As someone who does not 'look' like the typical person who fulfils a certain role because of your socioeconomic status, ethnicity, gender or some other characteristic, there may be a steeper road in your journey; however, it is essential to remember that you can add so much value when you succeed. Why? Very often the jobs we do directly or indirectly involve serving other people in society. In terms of their needs, those people are arguably better understood by others who are like them. Can people with a high socioeconomic status really know how to distribute public services in a way that best serves people all across the income distribution? Can men really know how to write, direct and produce entertainment that is embraced equally by both genders? Can executives at retail and services companies really understand global tastes and preferences if they all come from the same geographic location?

If there is an image in society for what a person who does a particular role should look like, remind yourself it is a *good thing* not to fit the mould. Not doing so gives you a vantage point that others in that role do not have. It gives you a competitive edge. Diversity makes good business sense – it's not just a warm and fluffy word.

If you are different from the people who have traditionally pursued your goal, keep in mind that it is a good thing!

Who better to rock the boat than you? Make it your mantra, embrace the lessons from Chapter 3 – remembering that self-belief is malleable – and keep moving forward.

But how can you deal with those who interview you, those you need to fund your business idea or those you rely on as advocates holding these same images of what the usual mould looks like – and, worse, acting on them?

The easy (but utterly depressing) answer? You have to be better than everyone else.

Evidence from behavioural science does suggest that those who do not fit the mould can make it, but they need to be better than those who *do* fit the mould by a decent amount. It is pretty awful to be advised simply to be more than twice as good to get the same opportunities. In fact, it is grossly unfair. There must be an easier way! But while we wait for the world to change, is there anything else that you can do to tip the odds back in your favour?

Yes. There are lots of things you can do. Chief among them: research. You should research the signals that are associated with the job or skills ME+ will do or is looking to acquire. What does this mean? You know you will be great in the job, but the people you want to hire, fund or take you on as a consultant or freelancer do not have the same information as you. You can get this information to them by acquiring signals related to the job you want to do.

In the same way that stereotypes and the representativeness heuristic cause people to associate certain types of people with specific roles, there are also certain signals that will identify you as being a good match for that role. These signals include attending certain conferences, and networking in certain circles. These are all things you can do in the short term. Research the signals for your big-thinking goal and any associated major milestones. If you do not find the information easily, ask your new networks (see Chapter 2). Then set about acquiring as many of these signals as possible.

Along with these signals, make your skills, abilities and talents crystal clear to the world. Make them salient. As previously mentioned, you can do this by having an elevator pitch that is short and sweet, which tells people what you bring to the table. You can also do this in a brief biography at the top of your CV, LinkedIn profile, or somewhere prominent on the application form or tender you may be filling out.

> Remember, reactions to stereotypes are mostly unconscious, so investing in signals helps people to recognize you quicker as an expert in your field.

### *INSIGHT 2: EVERYONE'S ADVICE IS NOT CREATED EQUALLY*

I met Amita at an event at a financial services firm, where I was speaking about behavioural biases in feedback. Amita had just gone through a development review. Various versions of the development review are carried out in workplaces all over the world. Many of you will have experienced one.

The idea behind a development review is positive. Employees get a chance to reflect on what has gone well – and not so well – within regular time intervals (often a year). Unfortunately, the quality of development reviews varies depending on who is doing it. Amita's had been a very negative experience, which she told me about over a glass of red wine and a plate of creamy blue cheese.

Amita had been told to work on her accent, under the guise of helping her with presentation skills. She was rightfully upset, as her accent was an inherent part of who she was. What's more, Amita already spoke with such clarity that

I could not see why someone would think that 'working on her accent' would help her get her messages heard better. Being told to work on your accent is different from being told to slow down so people have a chance to digest your messages, or being advised to project your voice so that people can hear what you have to say.

I identified with Amita as I had been given similar 'advice' by a professor a few years before. (If you have yet to hear me speak, I have an Irish accent.) What was interesting was that this professor seemed to be coming from a good place. I didn't sense any malice or ill will beneath their motivations. There was no spite. They genuinely thought that it would help me be more relatable when speaking about my research in public forums. In this case, their notion of 'relatable' seemed to be based on norms of who we more commonly encounter on TV and radio.[6] Like Amita, I was rightfully annoyed. My accent, like Amita's is to her, is an authentic part of who I am. While I am happy for it to continue being shaped by where I live, I am never going to cultivate a different persona to fit in with a social norm. And neither should Amita.

Other advice that I have got throughout my career and have discarded includes 'take yourself more seriously' and 'be less direct'. My tendency to deliver messages with no frills and my ability to laugh at myself are part of who I am. If I am to succeed, it will be with these character traits in place. I have many traits that I am happy to work hard to change – as I've talked about in this book, I am in an ongoing battle with my impatience and need for immediate gratification. I have worked hard over the years to boost my resilience, and I continue to work hard every day on enhancing my ability to explain difficult behavioural science material in an understandable way. It isn't useful for me to be told 'change your accent' because it's impossible – and even if it wasn't, I'm not going to do it anyway.

When receiving feedback, the first question to ask yourself is what aspects of yourself you will accept feedback on. Having a keen awareness of the characteristics that you will not compromise on will help you to avoid falling into the trap of pursuing activities that encroach on your authenticity. From time to time, you will get advice that is flawed. It will be based on constructed social norms from people with biases and blind spots. Knowing your boundaries allows you to stay true to yourself.

While I have had numerous enquiries about my ability to facilitate a course that would make employees more confident, I have never once been asked to facilitate a course that would allow introverts to participate in meetings in a manner they feel comfortable with. I have also never been asked to facilitate a course for extroverts that would make them more conscious about taking all of the air time in important conversations. Why is that?

Society accepts that competitive extroverts are allowed to talk up in meetings. They become the model. But what if being an introvert is an inherent part of who you are? Do you really want to change a core part of yourself to fit in with others? That sounds like a miserable existence.

Before you open the door to feedback, reflect on the aspects of yourself that make you *you*. This will help you filter criticism, and pursue only the pieces of advice that move you forward in a way that is in the direction you want to travel. Never trade authenticity for approval.

So you are in the room. You are about to receive feedback. What should you know?

I have one major rule on feedback:

If someone offers you feedback, you should listen simply because they are spending their most valuable resource – their time – to give it to you.

There is one big proviso. If you receive negative feedback and cannot see yourself in it (this can happen: everyone has an ego), get a second opinion. Ideally, get three. Why three? Because you need to figure out if it is your biases that are stopping you hearing legitimate feedback, or if the behavioural biases and blind spots of others are affecting what is being said. The three people should be as independent as possible from each other. That is, they should not know each other, or at least not converse regularly.

What then? If there is agreement among your three chosen people, view it as a trend and take it seriously. As I've said before, if you are dead, you really should lie down. It is time to address the issue(s) that they raise.

But what if the feedback of one person isn't echoed by the other two? Discard it. You have experienced feedback that is tainted by behavioural biases and blind spots. If it is from somebody you can learn a lot from, it is fine to go back – but with a poop filter. The second time around you should not approach them. If the nay-sayer actually knocks on your door touting pearls of wisdom, ask them for facts to back up their words. Third time? Don't answer the door.

Whose opinion should you care about? Those who are willing to take the time to give feedback that will improve something that is important to your big-thinking plan. This might include a product you are launching, skills you are honing or a network you are building. Over time, you will figure out who they are, particularly if you adopt the three-person rule mentioned above. The people who you listen to regularly should be authentic in their motivations to move you forward.

> Overall feedback is not a democracy. That means that all votes do not count equally. You will figure out whose feedback matters more over time.

When searching for feedback that will help you advance your strengths and reduce your difficulties, you are putting your head above the parapet. By doing so, you may attract the attention of people who take joy in cutting you down to size. You are experiencing ***tall poppy syndrome*** – the tendency for people to knock down others who are achieving great things. Of course, what is thought of as 'great' is subjective, and simply moving from a status quo is enough for you to be viewed as a tall poppy in some circles.

Tall poppy syndrome has been found to affect a variety of groups, such as owners of start-ups, established business-owners, and high-achieving women and managers.[7] It is therefore important that you always filter the feedback you receive, and stick to the three-person rule of thumb.

### *INSIGHT 3: AVOID BEING LABELLED INCORRECTLY*

Jim was turned down for promotion two years ago and got a bit bummed out about the situation. I met him for coffee at a time when he had begun to decompress and had received feedback from people he trusted. The primary reason Jim failed in his promotion application was that he was seen as unreliable by one of the key senior executives in his organization. Jim realized that the only time he'd worked with this senior executive had coincided with a train strike on his commuter line. Jim could never tell how long he'd have to wait for his train to show up to start his long commute from the outskirts of London to the city centre.

Unfortunately, Jim being late to meetings due to the train strikes had been mistaken for a lack of punctuality and dedication. Nobody saw Jim standing in the cold waiting for a train that never came on the dark winter mornings. All they'd taken notice of was Jim walking in late some mornings, and the reasoning he gave had fallen on the deaf ears of the time-poor people in the room.

Have you ever had an occasion where the narratives surrounding you seemed a bit out of tune with the person you are? Have you ever thought, 'I don't know where you got an idea like that from?' You may have well been a victim of ***fundamental attribution error***. You can – and should – nip this in the bud.

Fundamental attribution error causes us to attribute a person's behaviour to their identity rather than the situation. For example, Jim's bad luck (situation) was attributed to a lack of punctuality and dedication (behaviour he can control).

Perhaps you ran over a deadline one time because it fell over a period of ill health? For those relying on you, it can be easier to assume that you are careless rather than blame the situation. In the same way, getting off on the wrong foot with someone once may ruin the potential for a working relationship that has great synergy. Wrong feet happen innocently every day when someone interrupts us in a meeting, doesn't respond to an email or excludes us from a brainstorming session. Fundamental attribution error causes an immediate reaction of damnation to hell, rather than a more considered response that takes seriously the possibility that this person may be having a rotten day and just temporarily dropped the ball.

Fundamental attribution error is more likely to happen when we don't know a person that well, or don't care to know them because we've failed to gel in the past.

At that point, confirmation bias steps in, ensuring that we search for and recall additional information in a way that confirms a particular belief we hold. In Jim's case, this would mean that the senior executive's ears pricked up when other colleagues talked negatively about Jim. Conversely, the senior executive's ears would have closed when more positive anecdotes about Jim were being relayed.

Rigorous research shows that fundamental attribution error corrupts high-stakes decision-making. Let's say you are starting your own company and have a view to scale beyond the monies you personally have – you are probably researching access to venture capital. Beyond money, venture capitalists often provide expertise and capabilities that give a competitive advantage to the start-ups they back. They also provide a signal to other investors that those they back are high-quality and worth watching. This signal can potentially cause a virtuous cycle that ensures a backed start-up gets an unprecedented crack of the whip at success.[8] A question then arises as to how good venture capitalists are at picking start-ups to back in these high-stake decisions. After all, they could make or break a company!

A 2004 paper by Joel Baum and Brian Silverman highlights that while venture capitalists are pretty good at picking certain winning traits, fundamental attribution error is alive and well. Specifically, it causes them to overestimate the human capital in the start-ups they back. Basically, if the companies they are vetting have experienced good luck, it is attributed to the people involved in the company rather than being in the right place at the right time.

What does the fundamental attribution error mean for your big-thinking journey? It implies that if you get lucky, that luck is going to be attributed to you – with the knock-on effect that your journey is accelerated. On the flip side, this means that if you hit a bit of bad luck, the negative outcome could be attributed to you rather than the random event that caused it. For example, let's imagine you are making a product and a company in your supply chain is exposed for paying its workers below the minimum wage. You have done due diligence that you can easily demonstrate. However, your customers and investors will associate these types of practices with your company. This bad luck damages your reputation and loses you money when they stop backing you.

It should also be noted that fundamental attribution error cuts both ways – and who knows? Maybe good luck will come your way and you will get to ride the wave of a positive image shock because of it . . .

***TOP TIP: CIRCUMVENTING FUNDAMENTAL ATTRIBUTION ERROR***

This isn't easy, and relies on your communication skills.

When you have bad luck, communicate how your outcome on this particular occasion was down to randomness rather than your skills and capabilities. If you are good at storytelling, you can wrap it up in an amusing anecdote. If not, stick to the facts and make clear you respect the other person's time. Lightning doesn't normally strike twice, so reassure your stakeholders that you are optimistic for a better outcome next time.

### *INSIGHT 4: CASCADES*

I recently attended an event to hear senior people in finance talk about how to ensure inclusion of all talent in banking going forward. The panel members were leaders from a variety of industries, and all of them spoke at events like this pretty regularly.

I am particularly interested in inclusion and ensuring that people get opportunities based on their skills and abilities alone. I was excited to be there and meet some new people, many of whom could rock the boat in their own organizations if they desired.

The conversation started off with a couple of people emphasizing how well their firms were doing on inclusion (though you're not going to change the world if you already think it's great). The third person to speak emphasized confidence and an ability to network as what people really need in order to be included. 'Come to events like these,' they said. 'Take responsibility for yourself. Spend time with us. We are here and want to meet you.' Now, I am all for people taking responsibility and determining their own future. But responsibility is a two-way street. We cannot put our heads in the sand and assume the playing field is level. If you are in a position to level the playing field, you have a duty to do so.

You may shrug and think, 'It was one opinion. What was said next . . .?' Actually, not a lot else *was* said, thanks to the ***informational cascade*** this speaker caused. An informational cascade occurs when we follow the lead of the person who speaks before us, and don't reveal our unique thoughts that could add real value. Why do we do this? When we discuss information that is familiar and feels right to the group we are in, we are liked by those around us as we are all on common ground. Challenging thoughts cause discomfort.

The person who spoke third was clearly looked up to by others on the panel, and as such they had started a reputational informational cascade. I had come along that night to get some fresh insights. But I was disappointed. The overall discussion did not reflect the knowledge in the room.

There are two main situations in which informational cascades may hinder your progress. The first is when you are presenting to a group of people, who will then deliberate on whether you got to some desired outcome or on how well you performed. You may experience this if, for example, you are pitching a project idea to a client, showcasing your business idea to potential funders, presenting a new way of doing things to senior management or defending a piece of work that you are being assessed on. If one person says something negative, the others might follow with other negative things.

The second is when you have a voice in a discussion that is important to you. Your performance in this meeting may be relevant for your big-thinking journey if you need to show leadership potential, creativity or innovation. If you are part of a start-up with two or more other owners, group meetings often decide what your product looks like. Essentially, as I'm sure you are aware, important stuff is regularly decided by group deliberations. Are you certain your voice is being heard equally with everybody else's, or is one person or one viewpoint dominating the conversation?

There are two important things to remember. First, important decisions that affect your progress are going to happen in meetings that you are part of. Second, the decision-making process in these meetings is going to be plagued by biases.

Are you surprised? Did you assume that group decision-making would lead to better outcomes than decisions made by individuals? Two heads are better than one, right? If one person has a blind spot, it's likely that the other person doesn't and so cancels it out. You expect, then, that the outcome from a group would be greater than the sum of its parts.

But for this to hold true, everyone needs to participate freely and have their voice heard. Everyone needs to be motivated by goals that are collective rather than individualistic. Empirical evidence from the lab and field suggests that this is not always the case.[9] In fact, most of the time meetings are affected by ***groupthink***.

One of the first major problems of groupthink is that it causes people to focus on shared information – as I experienced at that panel event – just so they can feel good about themselves. In the next meeting you are in, sit back and wait for the cascade.

When we are in a group setting, it makes us feel good about ourselves to talk about things that are familiar to everyone at the table. There is no discomfort. No uncomfortable pauses. Everyone is on the same page.

What does this imply for decision-making? You can have the most diverse and intellectual team in the world, but if they don't reveal information that is unique to them as individuals, the quality of group discussions will be poor. Spending too much time in group discussions reiterating what is already known is clearly a waste of time. Focusing on well-known information may make us feel good about ourselves, but that is where the benefits end.

The second major problem is that many of the cognitive biases that affect our daily decisions are actually *exaggerated* when groups meet. We have already met a myriad of these biases, which include the planning fallacy, representativeness heuristic, sunk cost fallacy and framing. Along with exaggerating these individual biases, groupthink causes an over-focus on information that members of the group have in common.

How can you fix groupthink when you are not leading the meeting? If you are a participant (rather than helplessly there to hear the panel's feedback) you won't gain many supporters by blurting out an opinion that is very different from the group's halfway through a cascade. So what can you do? It may help to start with reiterating some shared information, so you stick with the group's unconscious etiquette of saying the same point over and over again. No need to entirely spoil the party. Re-emphasize a point that has been made already that you genuinely liked.

Next, state your unique opinion in as few sentences as possible, tacked on to the end of your reiteration. You will also help your case if what you say is based on facts and evidence rather than personal musings. If there is hard evidence that signposts your idea is the right one, the group needs to hear it. Too many people rely on personal anecdotes and gut feelings when responding in meetings, and these people are hard to take seriously. If you really care about an issue, do the preliminary work and change minds with hard facts and data.

Assuming you know ahead of time the people who will be at the meeting, also make an effort to appeal to ego by personalizing your pitch to the tastes and preferences of the people in the room. If you are proposing something entirely radical that departs from shared information and viewpoints, this gives you the best chance of cutting though the groupthink.

Once you have had your say, rather than allow the cascade to flow at the chair's will, nudge somebody specific to speak next. You can do this by saying something like, 'The second point I made could benefit from opinions from my colleagues in the room, such as [insert name here], because . . .' One great tip for meeting leaders to break a cascade in their meeting is to call colleagues in random order (rather than allowing people to speak by raising their hand). If you aren't leading the meeting and don't have the luxury of choosing the order of speakers, you can still nudge who gets to speak after you. By relaying that you want to keep the conversation centred around your unique insights, you make the points you raised more salient. You also increase the likelihood that any subsequent cascade will be focused on information relevant to the topic discussed.

You could also go one step further. Let people know that because time is sensitive, after the meeting you would like to receive written feedback from the entire group. This serves two purposes. First, it allows for introverts and others who are not usually heard in meetings to become a real part of your discussion, giving you more diversity in the feedback that you receive. Second, if agreed by the chair, a decision won't be made until the next meeting. Putting some time between raising a new idea which is counter to the cascade and when the option to 'go with' is chosen will take the emotion out of the decision and give your idea the biggest chance of success.

If you are in a meeting where you are being judged 'live' and have an opportunity to give feedback, your power to change a cascade is more limited but the strategy is the same. If the cascade is positive, just let it flow. After all, you are there to have a good outcome. If the panel need to engage in shared-information back-scratching to get you there, so be it. We all get our jollies somewhere. Chalk it up to luck, and thank the stars.

If the cascade is negative, raise a new point in your reply, and nudge a particular panel member to speak next by calling them by their name and asking for their reaction to what you have said. Remember: put emphasis on facts and hard data where possible.

But what about the occasions when we are to be judged by a panel and do not have a voice in the ultimate decision-making process?

### *INSIGHT 5: JUDGEMENTS*

I met Henry at a large conference designed to bring lawyers who support financial services together. I was giving an overview of how behavioural science insights can help teams work better. During the live Q&A, Henry threw me a curve-ball and asked about pitching. He specifically wanted to know the best position in the order to request when pitching for new business with his own team. This was not a question related to my presentation, but I recommended he go last if offered the choice. Provided, that is, the last position was not just before lunch.

Henry wrote to me about eight weeks later and said he had tried this and it had worked. He had secured new business. I was quick to respond that a one-time success is not a winning streak and he should audit other outcomes going forward. However, Henry had got me interested in thinking about what determines whether someone is successful when they pitch, interview, or perform 'live' and face a panel of judges. Turns out this is a pretty interesting area of research in behavioural science.

We are constantly being judged in many areas of our life . . . When we interview for a job. When we submit a piece of writing. When we give a public talk. When we pitch our best idea. When we debate, audition, speak up in a meeting, or even when we meet up for coffee with a colleague. In all these situations we are being watched, and someone else determines if we are successful. Someone else determines if we are to be taken seriously. Even if we come fully prepared, the process of judging is riddled with behavioural biases and blind spots. But can we tip the odds in our favour?

Planning on delivering a competitive pitch for funding? The time or place in the order in which you get to present to your funding panel has been shown to make a real difference to the outcome. If each person presenting is rated with a score, you may be better off presenting as late as possible in the day.[10]

If it's a situation where rating scores are not being calculated officially, like in an interview setting, there are two effects to keep in mind if given a choice of slots. The first is ***recency effect***. Some research suggests you are better off going as late as possible, as this way you remain fresh in the judge's memory. However, pulling in the opposite direction is ***primacy effect*** – the person who is seen first is judged most accurately.

If you know you have a stellar idea, you should always present first. But you should choose to go last if you don't have 100 per cent confidence in your idea, and if you know that the judges will cross-compare at the end of the day. This harnesses the well-known ***peak-end rule*** that the most emotionally intense points and the end of an experience are most memorable. You are more likely to be successful if the judges recall what you actually said, and going at the end ensures that happens!

The slots you definitely want to avoid? Try not to get stuck in the middle unless you are certain your pitch will be the peak of the judges' day.[11]

> ***TOP TIP: THE PEAK-END RULE AND PITCHING***
>
> In Chapter 3 we discussed the role of the affect heuristic (our emotions) in our decision-making. The upshot: our emotions weigh heavily in our decision-making. This also means that emotions influence how a panel, audience or judge perceive you. So what does this mean for your pitch?
>
> 1 Take care to avoid time slots where the judges are more likely to be grumpy, like just before lunch or when there won't have been a break for a while.
> 2 Remember the influence of emotions when you are preparing your pitch. Peak-end rule implies that pitchers who emotionally connect to the judges are more memorable. Connecting your pitch to a bigger meaning via a simple narrative will give the judges the best chance of connecting emotionally to you and your ideas. If you are pitching for investment or a consultancy gig, use stories to bring to life the added value that your product or service will bring to the world. If you are pitching for a job, use stories to help the panel fully understand your relevant work experience. If you are pitching for a stretch project at work, use stories to explain what taking responsibility for this project will mean for you professionally.

### *INSIGHT 6: ARE YOU IN THE IN-GROUP?*

I met Rob when I was doing a series of round tables on behavioural science and culture. Rob evenly shared the responsibility of childcare with his wife, and he had embraced agile working with gusto. He did this to the extent that he never went to lunches or coffees with his colleagues, and on the days he was in the office he worked through breaks and munched homemade sandwiches. I learned this from Rob himself, who on the third day of my round tables had made a special effort to come and meet me and the others for lunch. Rob made a big deal of underscoring what an unusual event it was for him to venture out for lunch, and how special I should feel. Rob also reckoned he was an innate behavioural scientist and took an extraordinary interest in my work, asking me an array of questions and listening earnestly to my responses. He even asked me to go to the early-bird dinner he organized monthly.

What became clearer during the extra-fun dinner I attended was that Rob was incredibly well liked by his colleagues. This happened despite him being largely absent from his workmates' routine activities. It wasn't just social events; a handful of his colleagues relayed that Rob always helped them with their work when called upon. This practice was also reciprocated. Rob was weakly tied to the in-group and pretty much everyone else he needed to collaborate with at work, but he still garnered the rewards of respect and collegiality you might usually expect to be reserved for those with much stronger links.

For those of us navigating a job with co-workers around us daily, you will notice that some colleagues appear closer than others. If you are doing a university degree, you will notice groups of classmates eating together or going to coffee more often. If you are renting temporary office space or hot-desking in a serviced office space, you will notice that some fellow renters have gelled more than others. If you are networking, you will notice that some circles tend to move together on rotation much more regularly than others. If you are at the helm of a start-up, some of those on the journey with you will get on better than others.

As humans we tend to form in-groups, with those in the group being more likely to be part of social events, sporadic gatherings and conversations.

Does it matter?

On the surface, no. While some people suffer from the fear of missing out, I personally suffer from the fear of being included too often. I am probably not alone. A lot of people like their own company and dread weeks when their social calendar is back-to-back, especially if it is work-related. I have no problem with people arranging a variety of activities and not including me. I wish they would do it more often. However, with all of the cognitive biases floating around, could close in-group dynamics cause you to be excluded from opportunities that matter in your big-thinking journey?

The simple answer is 'yes'.

A myriad of biases ensure that in-group members look after their own. This includes informing them of opportunities when they arise. The ***familiarity effect*** ensures that individuals that are in the in-group are favoured. The ***halo effect*** also comes into play here – if someone has the positive attribute of being a friend or confidant, other positive attributes like skill, ability and talent are more likely to be associated with them. ***Intergroup bias*** also causes members to evaluate those in their own group more favourably. In periods of uncertainty, people who are in the in-group are more likely to stick together, with the potential to leave others out in the cold when times get tough.

I have no time for toxic in-groups that exclude people from meetings and conversations that they should be part of. This is a clique. If you feel that you are being excluded by a clique, it is important you call it out. You will probably be met by a defensive reaction, but exclusion is exclusion however it is dressed up.

Toxic in-groups are distinct from collegial in-groups. As humans, we need to connect with each other. Collegial in-groups form when groups of individuals in close proximity spend time together and hone relationships that contribute to a common good. At a university, in your serviced office space, at networking events or at your regular day job, you should make time to be part of these groups.

Why? First, it is good for you to expose yourself to others and their ideas. It helps you grow. Second, having a good social network enhances your well-being.

It also doesn't have to be all or nothing. There is ample evidence that being a weak tie – that is, being an acquaintance rather than a close friend (i.e. a strong tie) – is beneficial in terms of advancing career goals and access to opportunities.[12] Throughout your big-thinking journey, make an effort to connect to collegial in-groups either as a weak or a strong tie.

Your progression means being nice to people, so get on with it!

### *INSIGHT 7: GETTING SMALL YESES*

Kaitlin was struggling at work. She had not received a bonus or a promotion for last year's efforts. What was worse was that when Kaitlin asked her manager and the colleagues she worked with regularly for help in getting more experience, or to be included in stretch assignments, she was routinely told no.

Kaitlin saw the writing on the wall, and put herself on the job market. When I met her, she was enquiring about doing an executive master's at the LSE. She was at the end of her tether and wanted some way for people to see her differently. In this respect, a degree can indeed signal that you are on an upward trajectory, but doing this alongside a job where she didn't feel valued made it unlikely that Kaitlin would thrive in a master's programme.

Usually a meeting like this one is spent outlining the overall programme structure, and the courses that Kaitlin would get to study. But it was clear this wasn't the right road for Kaitlin. Instead, we spent the meeting thinking through shadowing and secondment opportunities at her current firm that would expose her to a different set of colleagues. Within six months, Kaitlin was seconded into a more senior role.

Embedded within this suggestion was my realization that Kaitlin needed to accumulate some small yeses at work to get her off her plateau. Her current status quo was being told no to any asks. And an added benefit of a secondment was that she could later benefit from the ***incumbent effect***. Once Kaitlin was in a job at a higher level, she was more likely to be seen as suitable for an equally senior role.

This anecdote has a happy ending. Two years after I met Kaitlin, she was promoted – and received a decent bonus to boot!

Kaitlin had broken her trend of being told no and begun a new trend of being told yes. Getting the first yes was the key to breaking her plateau, as small yeses are cumulative. Being able to illustrate your first, second and third yes is proof that you have talent and ability, particularly if the opportunities you have been given come from three different people.

Are there behavioural science lessons that can help you get new people around you to say yes? There are – so let's explore flattery!

Economists can be cruel. To clarify, I mean academic economists. Known for tough environments that are less appealing to women than men (which is also credited as a reason why so few women stay in the field),[13] flattery is seldom found in the corridors of top economics departments. So it was a pleasant surprise when I started having conversations in industry because the compliments I received increased exponentially. I like to think that some of them (hopefully most) are genuine, but it happens so frequently and roughly half are quite generic, which makes me pause and consider whether the ***Barnum effect*** is at work. This is the phenomenon that occurs when individuals believe that personality descriptions apply specifically to them, despite the fact that the description is actually pretty generic. In other words, it is meaningless flattery. Yes, there is evidence in behavioural science that suggests meaningless flattery works!

You can use the Barnum effect to help build a rapport with others.

Why does it work? Simple. The Barnum effect appeals to ego. As humans we like to feel good about ourselves, and ego ensures that we give more time to people who enable that. This is the explanation given by Craig Landry and colleagues in their 2006 study, which found that male respondents give more to charity when approached by attractive females in door-to-door fundraising. The authors also suggest that the additional generosity was prompted by a need to sustain ego and a positive self-image.

So what does this mean for you? It means you should make requests more pleasurable by helping people feel good about themselves. Ideally, you will have something authentic to say to the person you are speaking to that will enhance their self-image and make the discussion easier. A genuine compliment can go a long way! But if your mind goes blank, a generic compliment can be a viable substitute. Keep a few in your back pocket! The Barnum effect ensures they will likely be well received. But be warned, it's a coin toss. If you meet someone well versed in the Barnum effect, it may come across as saccharine or unprofessional. Genuine compliments and interactions are always preferred!

**TOP TIP: ASKING FOR AN OPPORTUNITY**

1. Remember the lessons from Chapter 2 regarding asking for help (see p. 51)? The same applies to opportunities! Frame the request as a win-win, outlining the costs and benefits in a factual manner.
2. Draw on lessons from the judgements section of this chapter (see p. 199). Use narrative to connect people to the mood you want to convey.

If you are trying to get a 'yes' vote for an idea, talk about it regularly and often. Why? The ***exposure effect*** ensures that if people are exposed to something, they are more likely to endorse it. It also demonstrates that there is a method in talking to others about your ideas. A happy side effect is that it opens the door for feedback that will help you refine your ideas.

You can also leverage ***commitment bias***. If there is someone in a meeting you need a yes from and you sense the mood is right, put them on the spot for an answer. Commitment bias ensures that once someone has publicly committed to endorsing you, it is difficult for them to retreat from that support. Cognitive biases also ensure they will likely feel good about this endorsement. Win-win!

So how does it work? Once people make their mind up,

they don't like changing it and confirmation bias sets in. As new information comes along, they discount information that proves them wrong and over-focus on information that reaffirms their endorsement.

If this all sounds a bit Machiavellian for your taste, don't worry. Mine too. I am someone who is prone to ***reciprocity bias*** – sometimes to my detriment, but often to the gain of yeses. Essentially, I begin by treating others how I like to be treated, and over time I find that this tendency results in a further tendency to gain acquaintances and confidants who are happy to support my various plans, with me reciprocating when needed. A different approach to the Barnum effect, and much easier for those of us who can't stomach office politics and BS (and I don't mean behavioural science)!

### *INSIGHT 8: WHAT TO DO WHEN FACED WITH A NO!*

I met Peter just as his conference company was beginning to garner success and he knew he was going to make it financially. We were meeting to discuss the possibility of me speaking at one of his events, and that morning Peter was a fireball of energy. He talked fast, and spent a lot of time describing how he had ended up being successful, and how he still couldn't believe it. He also talked at speed about teaching his two young children to strive for entrepreneurship. I asked what the main lessons he was imparting to them were. He focused on two: first, that you need an idea that adds value to the world; and second, you need to keep going despite being told no. I couldn't have agreed with him more.

Peter had spent many months trying to make appointments with people who could ensure his business succeeded – essentially sponsors and speakers. He had failed to get many meetings. He also got told no at a lot of the meetings he did manage to arrange. But he kept going because he knew that he had a business that added value. Eventually, Peter got a yes. When the rain finally came, it poured.

> As you navigate your big-thinking journey, at times you will be held back by a vote of no confidence. If you are not being told no, getting rejected or failing regularly, you are not challenging yourself adequately on your journey. Buck up!

When you are told no, you may find evidence of glaring mistreatment and be filled with certainty that the people blocking your path are plagued by behavioural biases and blind spots. What should you do about this?

There are two main options at your disposal. First, speak with the people who turned you down. Relay your disappointment with their decision and ask them to take another look at the value your idea could bring. As we discussed in Chapter 2, the bizarre thing about human behaviour is that, when you ask for help, you are unlikely to be turned down twice by the same person. What often stops us trying a second time is the saving face effect. So consider putting your pride to one side and having a direct conversation where you ask for the decision to be reversed.

Second, you should explore revising your idea, taking into account any feedback you have received. After revising, try asking again. If that doesn't work, look for other doors that you can knock on that have different people behind them. When faced with people with behavioural biases and blind spots, remember that there are many more people in the world without the hang-ups that you are experiencing. It is never the case that you have to be reliant on one person or one group of people to move you forward. You may need to do some work to figure out who the next people you contact are, but don't ever get stuck on having the same door slammed in your face. Insanity, after all, is doing the same thing over and over and expecting a different result.

Think of your big-thinking journey as a game of snakes and ladders. A 'no' vote is like sliding down a snake. It's a setback. But if you persevere, you'll find a ladder that helps you make up what you lost. Today and in the future you will still encounter snakes, *but* they are declining in numbers. There are many more ladders than there used to be, and once you succeed the ladders will become more frequent if you remember to pay any help you receive forward. You just need to turn up regularly and take your small steps to discover the ladders available to you now, and keep going if you end up slithering down a snake.

### *INSIGHT 9: PLEASE SHOW UP FOR OTHERS*

I have given many talks to groups at firms. When I started out I was mostly invited to speak on gender behaviour gaps. The interesting thing for me? The majority of the audience were women. Actually, I would say that when I first started giving these talks more than 95 per cent of the audience were women.

Does it matter? Yes.

We should care about circumventing the biases other people experience. These biases arise when we assign kudos to people based on characteristics that do not correlate with their ability, skills and talent. As an individual, it is not nice to be on the end of other people's biases and blind spots. So while you pay attention to your own journey, and circumventing the biases of others which affect you, also pay attention to levelling the playing field for colleagues and acquaintances who may be facing a similar battle in a different theatre.

What can you do to help?

Across the world, firms, universities and public bodies have created affinity groups based around gender, race, ethnicity, LQBTQ+ identities and more. These groups are great forums to share common experiences and highlight concerns, in addition to – when run well – providing a space with high levels of ***psychological safety***. Psychological safety implies an environment where people are secure in the knowledge that when they speak up there will be no punishment or humiliation.

But it is important that, when there are open events, others who do not identify as being part of the group show up. Why? If we only show up for the group we belong to, there will always be winners and losers, and unequal systems that reward characteristics that are unrelated to ability, skills and talent will continue to be rewarded. We should champion change in areas that we do not gain from, too. If enough of us take the time to learn about how other groups may be struggling, real change can happen.

> Change happens when a critical mass of people are all doing the same thing and a tipping point is reached.

A ***tipping point*** is behavioural science speak for the moment when the number of small changes becomes significant enough to cause a much bigger shift. The important thing is that we listen to each other, and really try to walk in the shoes of other people from time to time. Just as you will be asking for help, mentorship and opportunities on your medium-term journey and expecting some yeses, in return you should be giving some yeses to folk that ask for *your* help along the way. I am certain that you will learn something from the experience!

### *INSIGHT 10: KEEP IN TOUCH*

It may feel a bit disheartening to learn how many external biases you may have to battle on your big-thinking journey. Perhaps you already knew that other people's biases were holding you back, or perhaps this was all news to you. Whichever it is, take a second to consider how much they are holding you back versus how much you are holding yourself back. For me, I know that my own versus others' biases are 80:20. What do you think your ratio is? This exercise should help you see that a decent amount of your journey is within your own control.

In this chapter, I have addressed the major occasions where I expect you will encounter biases and blind spots in others on your big-thinking journey. I hope the insights are also transferable to occasions which are not explicitly covered. But if they aren't and you can't find answers by seeking help from your existing network, I would love to help you. At the back of the book, I've noted how you can get in touch with me so I can continue to help you move forward. What's most important is that you are not waylaid for too long on your journey to ME+.

## HOW CAN YOU END OTHER PEOPLE'S BIASES AND BLIND SPOTS?

Learning how to circumvent other people's biases and blind spots can help ensure a smoother road on the journey you have committed to take. Remember Alex, the entrepreneur who was refusing to listen to feedback? When I met her in

2018, she was turning a blind eye to her own disorganization, which was holding her back. However, as I demonstrated, Alex will also almost certainly face the biases of others. Given that far fewer women than men are entrepreneurs, mechanically Alex does not look like the average person in that role. She needs to pay attention so that a falsely perceived lack of 'fit' does not also delay her progress.

The ten behavioural science insights provided in this chapter can help Alex. They can also help you on occasions where you encounter the biases of others. I encouraged you to read this chapter from start to finish. Each insight related to a potential major occasion in your journey when you may be confronted with the biases and blind spots of others. You can call upon the insights as you need them, but I do hope you never do!

Let's recap them now . . .

***INSIGHT 1: HALTING UNCONSCIOUS BIAS, THE REPRESENTATIVENESS HEURISTIC AND STATISTICAL DISCRIMINATION***

You can give certain signals that will identify you as being a good match for a specific role. Research what the signals are and acquire as many of them as possible.

***INSIGHT 2: EVERYONE'S ADVICE IS NOT CREATED EQUALLY***

If feedback does not ring true, adopt the three-person rule and see if they all say the same thing.

***INSIGHT 3: AVOID BEING LABELLED INCORRECTLY***

Fundamental attribution error causes bad luck to be considered part of your persona by others. Hone your communication skills and ensure key stakeholders are always kept in the loop concerning any setbacks.

***INSIGHT 4: CASCADES***

An informational cascade happens when a group gets together and focuses on what they already know. Pay homage to the shared information before you outline a different course. This will ensure that you're heard. Put particular emphasis on data that backs up your ideas.

***INSIGHT 5: JUDGEMENTS***

When your journey relies on being judged by strangers, it is best to take the last slot of the day. Use narratives to connect the benefits of your idea to the real world, ensuring that you end your presentation well to leverage the peak-end effect.

***INSIGHT 6: ARE YOU IN THE IN-GROUP?***

Developing relationships throughout the course of your journey is important. It doesn't have to be all or nothing. Invest time in developing weak ties who you can learn from, and benefit from reciprocity.

***INSIGHT 7: GETTING SMALL YESES***

To make a yes more likely, appeal to the other person's ego with a genuine compliment. Talk about your ideas regularly, as exposure makes them more likely to be adopted.

***INSIGHT 8: WHAT TO DO WHEN FACED WITH A NO!***

When faced with a no, remind yourself that there is learning in failure. You can choose to ask for the decision to be reversed, adopt the feedback you received, or find a new door to knock on. The most important thing? Never give up.

***INSIGHT 9: PLEASE SHOW UP FOR OTHERS***

Pay attention to levelling the playing field for colleagues and acquaintances. Change happens when a critical mass of people are all doing the same thing and a tipping point is reached. Every person who adopts this ethos therefore gets us closer to a more positive status quo. Be one of those people.

***INSIGHT 10: KEEP IN TOUCH***

If you find yourself dealing with a behavioural bias or blind spot that is truly unrelated to what is covered in this chapter, drop me an email and we can try to figure it out together.

Remember these ten insights throughout your big-thinking journey when you run into other people's biases and blind spots, or when preparing for any major milestone that requires interactions with others. I know for sure that if you commit to this strategy, you'll be far more likely find yourself on a smoother path!

Happy circumventing!

Before we move on, make sure that you:

- Have read through the ten behavioural science insights.
- Spend some time to anticipate any occasions when you think you may need these insights. Set reminders in your diary so you remember the relevant insight(s) when you're approaching the event.

### FIVE FAB BEHAVIOURAL SCIENCE CONCEPTS MENTIONED IN THIS CHAPTER

1. **Unconscious biases:** Learned stereotypes that are ingrained and which influence decision-making via System 1.
2. **Tall poppy syndrome:** The tendency for people to knock down others who are achieving great things.
3. **Fundamental attribution error:** This causes us to attribute a person's behaviour to their identity rather than the situation.
4. **Informational cascade:** A phenomenon in which individuals make the same points in a meeting repeatedly.
5. **Peak-end rule:** Implies that people judge an experience based on their feelings at the peak (most intense point) and at the end.

# CHAPTER 6

# ENVIRONMENT

'It's been a hell of a day,' I mumbled to myself, putting my key in the front door. It was January 2020, and from the moment I put my feet on the ground to salute the sun, to the last steps of my journey home, it had been awful. In fact, I had spent the whole day shovelling poop, only for various people to pick it up and start throwing it at each other again. I was exhausted. I was glad to be home.

Each and every day, I am lucky. I get to decompress in an environment where I know that I will be happy, healthy and safe. Whether it's crashing on the couch with my bulldog Kacey, soaking in a hot bath, or reading novels in my love seat, there is something about getting to spend time alone in my sanctuary that can ease the stresses of even my worst days. Waking up each morning and reminding myself that I will get to relax at the end of the day allows me to roll with the punches (or poop!) the day throws at me.

It is essential to find a space – and earmark some time – for rest and relaxation.

This may be an entire house if you live alone, your bedroom if you house-share, or just a nook somewhere at home if you have a gaggle of toddlers to raise. The surroundings that we find ourselves in, whether consciously or unconsciously, affect our behaviour in myriad ways, including our performance, stress levels and happiness.

In behavioural science there is a well-worn adage that ***context matters***.[1] How we behave is affected by the cues we experience on a moment-by-moment basis in our environment. We process these cues unconsciously. For example, people buy more French wine when French music is playing in a store, and more German wine when German music is playing.[2] Why? The music acts as a subconscious cue, ***nudging*** a person towards a particular choice. But we are blissfully unaware of the cue.

External stimuli alter our mood and the decisions that we make without us even knowing it, and stimuli are all around us, both strategically placed (like the music in the shop in the example above) and totally accidental. At the LSE, one of our student prizes even has the name 'Context Matters', to remind students to think about the context in which they did their research when interpreting their findings.

All of the preceding chapters have needed you to be on high alert. In order to make the messages of these chapters work, it was necessary to take continuous small steps. You were experimenting to see what behavioural science insights would help you change your own behaviour, and trying to circumvent the damaging effects of other people's biases and blind spots. But this chapter is different. It is about making decisions about the environment in which you do your work.

The great thing about taking steps to change your environment is that often you can make a structural change once, and reap the benefits for years to come.

You don't need to consciously take actions to choose aspects of your environment every day.

The main aim of this chapter is to outline environmental tweaks that will help you work better and faster. A tweak is a change to your environment that you make once, as compared to small steps that you take repeatedly. These tweaks are mostly easy to do and it is relatively easy to figure out if a tweak gave benefits, as its effects should be felt almost immediately.

But there is one exception . . .

You will have to work hard to make your environment interruption-free. This can be tedious at first, and battling online interruptions is the ultimate challenge. You may find yourself repeatedly falling victim to the ***intent-action gap***, which describes the gap that so often emerges between the actions people say they are going to take and what they actually do. To reflect this, the ten behavioural science insights are split into two distinct sections.

The first section represents the small steps that can be made to help you avoid digital interruptions. Consistent with the space it takes on the page, this change may take a while to embed in your life and requires repetitive actions. We will tackle this first, following the advice of Brian Tracy, a thought leader in individual personal development, who tells us to 'eat that frog' – meaning it is always best to start the day with the hardest task on any list.

The second section represents general tweaks to your environment that should help you work better and faster. These are written as rapid-fire insights for you to consider and should be relatively easy to try out. At the end of this section you should commit to rolling out at least one of these nine insights in your own life now. But, over time, you may wish to incorporate more.

As you work through the two sections, remember that the lessons from behavioural science relate to the average person in a particular population. This means that not all of the suggestions will necessarily work for you. Pay attention to whether the tactic(s) you do choose to adopt changes the level of digital disruptions you experience in your work environment. If not, try another tactic and evaluate the effects again. For the rapid-fire insights, introduce each environmental tweak into your life in a trial-and-error manner, and give it one week to start seeing benefits. This means that you ultimately keep only what is successful and discard the rest. By the end, you will have adopted a combination of insights that work best for you.

Are you ready to get the behavioural science designers in?

### *INSIGHT 1: INTERRUPTIONS*

I struggle to ignore distractions. A ding on my smartphone to signal a social media notification or text message jolts me out of flow. If I'm not paying attention, I can find myself mindlessly surfing the internet. A knock on my office door can cause me to return home with the same to-do list I started my day with. My System 1 even decides to check my email on autopilot, setting me up to be distracted by the random thoughts and requests of colleagues and friends.

In 2018, after a particularly bad day of distractions, I decided to do an audit. I counted and logged the number of distractions that I experienced over seven one-hour slots that fell between 10 a.m. and 5 p.m., my core working hours for one day. The final tally was 5, 9, 4, 7, 5, 3, 11 – 44 distractions in one working day! That was the day I decided to do something to stop distractions for good.

Interruptions are a problem for all of us. In order to work

out just how much they are affecting you, I suggest you do your own workday audit. Interruptions nobble the most precious resource you have: time. They are the ultimate time-sinker. Thanks to an ability to be contacted in person, on the phone, or via email, WhatsApp, Skype, Messenger, LinkedIn, Twitter, Slack, Teams, Zoom and Meets, as well as an ever-increasing list of other mediums that I am blissfully unaware of, we relinquish control of our time to the whims of other people.

> We unconsciously meander into environments that facilitate an excessive number of interruptions.

The cost? Our flip-flopping attention makes it hard to get anything groundbreaking done. Or, indeed, *anything* done at all.

In Chapter 2, we spoke about achieving a state of flow. Flow enables focused work. When you are in flow, time flies. You are immersed. You do your best work. For most of us, this type of immersion involves an activity that flexes significant cognitive muscle. When I achieve flow, I access my most creative and innovative ideas. I am more productive. I can even achieve flow when I batch-respond to emails offline. This means that I go offline, respond to all of my unanswered emails, and leave the room when I turn my Wi-Fi back on. I don't see any responses until I sit down for the next batch. By batching, I am in tune with one task. I am out of tune with the rest of the world . . . until I am interrupted.

Does it matter if we allow ourselves to get interrupted? Yes! Whether you are designing a new product, coming up with a creative solution to a problem, or learning a new skill, you need periods of time without interruptions. Even the briefest of interruptions – like responding to a beep on your phone – can derail flow and cause you to make mistakes when trying to concentrate on something challenging.[3] Interruptions don't just take up time in the moment. They also cause a need for more effort (and time) to return to the same level of flow you experienced prior to the interruption. Interruptions also negatively affect your well-being. They have been linked to irritability, depression and lower levels of job satisfaction across a variety of worker types and contexts.[4] Everyone needs to have some time in their day that is in an environment free of interruptions.

But how can this be achieved?

It is up to you to purposefully design and seek out an environment that serves you well.

One of the biggest interrupters is firmly within our grasp to curtail: digital interruptions. We can turn off alerts and tune out the endless requests for our time. Remember, time is the only resource you cannot replenish. As such, you must set up environmental cues that allow you to protect your time during periods that you wish to avoid being interrupted.

In Chapter 3, the importance of curbing time-sinkers was emphasized as a way to carve out time for the activities that will move you forward quickly. For most of us, the biggest time-sinker is the time we squander online, engaged in a variety of useless activities.

How you set up your workspace can make you more or less likely to succeed in your quest for periods of quiet concentration. At one end of the spectrum, there are those of you whose personal area consists of a laptop. Your workspace venue is TBC each day. It could be a local café, a park, the kitchen table or even a long train journey. At the other end of the spectrum are those who have a devoted home office or a designated workspace in an office. Regardless, the first port of call is always to minimize online distractions.

> Any time we want to diminish a negative behaviour, we should try to increase its costs and decrease its benefits.

It is up to you to increase the hassle of going online when you want to do focused work. In *Make Time: How to Focus on What Matters Every Day*, Jake Knapp and John Zeratsky suggest turning all alerts off on your smartphone, removing email from your desktop and turning the Wi-Fi off to gain focus.

What are the mechanics in how this causes a change in behaviour? It increases the cost of accessing online distractions, and also reduces the pain (that is, you get a benefit gain) of having to grapple with your attention being constantly drawn to an enticing message or refreshing your Twitter feed.

Following their suggestions, I dutifully removed my email and social media apps from my iPhone, along with all alerts. This included phone call and message alerts, resulting in my phone never ringing (and I do mean *never*!). On my desktop, I removed email. I also programmed my Wi-Fi to forget the password that allows me easy access. This means that if I wanted to go online, I had to go downstairs where I had the password written down (my broadband provider handily insists that the password is weird, convoluted and difficult to memorize). Essentially, I increased the cost of accessing the distractions that affect me the most. I made my immediate environment a low-interruption zone.

So did it work?

At first, I found new distractions as I suffered through

withdrawal symptoms. I made tea, I decluttered, I tickled a bulldog who clearly wanted to sleep, and I damned Jake Knapp and John Zeratsky to an equally miserable existence and boring environment.

But I persevered.

I will confess to persevering only because the hypocrisy of not persevering weighed heavily on me (increasing the psychological cost of quitting). As a commitment device I had told several people that I was making this change. This was a case of the saving face effect working in a *positive* direction.

One week later, the penny dropped. My productivity began to increase exponentially. I was happier and much less stressed. A mantra that I am not a heart surgeon or president of a small country reminded me that being offline for sustained periods would not cause any real harm.

How did I manage with work emails? I am not totally irresponsible. I retained an email app on an old iPad and answered diligently from there once a day. I did this at 6 p.m. every evening. I chose this time strategically, as I knew I was less likely to get distracted by ping-pong responses. If an email required me to do some work to respond, I scheduled it in a queue for some time over the next week, depending on how important I perceived it to be. If I was able to respond to the email quickly, I did so immediately.

Not checking emails on a moment-by-moment basis required real self-discipline because I am a self-confessed addict when it comes to continuously refreshing my inbox. It is something I do unconsciously. You may have a similar online addiction that you need to crack. It may not be a communication tool – it could be gaming, shopping or checking the news.

So what can you do?

Only allow access to your time-sinker from one device. And place that device out of your immediate environment when you need an interruption-free zone. Voila! You have mechanically engineered an interruption-free environment. And what happens next? Your System 1 (your fast brain) will begin to associate that device with the time-sinking activity, making it a new habit to engage in this way and reducing the likelihood that you unconsciously engage in your time-sinker via some other mechanism. This is what I did when I only allowed myself to check emails on my iPad. I also only engaged with social media and messaging on this iPad. I essentially decided to become a person who only engages in online communication once a day, via this iPad.

In the beginning this was very conscious and deliberate. I struggled to not check my emails on my phone or laptop, as I had done routinely for years. On some days, I allowed myself to break, but as a compromise I made sure to fetch my iPad and checked from there. Although in general I was checking more regularly than I'd have liked, I was still solidifying the fact that this was an activity that was associated with the iPad. At some point, my new habit crossed some invisible behavioural science threshold, and being a once-a-day email checker became a part of my identity.

I am always fascinated by how one small change can bring about unexpected consequences or an ***externality***. The majority of people who cluttered my inbox were fine with a slower turnaround. They even got the hint and emailed me less. A minority, not so much. These people took to reaching me in various ways, stopping short only of sending a carrier pigeon. One colleague even insisted that I could open a separate email account to receive emails from priority people. How did I respond to this? At 6 p.m. I wrote a reply letting them know it was super sweet that I was missed, but a separate account would likely be a backward slide in terms of my email addiction and I wasn't prepared to risk it. I thanked them for being understanding as always, and promised to call at 6 p.m. the following day from my iPad. Labelling them as 'sweet' and 'understanding' in this case was a Barnum effect appeal to ego, but thankfully it worked. Freedom!

Okay. I appreciate that some of you will engage in work where it is not possible to allow a twenty-four-hour turn-around on all responses. You may need to react three, four or five times a day. In this case, a priority email account may actually be useful for you. Or you might want to find another very specific way that people relevant to your productive and necessary work can contact you urgently. However, if you truly believe that you need to be sitting on email or some other form of online communication all day long, please question your rationale. Aside from emergency switch operators or folk working in a call centre, it is pretty hard to believe that being constantly on call is the best use of your time.

Don't believe me? Start stealing one hour away from online distractions each day and monitor two things. First, did the world stop moving? Second, did you get something worthwhile done in the time you stole away?

Whether you are sitting in an open-plan office, working in a local café or cocooned in a home office, it is important that you prioritize some time for your small steps. Do this intentionally.

Make a commitment right now to engage with online communications differently.

That commitment should move you from reacting to frivolous online time-grabs that serve as time-sinkers, towards more intentional interactions that provide benefits without distractions.

As a starting point to battling online distractions:

1) What is your biggest digital distractor? ______________

2) Set up your digital environment so you only engage with this distractor through one device. What device will you use? ______________

3) Make a commitment to only engage with that device at particular times of your day. What times will you agree to? ______________

## RAPID-FIRE INSIGHTS

In 2018, I kicked my digital distractions habit. Given my success, the concept of making small changes to my environment that would have disproportionate effects on my productivity continued to pique my interest. I approached my exploration of additional environmental tweaks from a cheap and cheerful DIY perspective.

I am willing to bet that interacting intentionally online, rather than allowing sporadic distractions to grab your time, will do the heavy lifting in terms of carving out hours to devote to your big-thinking journey. It will also mean that networking is more pleasurable as you concentrate fully on the person in front of you. As you come out of your online existence and into the physical world, it is worth looking around you with a question in mind: *Does this physical space help or hinder my ability to think big, take small steps and build the career I want?*

> The environment in which we live and breathe directly affects our performance, motivation, perseverance, and the choices we make at any given moment.

It is important that you choose to spend as much time as possible in an environment that nurtures both you and your ambitions. This is good news for the times we can readily modify our physical space and choose who we work with.

Learnings from behavioural science provide ideas about what environmental tweaks may help reinforce your small-steps habit. Remember, behavioural science studies typically focus on average effects that relate to one particular population. You may be different from both the average and the population in question. However, with certainty, I can say that your environment does change how you behave, your mood and your ability to focus. So let's explore nine rapid-fire behavioural science insights so you can get on with seeing what works for you!

### *RAPID-FIRE INSIGHT 1: AIR*

The ideal workplace has good airflow. Why? Good airflow has been convincingly linked to better performance in the workplace, with poor ventilation linked to absenteeism.[5] If you work in an office, or simply do not have the luxury of this choice, make an effort to work in a well-ventilated area or at least go outside a few times during the working day. A friend of mine swears by taking a notebook and pen and sitting outside on a wall among all of the London concrete at lunchtime. This hour gives him the space to take stock of his day so far. It also allows him to set intentions for productive work in the afternoon. All of this while enjoying the hustle and bustle of people-watching!

A wonderful new friend of mine told how, for as long as she can remember, she always chooses cafés with outdoor space and beautiful surroundings in which to enjoy a break over a cup of tea. She reasons that her beverage may be double the price, but the value added to her well-being far exceeds the hefty mark-up.

Can't find an hour to take a breath outdoors? Plan to take a work call in an outdoor space, or arrange to have a meeting in an airy coffee shop. We devote too much time to useless meetings these days anyway, so we may as well do them in nicer surroundings. At the LSE my office is not well-ventilated. My solution? I choose to hold meetings in a variety of places, including public spaces. Where there's a bench, there's a way!

### RAPID-FIRE INSIGHT 2: GREEN

If you really can't get outside during your working day, take a trip to the local garden centre and bring the outside indoors. Adding plants to your work area has the potential to augment your attention and productivity levels. A green companion is also beneficial in terms of reducing the ill effects of staying indoors too long, such as stress and fatigue.[6]

Now all you have to do is keep the plants alive! If that's beyond you, try a cactus terrarium. Mine even came with ornamental meerkats.

### RAPID-FIRE INSIGHT 3: NATURAL LIGHT

Prioritizing spending time in spaces with good airflow has the added advantage that you are more likely to experience natural light. Sitting on a park bench and writing this chapter may seem like an odd choice for someone who has the option of a private place to work, but the benefits I receive from working in an environment with natural light even include better cognitive performance.[7] I certainly notice that my mood and focus are more on point. I also experience less cabin fever and related fatigue, which tend to strike when I work indoors all day.

### *RAPID-FIRE INSIGHT 4: ARTIFICIAL LIGHT*

Don't have either the inclination or the option to sit outdoors? I live in the UK, so 75 per cent of the year I would be blown away by a westerly wind if I perched on a park bench. If you do have to expose yourself to artificial light for long periods of time, there is evidence that you should choose brighter options if you need to concentrate on a specific problem or task, and dimmer lights if you need to get your creative juices flowing.[8] Experiment and see if this works for you!

### *RAPID-FIRE INSIGHT 5: TEMPERATURE*

Group meetings can be places where we collaborate and push boundaries; we can come up with fantastic ideas or new ways of thinking. With the right group of people who feel psychologically safe and share common objectives, magic can really happen. Groupthink is nowhere to be found. Still, always remember to take the temperature of the room . . . literally.

When people are hot and bothered, they have been shown to be less productive and cooperative.[9] It is the same when you are working on your own.

> Typically, people will find flow easier when the room temperature is between 16 and 24 degrees Celsius.

The exact temperature that is the most conducive to productivity is personal, so why not find out your own range! Buy a cheap and cheerful thermometer and experiment with what temperature you feel most comfortable working in.

### *RAPID-FIRE INSIGHT 6: NOISE*

Of course, sitting in a beautiful café or any public space brings the real risk of unpredictable noise that can act as an interruption. Whether you are distracted by the hustle and bustle around you or can tune it out depends on the person. However, the evidence is clear that quieter surroundings promote motivation[10] and productivity.[11]

> It is up to you to make the effort to work in an environment that is quiet enough for you to focus when you need to.

Controlling the noise in your workspace is easy if you have an office of your own. If you work in a noisy environment, noise-cancelling headphones can help. For those of you who work in an open-plan environment, invest in some kind of sign or signal that you place on your desk to indicate that you should not be disturbed, like a 'Do Not Disturb' sign or a miniature traffic cone or a flag.

If you are working out and about, it is easy to find information online about times when cafés are busy, allowing you to plan your concentrated work around times that are quieter and when you can secure your favourite table. In the same way that you make efforts to plan meetings with colleagues or your new network, pay attention to the plans that you make with yourself for productive time.

### *RAPID-FIRE INSIGHT 7: A SPACE OF YOUR OWN*

A lot of you will have a designated space – whether it's a desk in an open-plan space, a nook in your bedroom, or an entire office. This is the place you go to in order to engage in continuous learning or other focused work. If you do not have an obvious space, try to ring-fence an armchair in the corner of a room or something similar. Remember that routine behaviours build habits. In this case, repeatedly going to one particular space, where you always work on the same thing, causes System 1 to automatically associate that space with that activity.

Why does this matter? It allows you to settle into your tasks and achieve flow more quickly. You can also use this designated space to carry out the weekly planning for your big-thinking journey.

### *RAPID-FIRE INSIGHT 8: CLUTTER-FREE*

Once you have identified your space, it is worth keeping it clutter-free. This helps you avoid being distracted.

A clear space = a clear mind.

If you take the time to visit me at the LSE and pop in unannounced, you will notice that one of my difficulties in life is that I tend to be messy. But I am much happier in less cluttered environments – and it is not just a matter of happiness. I am also better able to concentrate and more productive when my workspace is tidy. I can more easily put my hand on what I need. So I wasn't surprised to see emerging evidence that links clutter to higher levels of distraction.[12]

Decluttering any devoted workspace that you have will make it easier to achieve flow when you need to get in the zone. For those of you who, like me, are naturally on the messier side of things, this will involve recycling and selling some of your possessions. When doing this, be careful not to fall into the ***endowment effect*** trap. This operates by causing an emotional attachment to your possessions and describes the tendency for people to overvalue things that they own. If you have ever sold your house, it probably caused you to overvalue the painting and decorating that you did when talking to the estate agent about the valuation. It is also what is causing you to hold on to old books, clothes and knick-knacks that are no longer of use and might find better homes elsewhere. But once you toss something, you will adapt quickly to the loss. Remind yourself of this so you toss more rather than less, and give yourself that clutter-free zone.

### *RAPID-FIRE INSIGHT 9: COLOUR*

In the process of decluttering your space, there is also an opportunity to freshen up your walls. Research on colour suggests that the colour you put on the walls of your personal workspace may help your performance. However, there is no one colour that has been shown to reign supreme. Along with personal tastes there is also evidence to suggest that the colour you want to surround yourself with depends on what you are trying to achieve. Blue walls enhance creativity and systematic thinking, as well as cognitive performance.[13] Red walls, on the other hand, have been shown as advantageous when focusing on detail-oriented tasks.[14] Red has also been shown to be useful on occasions that call for guts, gumption and a competitive spirit. In a 2005 study, Rowe and colleagues illustrated this in an innovative way by exploring the fact that in the 2004 Olympic Games, competitors were randomly assigned red or blue attire in the wrestling and boxing competitions. The random assignment ensured that there were no systematic differences between those that were wearing red as compared to those in blue. (This could happen if those of higher skill or a more competitive spirit more regularly chose to wear red.) What did they find? Those wearing red are twice as likely to win as those wearing blue.[15]

It is not just the colour that has been investigated with respect to performance, either. How vivid a colour is has also been shown to affect outcomes. In private study spaces, vivid colours have been shown to increase performance over pale colours.[16]

Overall, the literature on colour doesn't offer definitive guidelines on how we should decorate our personal spaces, and an evidence base on colours outside red and blue is not yet established. But research does show it might be worth putting red on one of your walls if you want to evoke a competitive spirit, and opting for blue if what you want is to achieve calmness or lower levels of anxiety.

## HOW WILL YOU DESIGN YOUR PHYSICAL AND DIGITAL SPACE?

Tweaking your environment by drawing on insights from behavioural science can stack the odds in your favour and help you realize your goal. This chapter has been about identifying these tweaks. After discussing how to minimize online disruptions at length, I ran through nine rapid-fire insights to help you create an environment that will make you more focused and productive, in which to take regular small steps and engage in activities that allow you to realize your big-thinking goal.

Let's recap these insights now . . .

***INSIGHT 1: INTERRUPTIONS***

Commit to allowing virtual disruptions from only one device, which you place out of mind and sight when trying to achieve flow.

***RAPID-FIRE INSIGHT 1: AIR***

Seek out spaces with good airflow throughout your day to improve your performance.

***RAPID-FIRE INSIGHT 2: GREEN***

Add plants to your work area to augment attention capacity and productivity.

***RAPID-FIRE INSIGHT 3: NATURAL LIGHT***

Prioritize spending time in places with natural light to improve cognitive performance. If you are not blessed with great natural light options indoors, head outside.

***RAPID-FIRE INSIGHT 4: ARTIFICIAL LIGHT***

When working in a room with artificial light, choose brighter lights for concentration and dimmer lights for creativity.

***RAPID-FIRE INSIGHT 5: TEMPERATURE***

Pay attention to how your solo work and creative meetings play out at temperatures between 16 and 24 degrees Celsius, and adjust accordingly.

***RAPID-FIRE INSIGHT 6: NOISE***

Seek quieter surroundings to increase motivation and productivity for concentrated work.

***RAPID-FIRE INSIGHT 7: A SPACE OF YOUR OWN***

Secure a space of your own and program System 1 to automatically associate that space with concentrated work.

***RAPID-FIRE INSIGHT 8: CLUTTER-FREE***

Keep your workspace clutter-free to improve concentration. Watch out for the endowment effect, which can be the cause of holding on to clutter unnecessarily.

***RAPID-FIRE INSIGHT 9: COLOUR***

Experiment by surrounding yourself (this could be clothing or walls) with blue if you seek creativity, systematic thinking and improved cognitive performance. Switch to red if you want to focus on detailed-oriented tasks or to rally your competitive spirit.

In 2018, I (mostly) kicked my digital distraction habit by paying attention to my digital environment, and altered my physical environment to support more productive working practices. These changes meant I found flow much more regularly, which in and of itself brought joy.

Want to do the same? Commit to a tactic that will curb digital disruptions, and simultaneously choose a rapid-fire insight to try out. Pay attention, and mindfully acknowledge the benefits these changes bring. These benefits can include working better, faster and with more flow. If you see no sign of benefits after one week, modify the tactics you are using to curb digital disruptions and try a different rapid-fire insight. With trial-and-error learning, you are certain to find tactics that ensure you have periods free from interruptions and digital distractions. Equally, as you work through the rapid-fire insights, you will hopefully land on environmental tweaks that work well with your persona.

Eventually you should have trialled all of these insights, and be in a new steady state where the environmental tweaks that work for you are integrated into your daily life. Further down the road, they will fade into the background and simply be a structure that supports your big-thinking goal.

When I put my key in the door a few weeks after the poopy day that made me decide to change things up, I knew I was entering a house with a purposefully designed space that would give me the best chance of working more later if I cared to do so. I didn't work, though. Instead I turned off all of my devices and became engrossed in *Truth Be Told*, Apple TV's latest drama with the fantastic Octavia Spencer.

I also leaned on some behavioural science insights for honing resilience. These are the insights I will share with you next . . .

Happy designing!

Before we move on, make sure that you:

- Make a specific commitment to reduce the amount of interruptions you encounter daily.
- Select one environmental tweak from the nine rapid-fire behavioural science insights that you will roll out into your life tomorrow.

## FIVE FAB BEHAVIOURAL SCIENCE CONCEPTS MENTIONED IN THIS CHAPTER:

1. **Context matters:** The fact that how we behave is affected by the cues we experience on a moment-by-moment basis in our environment.
2. **Nudging:** Provides positive reinforcement that influences the behaviour of individuals.
3. **Intent-action gap:** The gap between what people say they are going to do and what they actually do.
4. **Externality:** A cost or benefit that affects a third party (who did not choose to incur that cost or benefit) because of another person's actions or change in behaviour.
5. **Endowment effect:** Causes an emotional attachment to your possessions.

# CHAPTER 7

# RESILIENCE

'You okay?' Kevin, a good friend of mine, asked in October 2004 as we pulled out of my driveway in Cork.

I was still waving furiously to my dad, even when he was out of sight. The tug on my heart was unmistakable, and it was consistent with the feelings I had felt over the last few weeks. Moving to Dublin to pursue a PhD had been bittersweet. The bitterness came from the loneliness I was feeling in leaving home. The sweetness reflected a brand-new chapter in my life. I would grow and change not just professionally, but personally.

I had high hopes that a change would do me good. The last couple of years had been tough. In January 2003, my cousin and good friend Emmett died at twenty-one from sudden arrhythmic death. Emmett played three sports and was visibly healthy, so to say this was a shock is an understatement. Then in September 2003, just after travelling to Barcelona with my mum for her sixtieth birthday, we found out she had ovarian cancer. It was very advanced by the time of diagnosis, and Mum sadly passed away in March 2004 after six months of being intensely ill. Shortly after that, my wonderful uncle, Emmett's dad, passed away from lung cancer, which was again diagnosed too late for treatment. To say that I had weathered an emotional storm in that short time period is putting it mildly. These three blows called for levels of resilience I sometimes did not have in plentiful supply.

But on that day in October, as I drove to Dublin with Kevin, I would need to summon resilience for something much more ordinary. Something that shouldn't have set my head swirling: the blow I was feeling from leaving home. I was in my twenties, so moving out was natural. Plus, I would see Dad again four days later when I visited for the weekend. And pretty much every weekend after that for the next year. Nonetheless, the emotional punch was real and had to be dealt with.

## DEFINING RESILIENCE

> Resilience is not just coping with major life stressors and tragedies. Resilience includes an ability to roll with the small, everyday punches.

Life's punches come in a variety of sizes. In this chapter we'll look at how behavioural science insights can help you handle everyday punches rather than the ability to handle major life stressors and tragedies, which is quite a different thing. The latter is indeed a key life skill, but it's way beyond the scope of this book, and I hope your big-thinking journey is free of these events. But I know for sure that you will have to face a variety of small blows as you pursue your new goal.

So what type of issues should you expect to deal with?

Depending on your level of resilience, you will define

'punches' differently. For someone with low resilience reserves, a work friend hurrying past them in the corridor rather than exchanging happy greetings as usual will be met with a worry that their friend was being rude or had slighted them intentionally. In contrast, those with high resilience reserves will assume that their friend is busy. They will not worry about the state of their friendship until the pattern is repeated. For them, there has been no punch because they don't sweat the small stuff.

For high-resilience people, being rejected for a job, freelance gig or having an idea batted down might be viewed as 'you win some, you lose some', and they will use the rejection as a chance to reflect on what went right and what went wrong. For those with low resilience, the confidence knock may stop them putting themselves out there again. They may even class the rejection as unfair and feel the world is against them.

Whatever you want to do with your life, I know one thing with certainty: there will be 'ups' and 'downs'. How you handle these ups and downs will impact your ability to progress.

How resilient are *you* to everyday punches? Look at the box below, and consider the lists of events that happen regularly in people's lives. I want you to imagine these events have happened to you and sort each of them into one of three categories, as follows, making the appropriate mark next to the event description:

1 *These things happen* – put an exclamation point next to the event.
2 *I will have regrouped and got over it in a day* – put a circle next to the event.
3 *This would really affect me and stop me in my tracks* – put a star next to the event.

**Taking exams . . .**

- You sit an exam and do not know the answers to a lot of the questions.
- You failed.
- You ranked in the bottom 20 per cent in your class.
- You missed an exam because of bad traffic and have to wait one year to retake it.
- You got a lower grade than expected.

**Public speaking . . .**

- You are sweating with nervousness before you go on to speak.
- A person tells you a point you're making is wrong.
- People are yawning throughout your talk and playing with their phones.
- You faint in the middle of giving your talk.
- You are asked a question you cannot answer during the Q&A.
- The feedback from your talk contains one response that provides detailed commentary on why you should be discredited.
- The feedback from your talk is largely negative.

**Trying to grow a new client base . . .**

- You send twenty emails to prospective clients and no one responds.
- You send twenty emails to prospective clients, and three reply with details on how your product/service does not match their needs.
- You send twenty emails to prospective clients, and five clients reply saying *thanks but no thanks* and that the product is simply too expensive.
- A first meeting with a prospective client gets off on the wrong foot.
- Your biggest client cancels their contract with you.

**Navigating the day-to-day work environment . . .**

- You have an important deadline, and a senior colleague whose input you need is not responding to your emails or calls.
- In an important meeting a colleague talks over you, and drowns out an important point you want to make.
- Despite requesting to be put on a plum project at work, you have not been chosen.
- A colleague misinterprets something you said to them in casual conversation – and, despite you apologizing and setting the record straight, continues their false narrative and complains to your boss.
- You have been paired with a poorly performing colleague for a particular project and they have dropped the ball.
- You emerge from your career development meeting feeling patronized and none the wiser about what it will take to get promoted.
- You are late on an important day at work because your train broke down.
- Your boss makes a mistake and takes it out on you.

**Searching for a new job . . .**

- You have written tailored applications for twenty jobs and have not got one call back.
- Despite an excellent first interview for your ideal role, you do not get a call back.
- The job you are competing for has a task-based assessment that you are pretty sure you just flunked.
- A job interview does not go very well.
- You miss a job interview because of being ill.
- You got the job you applied for but the pay is much lower than your current salary.

How did you do? Ideally, the majority of the events should fall into 'These things happen' or 'I will have regrouped and got over it in a day'. It is truly fantastic if this describes your current persona. But you're in the minority. If you had a few instances of 'This would really affect me and stop me in my tracks', don't worry. Most of us will overreact to temporary failures and get grumpy when our day is more unpleasant than expected.

After doing this exercise, you may realize you have more resilience when it comes to some of life's blips over others. In general, you can expect to be less resilient when you fail at something that plays a part in your personal narratives. You may be very upset by a colleague misinterpreting what you said to them. It could keep you up at night. In contrast, you may shrug off a train delay which causes you to miss a meeting as soon as you finally reach your destination. In this case, it is likely that you hold a narrative that you are a thoughtful colleague, but punctuality isn't part of your identity.

When we have bad luck or fail at something, we rely on resilience.

Luckily, there are some insights from behavioural science that can help build stores of resilience. These insights, if followed regularly, will allow you to be more resilient when you fail or have bad luck, and perhaps get you to a place where you do not notice everyday punches at all.

As in the other chapters, I will present ten behavioural science insights. These are insights that lend themselves to helping people hone resistance, while being relatively easy to integrate into even the busiest daily routines. Don't forget that while each behavioural science insight will help some of you, they will not necessarily help all of you.

Remember to evaluate the success of each item you adopt personally after a week. Keep what is working for you and discard the rest.

### *INSIGHT 1: RESILIENCE AND THE FUNDAMENTAL ATTRIBUTION ERROR*

As a thought experiment, imagine yourself walking a couple of streets from your house on a rainy day. You are heading to an important meeting. A car drives next to you going about twenty miles per hour over the speed limit, splashing you from head to toe. What do you do?

Many of us would curse under our breath. Some of us might curse aloud at the driver as they speed off. Would it change your mood? For how long? Minutes? Hours? Days? Many people would still be seething when they got to their destination, with this story dominating conversation on arrival.

There are many similar thought experiments you can do. A colleague arrives late to a meeting. A potential client makes a remark you perceive as rude. Being kept on hold during a call to the bank.

> Negative events – big or small – stay with us a lot longer than positive events of equivalent size.

Could some of these events be caused by fundamental attribution error, which we met in Chapter 5?

Let's go back and revisit the thought experiment with the puddle-splashing driver. What makes people so annoyed when they are splashed with a puddle? How would you rate the scale of your annoyance from 1 to 10 – where 10 is extraordinarily annoyed – if you were in this situation?

What are your assumptions about that driver? You probably view them as rude, arrogant and possibly even a bozo.

Any other adjectives spring to mind? Would the adjectives that you come up with change if you knew the driver was in a hurry to get to the hospital to see their dying parent? Would the adjectives be different if someone told you the driver was late for a job interview, having been unemployed for months, and they were stressed? Or what if there is another reason that evoked empathy in most of us without hard hearts?

If you had knowledge of the context behind their behaviour, would it have shortened the effect on your mood and changed your chain of reaction? For many, the empathy evoked by the puddle-splasher's circumstances would likely lessen the bad mood.

Why do we reach so quickly for the bozo justification when we are splashed? The answer is the fundamental attribution error. The act of the driver going through the puddle is being viewed as a reflection of the driver's personality rather than simply the situation they are in. Next time, question your anger and the underlying assumption that this is a driver that just doesn't give a rat's behind. I'll level with you: some drivers are bozos, and will take pleasure in soaking your cotton socks. However, an intensely negative reaction punishes you, and not the driver, by looming large over a portion of your day that would otherwise be productive.

Of course, in this example we will never see the puddle-splashing driver again. This means the impact of our reaction on our future relationship with them is irrelevant. But what happens if we succumb to fundamental attribution error when we react to an interaction with a client or co-worker? We may chalk up a first meeting with a new client to getting off on the wrong foot, without knowing that the client has been suffering from insomnia for the last fortnight. Or we may assume a colleague is being rude when they do not answer our emails. But perhaps they are dealing with a personal crisis.

Does it matter? I think it does. Just like you wouldn't want the permanent label of 'irresponsible' if you missed a meeting because of illness, or would like to be cut a break and allowed into an exam hall late if you experienced train delays, other people experience bad luck and have tough experiences that affect their day-to-day interactions. Next time this happens, remind yourself of fundamental attribution error and it may take the sting out of an initial interaction. It should help you move all of these types of occurrences into the 'These things happen' category, making you more resilient to everyday punches.

### *INSIGHT 2: DON'T LET FIRST IMPRESSIONS MATTER*

I once got to sit in on a meeting of senior managers in a midsized firm that involved a presentation from an expensive consultancy firm about diversity and inclusion. There were pie charts, pillars and mind maps. We had run about fifteen minutes over the allocated one hour, and it wasn't clear that the meeting was going to end soon, when a voice I didn't know said, 'If I hear about psychological safety one more time, I'm going to throw myself out the bloody window. This is all bulls***!' I looked around the room at the hung heads, clocked a couple of 'eeek!' faces, and watched as the Interrupter swung open the door and left. It banged shut behind him. The clearly mortified chair of the meeting apologized, and assured the presenter this was an anomaly and that the rest of us were fully engaged. We carried on. Yawn.

After the meeting there was a standing lunch, and nobody mentioned what had happened. This made me all the more curious about the Interrupter. When I had my palm-pressing time with the chair, I asked what the man's name was.

'Oh, that's Greg. Pay no attention to him. He's not a major stakeholder in our diversity and inclusion initiative. We don't need his buy-in. We are all committed to an inclusive workforce. It's great to have your input . . .'

He may as well have patted me on the head to make it flatter, but at least I now knew the name of the Interrupter, albeit it didn't have the same ring to it.

The Interrupter stayed on my mind. Perhaps I was captivated by the irony of screaming 'psychological safety is bulls***' in a diversity and inclusion meeting. Maybe I'm just nosy. Luckily for me, I was doing a short consultancy at his firm and had many chances to run into the Interrupter. The first time he seemed pleasant enough when he smiled and said hello. The second time we had a similar encounter. By the third time, when he offered me the last teabag in the staffroom, there was a sense of kindness that offset his cameo as the Interrupter, and I bravely asked if he had time to talk over his coffee (his second choice of beverage, as I nabbed the teabag).

I'm not a fan of chit-chat, so about fifty seconds into our impromptu discussion I asked what his problem was with psychological safety. What came next, I could not predict . . . He started to laugh. And laugh. And laugh. I stood there awkwardly for at least three minutes.

Once his sides were sufficiently split, he asked me to come meet his team.

What was striking about his team of twenty-plus people was that there were women and men in equal number, and a noticeable black, Asian and minority ethnic presence as compared to other floors. Everyone nodded happily at him. A few shouted jovial greetings. The atmosphere didn't have the same frazzled feeling I had picked up on some of the other floors in the same building. This was puzzling.

I would, in the week that followed, realize that the Interrupter's team was one of the best-performing in this company. This performance was measured in terms of income generated, but the team also consistently reported high levels of job satisfaction and happiness in pulse surveys.

I had judged the Interrupter incorrectly. How? My own biases and blind spots had constructed a false narrative about the type of person he was. First, I had suffered from ***illusory correlation***. I had falsely perceived a relationship between his tantrum and his attitude to equality at work. But no such relationship existed. This unconscious error had helped me construct an inaccurate narrative for the Interrupter. I thought blind eyes were being turned to his bad leadership because money was being made. The reality? The Interrupter was a man who cared deeply about diversity and inclusion. He was annoyed at his firm for using box-checking exercises to avoid the tough conversations about what was happening in other teams. He cared about diversity and inclusion, and that was evident in his actions. He had lashed out in the meeting because he felt that its purpose was virtue signalling rather than a call for real action.

But illusory correlation wasn't the only bias or blind spot that affected me that day. I was also affected by the ***horn effect***, a bias that causes one unpleasant experience to attach other negative attributes to a person without evidence.

First impressions are plagued by biases and blind spots. A negative first interaction like mine can easily be internalized as a punch, with a promise never to engage with the culprit again. Why not try to see negative first experiences as a 'These things happen' event, and save your resilience stores by avoiding the anxiety of worrying about them?

Giving people second chances and opportunities to clear up misunderstandings is one of the kindest things we can do as human beings.

For me, one of the best things I ever did was give the Interrupter an opportunity to give feedback on what I saw as bad behaviour. I learned a lot by engaging with him then, and we are still talking and learning from each other today.

Please do not misunderstand me here. I do not want you to put yourself in a position where you are consistently being exposed to bad behaviour by any one individual. That would make the big-thinking journey you are about to undertake miserable, and quickly erode your resilience stores. Rather, I am asking that you give second chances. Put the boot on the other foot; it will also be much easier for you to hone resilience if you know that second chances are possible when *you* make mistakes!

### INSIGHT 3: CELEBRATE SMALL WINS

Think back to the puddle-splashing thought experiment. Imagine yourself walking a couple of blocks from your house on a rainy day. You see the puddle and the approaching car too late to get out of the splash zone. However, the driver has seen you. They slow in ample time to avoid splashing you. What do you do?

For many of us, that is where this event ends. We will likely not remember it when we arrive at our destination. We might be less likely to wave our hand in gratitude in comparison with waving our fist in anger when splashed. How many of us would smile and wish the driver a nice day?

Okay! Okay! I get it – there is a cost to the splashing beyond an evil deed: you get a good soaking. No one likes being wet! But consider receiving a compliment from a client versus an insult. Increasing your earnings by £100 per week versus losing £100 a week. Whether it is a loss to our self-esteem or a loss to our pocket, loss aversion causes negative events to loom larger over our day when they happen as compared to comparable positive events.

Loss aversion, if left unchecked, causes any loss you experience to feel many times harder than an equivalent gain in emotional currency. We met anticipatory loss aversion in Chapter 4 as an explanation as to why people hold themselves back when going for a promotion or a pitch. In this case, people were holding themselves back because they were anticipating the losses that may come from failing. Now, the loss isn't imagined; it is very real. As a rule of thumb, you can expect to suffer a real loss twice as much as you would benefit from an equivalent gain.[1] So what does this mean for resilience?

Some of you will be taking risks in setting up a business. The business may excel for a while and then go into decline. Some of you will need to make downward moves in your organization to shift to a role that you find more interesting, and take a pay cut that bites. Recognizing that you won't acknowledge the joy of your ascent as much as you will feel the pain of your decline may be enough to make you stop, pause and acknowledge accomplishments when you *do* experience a success.

Keeping loss aversion alive in your mind can help in building resilience, as you are aware of its power to impact on you and can take steps to limit the damage. However, loss aversion is ingrained in us like any reflex, so this strategy will only get you so far. Shifting your attitude to balance losses and gains may be more easily done if you also make conscious efforts to shift your focus towards celebrating gains more regularly. How? On a daily basis, take stock of what has gone well. You can think of this as practising present-day gratitude because it relates directly to something that is happening now.

Can this simple exercise really build resilience? There is evidence to suggest that it can. One innovative study highlighted clearly the link between resilience and gratitude. Conducted by Rosanna Lau and Sheung-Tak Cheng in 2011, the participants – who were all Chinese adults aged fifty-five and over – were randomly divided into three groups. The first group was asked to write about life events that they were grateful for. The second group was asked to write about life events that they worried about. The third group was given a neutral task that did not involve any personal emotion. The researchers then assessed how anxious their participants were about dying – a topic that the researchers expect to be on their participants' minds – and found that those who had practised gratitude as part of the earlier exercise were far more resilient to contemplating death as compared to the two other groups.

Is there evidence beyond older adults? Yes, using a similar set-up. One such study was conducted by Robert Emmons and Michael McCullough in 2003. They focused on resilience in college students, and found that practising gratitude caused higher levels of life satisfaction, better mood and fewer headaches up to ten weeks after practice. These are big gains from a small action. Simple expressions of gratitude can really pay dividends in beefing up resilience reserves. What is more, expressing gratitude has also been linked to lower levels of depression – as well as increased happiness and better self-esteem.[2]

Consciously making a decision to acknowledge small 'wins' is a great way to start practising gratitude and increase resilience.

This doesn't need to be a big deal. You don't even have to write it down – although many people enjoy practising daily gratitude in this way. All that is required is taking five minutes each day (setting a regular time will help make it a habit), and purposely drawing your attention to all of the feel-good moments you experienced over the last twenty-four hours.

From big wins to small positive moments, drawing attention to these occurrences on a daily basis, however ordinary they are, engages your slow brain (System 2). Ensuring that these moments don't go unnoticed helps rebalance how you feel about losses when they do happen. This allows you to put negative occurrences into perspective.

We all have ups and downs, and it is good to curtail tendencies that focus too much on losses and ignore gains.

So start now, and write three small wins you experienced so far today:

1) ______________________________

2) ______________________________

3) ______________________________

### *INSIGHT 4: THE ABILITY TO THINK BIG AND TAKE SMALL STEPS IS A PRIVILEGE*

At seven years old, pizza and movies were enough to give me a respite from any stressful occurrence. As an adult in my thirties, I choose walks and Martinis when I need a timeout from routine stressful events, and three-day trips when things seem to be going haywire.

I would not notice unless I was paying attention to it, but being able to engage in time-outs like these is a privilege. It is also a privilege to be able to think big, take small steps and build the career you want.

You can help to hone resilience by reminding yourself how lucky you are to be able to think big and set about realizing your dreams, while also calling to mind that the knocks you receive along the way are just part of the journey. The sheer fact that you get to go on this journey is a privilege rather than a chore.

This is distinct from practising gratitude when you have small wins. There you are reacting to an event that has already happened. Here I am suggesting that you consciously practise gratitude for the choices that you have in your life, and specifically the choice to take small steps every day towards the big-thinking goal you want.

Around the world, there are millions of people who wake up and do not have the luxury to think big. Some are struggling to make ends meet. Others have their opportunities constrained by tradition or government. Others have to prioritize focusing on their own or a family member's health for now. Others aren't able to work.

> Thinking big and designing a plan to get there is something that you get to do rather than have to do.

We have already discussed the power of framing messages to other people in a positive way. For the small steps associated with your big-thinking goal, frame them as something that you 'get to do'. Doing so is a natural way to instil gratitude for the opportunities that you have. Remind yourself that you are always moving forward, regardless how small your steps are, once you are routinely engaged in the activities you identified in Chapter 2. Remind yourself that getting to engage in these activities is something to be grateful for in and of itself.

Practising gratitude in this way can hone resilience, and

also help weather the phases on your big-thinking journey when you have a steep learning curve or are tackling a lengthy project. It can also act as a reality check when something goes wrong, so you don't overreact and internalize stress, reducing your resilience stores.

### *INSIGHT 5: COMPARISONS MATTER*

I was asked to give a general interest talk to a large firm in 2015, on lessons from behavioural science and resilience. On the day of the talk, I had a high level of energy and I could feel it being reciprocated. I got to the part of my talk where I discussed the ***hedonic treadmill***, a well-known cause for why people do not end up happier when they move ahead in life in terms of income or other status-related goal – because there is always someone else who is achieving more or doing better. We are never done ***keeping up with the Joneses***. There is always someone – somewhere – you could perceive as doing better than you. In a world of Instagram, Facebook and Snapchat, finding them has become even easier.

Just then, I noticed a hand raised in the audience. It was a senior managing director. Grabbing the opportunity to take a big glug of water, I encouraged him to shout out his question with a wave of my hand.

'This has been the biggest difficulty managing people for me,' he said. 'Regardless of how well a person is doing, they are always dissatisfied come bonus day when I am forced to whip out the graph that shows them where their payment is, relative to colleagues who have the same position. Is the transparency worth the misery?'

These days, a call for transparency around pay has led to many big firms showing employees how they are doing as compared to their peers. Because few of us would be comfortable seeing ourselves ranked below average by our employer on any metric, this exercise can serve to make salient how far we are away from the Joneses in a very explicit manner. I am all for transparency around pay – it has been shown to increase the tendency for groups who commonly don't ask for pay increases to come forward more regularly, like women. However, making the day that performance pay is doled out a day to draw attention to relative pay does not make sense if you care about employee well-being and satisfaction. Perhaps this should be the day to draw attention to a graph that shows how far employees have come on their own career journey instead.

> You will draw less on your own resilience reserves if you focus on your absolute progress, and avoid comparisons with others.

This requires a mindset shift. Are you inclined to keep up with the Joneses? Do you compare your wins to those of people that you know or are exposed to regularly? Or do you view wins absolutely, by monitoring your own progress? If I compare myself to other people, I am making relative comparisons. If I am monitoring my own progress over time, I am making absolute comparisons.

It can be hard to focus only on absolute comparisons, but it will pay resilience dividends.

Imagine you are trying to lose weight. Relative comparisons would mean that you judge your progress compared to what others in your weight-loss group achieve each week. You would only be happy with a three-pound loss in weeks where others lost relatively less. Sound absurd? On too many occasions, we automatically measure our progress in terms of relative rather than absolute comparisons.

When you were younger and got your exam grades, did your parents ask you how others in the class did when they were reacting to your grades? Did you compare yourself to how well your friends did? If you were given a pay rise, and at the same time learned that everyone else in your workplace got more than you, would you be miffed? Would it take the shine off of your fatter pay cheque?

Focusing on absolute over relevant comparisons will help keep you performing better, speeding up your progress and maintaining your resilience reserves. Alongside my anecdotes are gold-star academic papers that support these sentiments and emphasize that relative comparisons hurt performance.[3] And if better performance isn't a reason to shun relative comparisons in favour of your own progress, then do it for your well-being.[4] What's the point in looking over your shoulder for someone else to compare yourself to? For a healthier attitude to progress, simply make salient your own progress compared to yesterday.

### *INSIGHT 6: REFOCUS YOUR ATTENTION*

The day that I experienced my greatest-ever embarrassment, the sun was shining, it was the height of summer and I was upside down. I was seven years old, and – hanging from the monkey bars – my tiny little face flushed red when I split my favourite shorts. Hoping nobody would see, I tried to scramble down but was met with a chorus of laughter from the fifty or so boys who attended the local school.

What are the earliest good life lessons you remember? For me, I learned that the best way to recover from an embarrassing moment in the playground is to find something else to take your mind off it. On that summer's day it was pizza and *Gremlins* (a movie that set out to be a horror but ended up being a comedy).

Turned down by a client? Rejected for a promotion? Had a writing submission ignored? Received a grumpy email from a colleague? Got into an argument with your business partner? When something bad happens, it can be worthwhile to take yourself out of that situation for a moment, and to do something else that takes your mind off it. When you do have to address the situation, your resilience reserves will have recovered somewhat. This also serves to minimize the likelihood of the affect heuristic, that mental shortcut that causes decisions and reactions to be impacted by emotions (which is not necessarily in your best interests).

### TAKING YOUR MIND OFF A STRESSFUL SITUATION

What do I do when I need to take my mind off things? It may come as no surprise that I have a ten-item menu to choose from, depending on the occasion:

1. Walking my dog Kacey in Richmond Park.
2. Bootcamp Pilates.
3. Reading fiction.
4. Having a Martini with a friend.
5. Immersing myself in theatre or a film.
6. Switching my phone off and wandering around London.
7. Finding flow with my research.
8. Getting a Thai massage.
9. Visiting somewhere isolated.
10. Visiting my family in Cork.

What should you do as a timeout? If you are someone that benefits from meditation, then go and do that,[5] but each person has their own thing. How we relax and gain perspective is personal, and discovering what works for you will help you endlessly in life. What you do may also depend on the magnitude of the failure or problem that you are dealing with. Most times I don't need to head to an isolated location and go off the grid! It can be enough to take Kacey to Richmond Park for an hour. Watching my bulldog's excitement as she finds a puddle to splash in or a dusty path to roll around in is all I need in those times. Being with Kacey, who is very much in the moment, puts me in the moment, too. It allows me to forget my troubles.

Take a moment now to write down your own ways of taking a timeout from the world:

1) ______________________________

2) ______________________________

3) ______________________________

4) ______________________________

5) ______________________________

6) ______________________________

7) ______________________________

8) ______________________________

9) ______________________________

10) ______________________________

In *Thinking Fast and Slow*, Daniel Kahneman writes, 'Nothing in life is as important as you think it is, while you are thinking about it.' If you allow a negative event that has occurred to occupy your mind, it will do just that – making a mountain out of a molehill. If you find yourself in an embarrassing situation, call to mind the spotlight effect (see p. 159). Odds are that other people are too busy fussing over their own mistakes and misdemeanours to care much about your cock-up. It's much easier to dust yourself off after failure when the realization dawns that very few people have noticed it.

To be clear, I am not suggesting that you go away forever. Nor am I suggesting that feelings should be buried deep down or that you deny yourself a moment to scream out in fury in the comfort of your own home. I am, however, suggesting that after experiencing an 'I will have regrouped and got over it in a day' or 'This would really affect me and stop me in my tracks' situation, you retreat for a while and focus on something else before taking any action.

If the failure or problem calls for decisions to be made, it really is better that you do not react in the moment. Just do yourself a favour and put some time between your heightened emotions and any binding decisions or actions. Most of the time, the big decisions in life allow for this breathing space, even if prompted by what seems at the time to be a catastrophe. So take that bit of breathing room. Don't send an angry email or throw a silly tantrum. It is fine to tell anyone asking you to react in the moment that you need some time to regroup, and it is not okay that they put you on the spot. Take that time to regroup, de-stress and build resilience.

### *INSIGHT 7: REVISIT YOUR TIME-SINKERS*

Yesterday, I ate takeaway for breakfast, lunch and dinner. I didn't go for a walk. I spent my time in unnecessary meetings, four of them with no agenda. People discussed their half-baked ideas. People spoke only to hear the sound of their own voice. I slowly lost the will to live. Last night I got four hours of interrupted sleep. My ability to buffer any stresses that may come my way today is pretty much zero. My resilience stores are truly depleted.

Yesterday I spent my most precious resource – time – badly.

In Chapter 3, you took some time to identify time-sinkers. You may have noticed that I identified unnecessary meetings just now. This is not to be mistaken with the time I spend speaking to people to explore collaborations, advance projects or just to connect. Those are interactions I cannot do without. Unnecessary meetings are something that I can most definitely live without.

You will have days when it seems like your time has evaporated into thin air. The knock-on effect is that you will not get any productive work done and you will not achieve flow. By the end of the day it will feel like nothing has been accomplished. When you are carrying this feeling, you will be less resilient and are less likely to roll with the punches. On these days, or perhaps one day after, it is worth doing a time audit of the day that you had, to identify the activities you engaged in that caused your lack of progress. Had you already identified these as time-sinkers in Chapter 3? Perhaps you had a blind spot and didn't identify them then? Perhaps these are activities you do not think you can get out of? Can you challenge this assumption?

> Identifying activities in your day that drain you, and cutting them down or avoiding them outright, will help protect your resilience levels.

It also frees up time to spend on the small steps you need to take to realize your big-thinking goal. Up to this point, these small steps have related to the skills that you wish to develop and the activities you want to be engaged in for your big-thinking goal. Now I would ask that you reassess how you are spending your time, and replace activities that drain you (like unnecessary emails) with things that replenish you. The cornerstone of this has to be eating healthy foods and moving your body more. If you eat better and get more exercise, you will find you have more energy and a clearer head. This can motivate a virtuous cycle where you become even more focused and confident in your ability to achieve your big-thinking goal, and also more resilient.

In the last section, you identified activities to engage in when you need a timeout. You chose these activities because engaging in them makes you feel better. Along with setting intentions to eat better and move more, why not incorporate one or more of these timeout activities into your weekly planning? You don't wait until your car breaks down to invest in its maintenance, so why wait until your resilience reserves are empty to top them up?

### INSIGHT 8: MEASURING YOUR RESILIENCE

As an academic, I get rejected a lot. It is part of the job. I write papers, and even those with high levels of creativity get rejected.

I say it is 'part of the job' because if you are an academic that is not getting rejected by journals, you are certainly not aiming high enough. It is easy to get published in a low-ranking journal, and much harder to get published in the very top international journals. I can say for sure that I have become much more resilient to rejection over the years because it has allowed me to stay in a job that I love. But is it possible to know how your resilience levels are improving? And can this knowledge help hone further resilience? Can resilience be measured?

In Chapter 3 we discussed that what gets measured gets done. By measuring and monitoring our progress, we are – by default – paying attention to it. Our progress has ***increased***

***saliency***. We are blatantly aware of improvements, and these gains help spur us on.

The same is true with resilience. In the same way that saliency helps you stick to your small-step activities because they are at the forefront of your mind, you will find it easier to continue investing in your resilience if you are aware that your reserves are increasing.

But to audit our resilience levels, we need to measure them. How that is done is not so obvious . . .

If you could buy resilience in a bottle, what would it look like? Would the ingredients be 50 per cent hardiness and 50 per cent mental toughness? Research suggests that people blessed with high levels of resilience are also likely to have these two personality traits.[6] You can measure how your resilience levels are changing by monitoring your scores on a brief resilience scale that captures these traits.

Owed to Bruce Smith and colleagues and introduced in 2008, the scale has six statements as follows:

1 I tend to bounce back quickly after hard times.
2 I have a hard time making it through stressful events.
3 It does not take me long to recover from a stressful event.
4 It is hard for me to snap back when something bad happens.
5 I usually come through difficult times with little trouble.
6 I tend to take a long time to get over setbacks in my life.

When considering these six statements, you should assess whether you strongly disagree, disagree, neither agree nor disagree, agree or strongly agree.

For questions one, three and five, scoring is 1=strongly disagree, 2=disagree, 3=neutral, 4=agree and 5=strongly agree. For questions two, four and six, the scoring is 5=strongly disagree, 4=disagree, 3=neutral, 2=agree and 1=strongly agree. The higher your score, the more resilient you are.

When beginning to audit your resilience levels, never make any judgement on where your starting point is. Improvement is always what you need to focus on. Remember that absolute – rather than relative – progress is what matters. Simply focus on truthfully scoring your responses to the statements above every six months, and pay attention to whether your score increases over your big-thinking journey.

The simple act of making your progress salient can keep you investing in your own resilience.

### *INSIGHT 9: REDEFINING PUNCHES*

We started this chapter discussing how different people will define what an everyday punch is differently. But people also change over time. One of the biggest things that has changed for me over the last decade is how I have redefined what an everyday punch is, allowing me to no longer sweat the small stuff.

Rather than measuring resilience in the manner described in the last section, you can also make your progress salient by reflecting on how your coping skills are changing in your regular weekly planning session. This is easy to do, and requires that you make a list of all of the negative things that have happened over the last week. As we did at the beginning of the chapter, categorize these events into 'These things happen', 'I will have regrouped and got over it in a day' and 'This would really affect me and stop me in my tracks'. You are increasing in resilience if you notice a relative increase in the first two categories, as compared to the number in the third.

Of course, as you increase in resilience, how you define a negative event will also change. If you notice that the list of weekly negative things is getting significantly shorter over the course of your journey, you can have faith that you are rolling with everyday punches much more often. This happens because events that made the list at the beginning of your journey, such as a colleague throwing an unnecessary tantrum or you getting negative feedback, are no longer showing up.

> The joy of not sweating the small stuff is that the small stuff is not even remembered. This frees up your time to focus on what really matters.

Do distinguish between rolling with the punches and allowing yourself to be punched unnecessarily. As a general rule, I don't blink if a colleague throws a tantrum. However, I am not someone to be held hostage, and if it is a regular occurrence I just silently write them out of my schedule.

### INSIGHT 10: SLEEP

*ZZZZZZZZZZZZZZZZZZZZZZZZZ.*

'Scientists have discovered a revolutionary new treatment that makes you live longer. It enhances your memory and makes you more attractive. It keeps you slim and lowers food cravings. It protects you from cancer and dementia. It wards off colds and flu. It lowers your risk of heart attacks and stroke, not to mention diabetes. You'll even feel happier, less depressed, and less anxious.'

The above paragraph is from *Why We Sleep* by Matthew

Walker. This book does a great job in detailing convincing evidence that sleep really is a panacea for many afflictions that affect our well-being. For the purposes of this book, healthy sleep habits make you more resilient. Sleep is also a good response mechanism when you have had a stressful day.

I do love sleep. I find it restores me when things get tough.

> After a good night's sleep, you should be better able to roll with life's punches.

A solid seven hours' sleep gives me the energy I need to be engaged when meeting colleagues, collaborators and students, and also makes me more likely to find flow in my continuous learning. The optimal amount of sleep may vary from person to person, but knowing how much sleep you need and putting structures in place to ensure you get it is a commitment to self-care that pays dividends in terms of resilience and beyond.

***TOP TIP: GETTING BETTER SLEEP***

To help you sleep better, choose one or more of the suggestions below to integrate into your routine. Like all of the behavioural insights we have discussed before, use a trial-and-error approach when trying these out:

1. Go to bed and wake up at the same time each night and morning.
2. Limit exposure to bright lights one hour before sleeping.
3. Commit to an unwinding period an hour ahead of bedtime that is free of screens of any kind.
4. Do not keep your phone or any other electronic device in the bedroom.
5. Avoid caffeine four hours before bedtime, and add a relaxing drink like hot milk or a herbal tea to your unwinding period.

6 Avoid eating heavy meals four hours before you go to bed.
7 Keep your sleeping area clutter-free.
8 Invest in breathable fabrics like cotton for your sheets, pillowcases, duvet covers and sleepwear.
9 Keep your room between 15 and 22 degrees Celsius, monitoring how you sleep within this range to isolate the perfect temperature for you.
10 Keep your room dark while you *zzzzzz*.

## PERSEVERE

Higher levels of resilience make you more likely to persevere. This particular life skill also correlates with higher levels of happiness, better mental health, fewer days lost to ill health, higher levels of innovation, and improved motivation. This makes investing in increasing your resilience levels very much worth your while.[7]

Back in 2004 when I made the move from Cork to Dublin, my resilience reserves were low. Lucky for me, my friend Kevin was in the driving seat (both literally and figuratively) that day to take my mind off things and assure me that the feelings would pass. It is worth emphasizing that at times when you aren't able to rely on your own resilience reserves, you can and should lean on a friend. Life is too short to always face the punches alone, particularly when we don't have to.

Of course, dealing with punches is not all bad. Being exposed to negative situations in itself builds resilience. Weathering storms brings benefits. It provides evidence of your coping skills. When you fail and persevere, you are building evidence that you are gritty. When you come out the other end of bad office politics with collegial relationships intact, you build evidence that you are respected. When you don't internalize someone else's negativity, you build evidence that you are strong. When you emerge from change intact, you build evidence that you are a survivor. Evidence creates a new positive narrative about your character that you then internalize.

This chapter has been about providing behavioural science insights that can help cultivate resilience. Let's recap them . . .

***INSIGHT 1: RESILIENCE AND THE FUNDAMENTAL ATTRIBUTION ERROR***

Next time you have a negative encounter, remind yourself of fundamental attribution error. It may help you downgrade the encounter so it doesn't affect your mood.

***INSIGHT 2: DON'T LET FIRST IMPRESSIONS MATTER***

First impressions are plagued by biases, blind spots and heuristics. Giving second chances and clearing up misunderstandings is one of the kindest things we can do as human beings.

***INSIGHT 3: CELEBRATE SMALL WINS***

Call to mind small wins on a daily basis.

***INSIGHT 4: THE ABILITY TO THINK BIG AND TAKE SMALL STEPS IS A PRIVILEGE***

Remind yourself daily that the sheer fact that you get to think big, take small steps and build the career you want is a privilege rather than a chore.

***INSIGHT 5: COMPARISONS MATTER***

Focus on absolute over relative comparisons to keep you performing better.

***INSIGHT 6: REFOCUS YOUR ATTENTION***

When something bad happens, take yourself out of that situation and do an activity that takes your mind off it, to circumvent the affect heuristic.

***INSIGHT 7: REVISIT YOUR TIME-SINKERS***

Guard your time from time-sinkers that deplete your resilience reserves. Reallocate this time to an activity that replenishes you.

***INSIGHT 8: MEASURING YOUR RESILIENCE***

Make the progress from your investments in resilience salient by auditing your resilience levels with a validated measuring tool.

***INSIGHT 9: REDEFINING PUNCHES***

Make the progress from your investments in resilience salient by paying attention to whether you are redefining what a punch is.

***INSIGHT 10: SLEEP***

Sleep.

Trialling these insights allows you to hone resilience. As your resilience reserves improve, you will notice that experiencing failure and problems in your journey becomes less of a big deal. You will see the learning in these new experiences instead. You will reframe what has happened as something challenging to overcome rather than a permanent obstacle. Dealing with punches is viewed as part of the ride. You take a punch, get up and move on. You adapt.

Happy honing!

Before we move on you should have:

- Made a list of the negative events that you experienced over the last week and sorted these events into three separate categories: 'These things happen', 'I will have regrouped and got over it in a day' and 'This would really affect me and stop me in my tracks'.
- Chosen one or more of the insights in this chapter to incorporate into your journey.

## FIVE FAB BEHAVIOURAL SCIENCE CONCEPTS:

1. **Psychological safety:** An environment where people are secure in the knowledge that when they speak up there will be no punishment or humiliation.
2. **Illusory correlation:** The phenomenon of perceiving a relationship between variables when no such relationship exists.
3. **Horn effect:** A bias that causes one unpleasant experience to attach other negative attributes to a person without evidence.
4. **Keeping up with the Joneses:** Using a comparison with others as a benchmark for your own success.
5. **Increased saliency:** Draws attention to the benefits of an action and makes a person more likely to keep on doing it.

# CHAPTER 8

# JOURNEY

Across the world, every day, people decide that they need to make a change at work. Many of you will have come to this book aiming to shake things up. You want to earn a living doing something *better* than what you do currently. What 'better' means will be personal to each and every one of you, but that doesn't mean that the principles to get there are different.

You may want to be happier at work, be more autonomous or do something that motivates you. You could be seeking personal fulfilment or looking for work that is socially responsible, or aiming for more money, status or power. You may want to work with people or work in solitude. You may want to be creative, innovative or work with numbers. What determines your wants are your values and preferences. These are different for all of us, and they change as we go through life.

The size of the goal you are shooting for will also differ. Some will plan to accelerate their career. Others will want to do a lateral move. More still will start a side hustle. Others will want to change career track altogether.

What you all have in common is that you are more likely to succeed if you put in place a plan that has structures to help circumvent your own biases and blind spots, as well as those of others.

Making the big-thinking journey a medium-term expedition is going to increase the odds of succeeding because the upheaval to your life is not too great. The core of this book set out a framework to help you do that, and there is value to returning to these pages throughout your big-thinking journey.

As you leave these pages you will have salient in your mind some well-defined goal to aim for, as laid out in Chapter 2. This is your big-thinking goal. You created it when you took the time to think big and decided on what work you wanted ME+ to be doing for a living. Linked to this goal you will have identified a set of activities that allow you to achieve it. These are the small steps, which if taken regularly will allow you to realize your goal. In Chapter 2, you also spent some time reflecting on the personal narratives that are holding you back. Once these narratives are identified, they can be changed by engaging in processes that align with the new story you want to write for yourself. For example, if you hold a belief that you always quit striving for goals that you set for yourself, focus on showing up for the small steps you also identified in Chapter 2. The small steps are then a process. By engaging in this process repeatedly, a new narrative emerges that replaces the older, negative narrative. Draw attention to the progress you are making by having weekly check-ins. Making the progress salient brings the benefits of the process to the forefront of your mind, motivating you further.

Time is your most precious resource. Spend it well. To give you time back so you can take regular small steps and realize your big-thinking goal, in Chapter 3 you identified your time-sinkers and made commitments to curtail them. To help keep these promises you made to yourself, you were given ten behavioural science insights. Do remember to pay attention to the effects these insights have on you as you incorporate them into your regular routine. You are unique and special, and different things work for different people. If you adopt an insight and it works for you, keep doing it. Otherwise, stop. This is trial-and-error learning.

As you finish this book you should recognize that your own cognitive biases will interfere with both your planning and the journey itself. Don't underestimate the challenge associated with curbing these biases. Many biases are engaged by System 1, your fast brain, at an unconscious level. You might be able to see logically how you could develop a bias, but it is difficult to stop automatic responses. To help yourself with this, you should have chosen some insights from Chapter 4 to integrate into your big-thinking journey. Doing so makes it more likely that your journey will be successful. Bon voyage!

Of course, it isn't all about you. In Chapter 5 we discussed how the cognitive biases of others can hold you back. Should you care? It is all very well to say no, you shouldn't – sod them! But what if the person – or persons – with the biases and blind spots can influence your progress? It is probably best to circumvent the issue, rather than suffering the progress blow. To help with this, Chapter 5 provided insights that will help you navigate around the biases and blind spots of others. You should refer back to these insights when other people get in the way of your progress. This includes hindering your ability to take regular small steps, and putting major obstacles in your way. Remember you can always reach out if you find yourself in a situation that seems insurmountable!

The environment that we live and breathe in most definitely affects our performance, motivation, perseverance, and the choices we make at any given moment. Learnings from behavioural science provide insights into what modifications may help reinforce your big-thinking journey. In Chapter 6 we covered tweaks that you can make to your own physical environment which can improve the chances of you reaching your big-thinking goal. The fantastic thing is that giving a small amount of attention to air, green, light, temperature, noise, space, clutter and colour can pay dividends. This chapter also covered changes you can make to your environment to stop digital interruptions – the ultimate time-sinker! You should now be leaving this book with a commitment to engage with online communications differently. We discussed picking your biggest distractor and intentionally setting up your digital environment so you only engage on one device and at particular times of your day. Trust me – it works!

And last but definitely not least, Chapter 7 discussed behavioural science insights that can help you hone resilience. Here we focused on developing resilience that will allow you to roll with everyday punches. Investing in honing resilience can also have positive impacts on your life outside your big-thinking journey. This core life skill correlates with higher levels of happiness, better mental health, fewer days lost to ill health, higher levels of innovation and improved motivation. Higher resilience levels also allow you to bounce back more easily from (or not even notice!) setbacks in your journey, setting you up to realize your chosen goal.

These six chapters, and the six key messages within them, are a framework for your big-thinking journey. Return to this book to remind yourself of the insights in each chapter from time to time. Although I have been writing with career-building in mind, the lessons in these chapters can also help you pursue other goals. For instance, Chapter 3, which discusses time-sinkers, is relevant when you need to make more space for family, self-care and your social life. Some of the messages on curbing your own biases in Chapter 4 are useful when trying to understand why you don't show up for yourself when you set health or financial goals. And paying attention to the tools described in Chapter 7 with respect to honing resilience will serve you well in all areas of life.

I hope the content of this book helps you reach your big-thinking goal with time to spare. It is exciting to set off on a career journey with intention. As I've emphasized throughout the book, any outcome is the product of luck and effort. So let me take this opportunity to wish you lots of good luck! I have every faith that you will put in sustained effort and meet your ME+ in the next few years. In the meantime, enjoy the journey!

On your journey, remember that those you meet along the way are also striving for their best lives. They have doubts, worries and feel pain just like you. Whenever you encounter people, you don't know what is going on in their lives. They may be hitting obstacles, or having a tough time. They may be falling victim to their own or others' biases and blind spots. They may not have high resilience levels. They may need you to help them with *their* journey. We've seen how other people can scupper your best-laid plans. For the people you meet, *you* are 'other people'. So when you meet others, pause. It takes just a moment to give a kind greeting. There is always room in your diary to lend a helping hand. Practise patience when others make mistakes. Respect them as you expect to be respected. Slow down and pay attention. When we are racing around, System 1 allows us to perform pretty well on autopilot, but it can also cause us to miss moments when other people need us to notice them. Those moments are worth giving time to.

Slow down, pay attention and always be kind.

Happy beginnings!

You can contact me by emailing g.lordan@lse.ac.uk

# Acknowledgements

The saying goes that it takes a village. For this book it took a city. London. I am particularly grateful to all of the people who have shared their stories and anecdotes with me in the City of London and beyond. It is learning of their experiences that has allowed me to get a clearer image of how behavioural biases hold people back in their careers, and what can be done about it. The number of people who have welcomed me into their offices and lives – across all levels of industry and beyond – since I landed in London in 2011, continues to astound me. Thank you for trusting me with your stories, pushing on my theories, and for your friendship.

Thank you to Michael Alcock, my utterly fantastic agent, and also his colleagues at Johnson and Alcock. Thank you to Teresa Almedia, who helped me for the last mile to finish on time. Thank you to Penguin Life for taking a chance on me, and Julia Murday for managing me through this process. Thank you to Jack Ramm and Lydia Yadi, my editors, who worked in the shadows to push this project to a different level. Thank you to all the other great people at Penguin who contributed to this book, with a special mention for Gemma Wain. I couldn't have asked for a better experience than I was given.

I am grateful every single day that I work at the LSE, and for the opportunities it has afforded me to meet the brilliant people who work within its walls. I would like to thank all of the colleagues who have supported me across the school over the years. Time is truly our most precious resource, and I have benefited greatly from taking the time of so many others at the LSE across a multitude of departments to discuss the ideas in this book and beyond. A good colleague has pointed out to me that if I forget someone I will be in trouble, so leveraging the Barnum effect, I will simply say a big thank you and 'you know who you are'. I will, though, specifically thank all of my co-authors, scattered around the world, for pushing me to do better work and actually finish papers! And also the behavioural science gang. I have been truly privileged to work with you as we grow behavioural science at the LSE together. A special mention goes to all of my students, and in particular to the first cohort of the MSc in Behavioural Science students, who joined us in 2019 and were with me while I wrote this book and through the COVID-19 lockdown. And also thank you to all of my colleagues who have helped work towards launching The Inclusion Initiative at the LSE.

I am indebted to my partner, Kieran. He has been a sounding board for my ideas, has read various drafts, never lets me down, and made me uncountable cups of tea while I worked every weekend and every evening on this book for months on end. Thank you. Dog lovers will understand why I can't leave these pages without mentioning Kacey, my beautiful bulldog, the perfect mascot. Walking and relaxing with her adds unmeasurable value to my life. Having her snoring next to me while I hit flow in my own work is the perfect background music.

I deservedly dedicated this book to my mum, who I continue to miss dearly. Mum paved the way for all of my opportunities in life, always cheering me on. To know her was to know someone who was extraordinary. I also need to thank all of my family and friends in my home town of Cork for their encouragement. I give special mention to Olive Desmond, my first boss, who all of those years ago showed me leadership through kindness. And to my dad and my aunt Marie, I could not have done this without you. You consistently welcome me home and take care of me whenever I want to drop by. You have been unwavering constants in my support system throughout my life, and this has meant the world to me. You are also fantastic company and I cannot wait to see you both soon.

And last but by no means least, I need to thank *you*. As a reader you have given me your time while reading this book. This has been my privilege. I hope you do think big, take small steps and build the career you want.

Happy endings!

# Notes

## *Chapter 1: Begin*

1 This comes through most clearly in research published by Dan Gilbert and colleagues in *Science* magazine in 2013. They studied more than 19,000 people and got them to report on how much they perceived themselves having changed in the past decade, and also asked them to predict how much they would change in the next ten years. People of all ages consistently said they had changed lots in the past but expected relatively little for the future. See J. Quoidbach, D. T. Gilbert and T. D. Wilson, 'The end of history illusion', *Science* 339/6115 (2013), pp. 96–98.

## *Chapter 2: Goal*

1 In behavioural science we know that most of us want to follow what the crowd is doing. This is called 'herding'. I therefore want to take this opportunity to tell you that 80 per cent of the readers of this book will likely complete this exercise – in an effort to harness social norms, and increase the likelihood that you will complete it, too.

2 It is even possible to consider the effects of stereotype threat by introducing an intervention to a random selection of

children that primes them explicitly prior to taking a maths exam. An example of an explicit prime is to include an illustration of a girl failing to solve a maths problem. A random selection of students taking an exam sees this picture, and gets a heavy hint that girls are bad at maths. This was the research approach taken in a study of 240 six-year-old children. The researchers gathered data prior to the maths test being taken or the picture being seen which indicated that there was no difference in actual perceptions regarding the mathematical ability of girls versus boys held by the children in the study. The authors highlight that, even without prior beliefs that girls are worse at maths than boys, being exposed to the stereotype threat caused them to perform worse than when they had no stereotype threat. See S. Galdi, M. Cadinu and C. Tomasetto, 'The roots of stereotype threat: When automatic associations disrupt girls' math performance', *Child Development* 85/1 (2014), pp. 250–263.

3 The heritability of intelligence is estimated to be between 20 and 60 per cent, depending on the life stage the sample is in. See C. Haworth et al., 'A twin study of the genetics of high cognitive ability selected from 11,000 twin pairs in six studies from four countries', *Behavior Genetics* 39/4 (2009), pp. 359–370; and also R. Plomin and I. J. Deary, 'Genetics and intelligence differences: Five special findings', *Molecular Psychiatry* 20/1 (2015), pp. 98–108.

4 The estimates range from 50 per cent down to 33.3 per cent. See D. Lykken and A. Tellegen, 'Happiness is a stochastic phenomenon', *Psychological Science* 7/3 (1996), pp. 186–189; J. H. Stubbe, D. Posthuma et al., 'Heritability of life satisfaction in adults: A twin-family study', *Psychological Medicine* 35/11 (2005), pp. 1581–1588; M. Bartels et al., 'Heritability and genome-wide linkage scan of subjective happiness', *Twin Research*

*and Human Genetics* 13/2, (2010), pp. 135–142; and J.-E. De Neve et al., 'Genes, economics, and happiness', *Journal of Neuroscience, Psychology, and Economics* 5/4 (2012), pp. 193–211.

5 See Daniel Kahneman, *Thinking, Fast and Slow* (London: Allen Lane, 2011).

6 See R. Koestner et al., 'Attaining personal goals: Self-concordance plus implementation intentions equals success', *Journal of Personality and Social Psychology* 83/1 (2002), pp. 231–244, for a discussion on why the commitment should be both challenging and attainable.

7 See Heidi Grant-Halvorson, *Reinforcements: How to Get People to Help You* (Boston, MA: Harvard Business Review Press, 2018) for a full discussion of studies that cover the psychology of asking for help, backed up by experimental evidence.

8 See V. K. Bohns, '(Mis)understanding our influence over others: A review of the underestimation-of-compliance effect', *Current Directions in Psychological Science* 25/2 (2016), pp. 119–123.

9 Vanessa Bohns has studied such requests, and her research illustrates that face-to-face requests for help are more likely to result in success as compared to email.

10 See D. A. Newark et al., 'The value of a helping hand: Do help-seekers accurately predict help quality?', *Academy of Management Proceedings* 2016/1 (2017).

11 See M. M. Roghanizad and V. K. Bohns, 'Ask in person: You're less persuasive than you think over email', *Journal of Experimental Social Psychology* 69 (2017), pp. 223–226. They show that, in general, people underestimate the probability of success for face-to-face requests, but overestimate the likelihood of a positive response from an email request.

12 When asking for help, we are essentially giving the other person a choice. They can say yes or no. Any choice can be framed

in a way that highlights the positive or negative aspects of the same decision, and framing it in a positive light means a person is more likely to say yes. For seminal work in this area, see D. Kahneman and A. Tversky, 'Prospect theory: An analysis of decision under risk', *Econometrica* 47/2 (1979), pp. 263–291; I. P. Levin et al., 'All frames are not created equal: A typology and critical analysis of framing effects', *Organizational Behavior and Human Decision Processes* 76/2 (1998), pp. 149–188.

13 See Y. Ioannides and L. Loury, 'Job information networks, neighborhood effects, and inequality', *Journal of Economic Literature* 42/4 (2004), pp. 1056–1093, for a review of a large body of evidence which emphasizes evidence of the benefits of social networks to search for and find jobs. Other convincing studies that link social networks to labour market outcomes include P. Bayer et al., 'Place of work and place of residence: Informal hiring networks and labor market outcomes', *Journal of Political Economy* 116/6 (2008), pp. 1150–1196; and J. Hellerstein et al., 'Neighbors and coworkers: The importance of residential labor market networks', *Journal of Labor Economics* 29/4 (2011), pp. 659–695.

## *Chapter 3: Time*

1 The *modh coinníollach* is a weird tense in the Irish language, which relates to affirmative statements in the conditional mood. It's used when you're talking about something that might or might not occur. For example, 'If I were a successful author, I would be very happy.' The *modh coinníollach* is still terrorizing Irish schoolchildren at exam time today.

2 There is an emerging evidence base that links social networking to poor mental health outcomes. For example, spending too much time on social networking websites (see K. W.

Müller et al., 'A hidden type of internet addiction? Intense and addictive use of social networking sites in adolescents', *Computers in Human Behavior* 55/A (2016), pp. 172–177), and being exposed to images that suggest that everyone else leads a better life (see H. G. Chou and N. Edge, '"They are happier and having better lives than I am": The impact of using Facebook on perceptions of others' lives', *Cyberpsychology, Behavior, and Social Networking* 15/2 (2012), pp. 117–121).

3 I would still find it hard to estimate the time-cost of constantly checking my email even with a minute-by-minute time audit. But I can say for sure that the endless checking of my emails prevents me from doing good work – so much so that on the days that I didn't intentionally stop checking my email, nothing really got done.

4 This lack of ping-ponging actually reduced my email flow, as fellow ping-pongers realized that I was no longer in their club. I assume they went off to ping-pong with others.

5 The personalization of interventions is still a young topic in behavioural science, but there is a growing literature that emphasizes its potential across a growing number of life domains. For example, personalizing feedback based on a person's behaviour and circumstances has been shown to be effective in cutting down smoking (see J. L. Obermayer et al., 'College smoking cessation using cell phone text messaging', *Journal of American College Health* 53/2 (2004), pp. 71–79; and A. L. Stotts et al., 'Ultrasound feedback and motivational interviewing targeting smoking cessation in the second and third trimesters of pregnancy', *Nicotine and Tobacco Research* 11/8 (2009), pp. 961–968) and managing diabetes (for a study of type 2 diabetics, see J. H. Cho et al., 'Mobile communication using a mobile phone with glucometer for glucose control in Type 2 patients with diabetes: As effective as an internet based glucose monitoring system', *Journal of Telemedicine and*

*Telecare* 15/2 (2009), pp. 77–82; and for a study for type 1 diabetic patients, see A. Farmer et al., 'A real-time, mobile phone-based telemedicine system to support young adults with type 1 diabetes', *Informatics in Primary Care* 13/3 (2005), pp. 171–178), as well as helping people lead a more healthy and active lifestyle in general (examples include a study by F. Buttussi et al., 'Bringing mobile guides and fitness activities together: A solution based on an embodied virtual trainer', *Proceedings of the 8th Conference on Human-computer Interaction with Mobile Devices and Services* (2006), pp. 29–36; and H. O. Chambliss et al., 'Computerized self-monitoring and technology assisted feedback for weight loss with and without an enhanced behavioural component', *Patient Education and Counseling* 85/3 (2011), pp. 375–382). HMRC also regularly personalize their letters to ensure that tax is paid on time (see the 2012 report from the Cabinet Office's Behavioural Insights Team, 'Applying behavioural insights to reduce fraud, error and debt').

6 Some great studies exploring the impact of peer effects on academic outcomes include S. E. Carrell and M. L. Hoekstra, 'Externalities in the classroom: How children exposed to domestic violence affect everyone's kids', *American Economic Journal: Applied Economics* 2/1 (2010), pp. 211–228; S. E. Carrell et al., 'Does your cohort matter? Measuring peer effects in college achievement', *Journal of Labor Economics* 27/3 (2009), pp. 439–464; D. J. Zimmerman, 'Peer effects in academic outcomes: Evidence from a natural experiment', *Review of Economics and Statistics* 85/1 (2003), pp. 9–23; and B. Sacerdote, 'Peer effects with random assignment: Results for Dartmouth roommates', *The Quarterly Journal of Economics* 116/2 (2001), pp. 681–704. There is also evidence to suggest that peer effects can change other outcomes, such as teaching quality (C. K. Jackson and E. Bruegmann, 'Teaching students and teaching each other: The importance of peer learning for teachers', *American Economic*

*Journal: Applied Economics* 1/4 (2009), pp. 85–108), the propensity to commit crime (P. Bayer et al., 'Building criminal capital behind bars: Peer effects in juvenile corrections', *The Quarterly Journal of Economics* 124/1 (2009), pp. 105–147) and the likelihood of smoking weed and drinking alcohol (A. E. Clark and Y. Lohéac, '"It wasn't me, it was them!" Social influence in risky behavior by adolescents', *Journal of Health Economics* 26/4 (2007), pp. 763–784).

7 See E. O'Rourke et al., 'Brain points: A growth mindset incentive structure boosts persistence in an educational game', *Conference on Human Factors in Computing Systems – Proceedings* (2014), pp. 3339–3348.

8 See J. Aronson et al., 'Reducing the effects of stereotype threat on African American college students by shaping theories of intelligence', *Journal of Experimental Social Psychology* 38/2 (2002), pp. 113–125; D. Paunesku et al., 'Mind-set interventions are a scalable treatment for academic underachievement', *Psychological Science* 26/6 (2015), pp. 784–793; and D. S. Yeager et al., 'Using design thinking to improve psychological interventions: The case of the growth mindset during the transition to high school', *Journal of Educational Psychology* 108/3 (2016), pp. 374–391.

9 See G. L. Cohen et al., 'Reducing the racial achievement gap: A social-psychological intervention', *Science* 313/5791 (2006), pp. 1307–1310.

10 See J. J. Heckman and T. Kautz, 'Fostering and measuring skills: Interventions that improve character and cognition', (No. 19656) National Bureau of Economic Research (2013); and D. Almond et al., 'Childhood circumstances and adult outcomes: Act II', *Journal of Economic Literature* 56/4 (2018), pp. 1360–1446, which provides a compelling argument backed by empirical evidence that soft skills can be changed throughout the life-course. Notably, the authors also suggest that these are far more malleable than cognitive skills in later childhood.

11 See G. M. Walton and G. L. Cohen, 'A brief social-belonging intervention improves academic and health outcomes of minority students', *Science* 331/6023 (2011), pp. 1447–1451, who leveraged administrative data for ninety-two freshmen students at a large university campus.

12 See A. C. Cooper et al., 'Entrepreneurs' perceived chances for success', *Journal of Business Venturing* 3/2 (1988), pp. 97–108.

13 In 2006, G. P. Latham and E. A. Locke reviewed over forty years of goal-setting research and concluded that once the person is committed to their goal, having a specific goal enhances a person's performance and also the likelihood of them getting to where they want to go.

14 See R. Koestner et al., 'Attaining personal goals' (2002); and E. A. Locke and G. P. Latham, 'Building a practically useful theory of goal setting and task motivation', *American Psychologist* 57/9 (2002), pp. 705–717.

15 See E. A. Locke et al., 'Separating the effects of goal specificity from goal level', *Organizational Behavior and Human Decision Processes* 43/2 (1989), pp. 270–287.

16 For the link to happiness, see Paul Dolan, *Happiness by Design: Finding Pleasure and Purpose in Everyday Life* (London: Penguin Books, 2014); for the link to motivation, see Emily Esfahani Smith, *The Power of Meaning: Crafting a Life That Matters* (New York: Crown, 2017). For the link to lower levels of stress and cynicism see Kim S. Cameron, *Positive Leadership* (San Francisco, CA: Berret-Koehler Publishers, 2008); D. Chandler and A. Kapelner, 'Breaking monotony with meaning: Motivation in crowdsourcing markets', *Journal of Economic Behavior and Organization* 90 (2013), pp.123–133; and B. D. Rosso et al., 'On the meaning of work: A theoretical integration and review', *Research in Organizational Behavior* 30/C (2010), pp. 91–127.

17 This draws on the framework laid out by Cameron in *Positive Leadership* (2008).

18 See R. Koestner et al., 'Attaining personal goals' (2002), which highlights that when people see that they are making progress towards a goal they subsequently perform better.

19 For example, see N. Rothbard and S. Wilk, 'Waking up on the right or wrong side of the bed: Start-of-workday mood, work events, employee affect, and performance', *Academy of Management Journal* 54/5 (2011), pp. 959–980. This study considers start-of-workday mood and looks to see how it affects call centre workers. The authors give clear evidence that the mood of the workers at the start of the day has a significant influence on performance quality and how the employee engages with customers. It is worth bearing in mind that your mood distorts how you see and act in the world. While you cannot always control your feelings, you can be more sensitive towards yourself when you are having a bad day.

20 The compromise effect has been well studied in marketing, and explains purchase decisions pretty well. It implies that if you are buying anything and are presented with three options, the majority of people will opt for the mid-priced choice. See, for example, A. Chernev, 'Context effects without a context: Attribute balance as a reason for choice', *Journal of Consumer Research* 32/2 (2005), pp. 213–223; N. Novemsky et al., 'Preference fluency in choice', *Journal of Marketing Research* 44/3 (2007), pp. 347–356; and U. Khan et al., 'When trade-offs matter: The effect of choice construal on context effects', *Journal of Marketing Research* 48/1 (2011), pp. 62–71. If humans tend to prefer a moderate option when making purchase decisions, what's not to say that we don't also prefer a more moderate option when allocating our time? Perhaps you have a hidden Goldilocks persona, and this approach will allow you to hit on a workload that's just right!

21 See Richard H. Thaler and Cass R. Sunstein, *Nudge: Improving Decisions about Health, Wealth, and Happiness* (New Haven, CT:

Yale University Press, 2008); J. Bhattacharya et al., 'Nudges in exercise commitment contracts: A randomized trial', *NBER Working Paper Series* 21406 (2015); and K. Volpp et al., 'Financial incentive-based approaches for weight loss: A randomized trial', *JAMA* 300/22 (2008), pp. 2631–2637.

## *Chapter 4: Inside*

1 Yes, we behavioural scientists do have an answer for everything! Don't believe our theory? Well then you must be biased! Handy, eh?

2 See Scott Page, *The Diversity Bonus: How Great Teams Pay Off in the Knowledge Economy* (Princeton, NJ: Princeton University Press, 2017).

3 See R. Stinebrickner and T. R. Stinebrickner, 'What can be learned about peer effects using college roommates? Evidence from new survey data and students from disadvantaged backgrounds', *Journal of Public Economics* 90/8-9 (2006), pp. 1435–1454.

4 See S. Pinchot et el., 'Are surgical progeny more likely to pursue a surgical career?' *Journal of Surgical Research* 147/2 (2008), pp. 253–259, which illustrates occupational inheritance for medical doctors; V. Scoppa, 'Intergenerational transfers of public sector jobs: A shred of evidence on nepotism', *Public Choice* 141/1 (2009), pp. 167–188, which looks at public sector jobs; B. Feinstein, 'The dynasty advantage: Family ties in congressional elections', *Legislative Studies Quarterly* 35/4 (2010), pp. 571–598, which considers positions in US government; and L. Chen et al., 'Following (not quite) in your father's footsteps: Task followers and labor market outcomes', MPRA Paper 76041 (2017), which highlights that children choose jobs involving similar tasks to those their parents do.

5 See R. Brooks et al., 'Deal or no deal, that is the question: The impact of increasing stakes and framing effects on decision-making under risk', *International Review of Finance* 9/1-2 (2009), pp. 27–50, and J. Watson and M. McNaughton, 'Gender differences in risk aversion and expected retirement benefits', *Financial Analysts Journal* 63/4 (2007), pp. 52–62, for evidence on gender; C. C. Bertaut, 'Stockholding behavior of US households: Evidence from the 1983–1989 Survey of Consumer Finances', *Review of Economics and Statistics* 80/2 (1998), pp. 263–275, and K. L. Shaw, 'An empirical analysis of risk aversion and income growth', *Journal of Labor Economics* 14/4 (1996), pp. 626–653, for evidence on education levels; J. Sung and S. Hanna, 'Factors related to risk tolerance', *Journal of Financial Counseling and Planning* 7 (1996), pp. 11–19, and D. A. Brown, 'Pensions and risk aversion: The influence of race, ethnicity, and class on investor behavior', *Lewis & Clark Law Review* 11/2 (2007), pp. 385–406, for evidence on ethnicity gaps in the US; W. B. Riley and K. V. Chow, 'Asset allocation and individual risk aversion', *Financial Analysts Journal* 48/6 (1992), pp. 32–37, and R. A. Cohn et al., 'Individual investor risk aversion and investment portfolio composition', *The Journal of Finance* 30/2 (1975), pp. 605–620, for evidence on differences by wealth.

6 See P. Brooks and H. Zank, 'Loss averse behavior', *Journal of Risk and Uncertainty* 31/3 (2005), pp. 301–325; and U. Schmidt and S. Traub, 'An experimental test of loss aversion', *Journal of Risk and Uncertainty* 25/3 (2002), pp. 233–249.

7 See M. Mayo, 'If humble people make the best leaders, why do we fall for charismatic narcissists?' *Harvard Business Review* (7 April 2018).

8 See John Annett, *Feedback and Human Behaviour: The Effects of Knowledge of Results, Incentives and Reinforcement on Learning and Performance* (Harmondsworth, Middlesex: Penguin Books,

1969) and Albert Bandura, *Principles of Behavior Modification* (New York, London: Holt, Rinehart and Winston, 1969).

9 See A. Kluger and A. DeNisi, 'The effects of feedback interventions on performance: A historical review, a meta-analysis, and a preliminary feedback intervention theory', *Psychological Bulletin* 119/2 (1996), pp. 254–284. This meta-analysis combines 607 effect sizes that relate to 23,663 observations in a statistical analysis that examines the effects of feedback on performance.

10 See V. Tiefenbeck et al., 'Overcoming salience bias: How real-time feedback fosters resource conservation', *Management Science* 64/3 (March 2013), pp. 1458–1476, which highlights that real time feedback changes energy intensive resource consumption.

11 See T. Gilovich et al., 'The spotlight effect in social judgment: An egocentric bias in estimates of the salience of one's own actions and appearance', *Journal of Personality and Social Psychology* 78/2 (2000), pp. 211–222.

12 For a good discussion on these two biases, see J. Baron and I. Ritov, 'Omission bias, individual differences, and normality', *Organizational Behavior and Human Decision Processes* 94/2 (2004), pp. 74–85.

13 See, for example, I. M. Davison and A. Feeney, 'Regret as autobiographical memory', *Cognitive Psychology* 57/4 (2008), pp. 385–403; T. Gilovich et al., 'Varieties of regret: A debate and partial resolution', *Psychological Review* 105/3 (1998), pp. 602–605; and M. Morrison and N. Roese, 'Regrets of the typical American: Findings from a nationally representative sample', *Social Psychological and Personality Science* 2/6 (2011), pp. 576–583.

14 See S. Davidai and T. Gilovich, 'The ideal road not taken: The self-discrepancies involved in people's most enduring regrets', *Emotion* 18/3 (2018), pp. 439–452.

15 For an example study, see D. M. Tice et al., 'Restoring the self: Positive affect helps improve self-regulation following ego

depletion', *Journal of Experimental Social Psychology* 43/3 (2007), pp. 379–384.

## *Chapter 5: Outside*

1 I would choose someone myself, but of course I don't want to isolate a specific set of readers.
2 Sadly for them, the £100 was hypothetical!
3 See S. J. Solnick, 'Gender differences in the ultimatum game', *Economic Inquiry* 39/2 (2001), pp. 189–200; and C. Eckel et al., 'Gender and negotiation in the small: Are women (perceived to be) more cooperative than men?', *Negotiation Journal* 24/4 (2008), pp. 429–445.
4 For evidence on age, see D. Neumark at al., 'Is it harder for older workers to find jobs? New and improved evidence from a field experiment', *Journal of Political Economy* 127/2 (2019), pp. 922–970; for evidence of gender in England, see P. A. Riach and J. Rich, 'An experimental investigation of sexual discrimination in hiring in the English labor market', *Advances in Economic Analysis & Policy* 5/2 (2006), pp. 1–22; and for evidence on women of child-bearing age, see S. O. Becker et al., 'Discrimination in hiring based on potential and realized fertility: Evidence from a large-scale field experiment', *Labour Economics* 59 (2019), pp. 139–152.
5 In the UK, for every ten male entrepreneurs there are about five female. In Australia, the US and Canada the ratio is slightly better, at 10:6. In the UK (see *The Alison Rose Review of Female Entrepreneurship*, 2019), only 1 per cent of all venture funding goes to businesses founded by all-female teams, inhibiting scale-up (see British Business Bank, Diversity VC, and BVCA, *UK VC & Female Founders* report, February 2019).
6 See D. O'Brien et al., 'Are the creative industries meritocratic? An analysis of the 2014 British Labour Force Survey', *Cultural*

*Trends* 25/2 (2016), pp. 116–131, which demonstrates that working-class persons are under-represented in the creative industries. Also see S. Friedman et al., '"Like skydiving without a parachute": How class origin shapes occupational trajectories in British acting', *Sociology* 51/5 (2017), pp. 992–1010, which demonstrates a similar conclusion specific to acting.

7 See J. Miller, 'Tall poppy syndrome (Canadians have a habit of cutting their female achievers down)', *Flare* 19/4 (1997), pp. 102–106; P. McFedries, 'Tall poppy syndrome dot-com', *IEEE Spectrum* 39/12 (2002), p. 68; H. Kirwan-Taylor, 'Are you suffering from tall poppy syndrome', *Management Today* 15 (2006); and J. Kirkwood, 'Tall poppy syndrome: Implications for entrepreneurship in New Zealand', *Journal of Management and Organization* 13/4 (2007), pp. 366–382.

8 Research shows that VC-backed start-ups outperform, comparable to non-VC-backed start-ups. See W. L. Megginson and K. A. Weiss, 'Venture capitalist certification in initial public offerings', *The Journal of Finance* 46/3 (1991), pp. 879–903; and Jeffry A. Timmons, *New Venture Creation: Entrepreneurship for the 21st Century* (Boston, MA: Irwin/McGraw-Hill, 1999).

9 For a fantastic summary of experimental and observational research related to groupthink, see Cass Sunstein and Reid Hastie, *Wiser: Getting Beyond Groupthink to Make Groups Smarter* (Boston, MA: Harvard Business Review Press, 2015).

10 See W. Bruine de Bruin, 'Save the last dance for me: Unwanted serial position effects injury evaluations', *Acta Psychologica* 118/3 (2005), pp. 245–260, for evidence from figure skating and the Eurovision song contest; and L. Page and K. Page, 'Last shall be first: A field study of biases in sequential performance evaluation on the Idol series', *Journal of Economic Behavior and Organization* 73/2 (2010), pp. 186–198, for evidence from TV talent contests.

11 For more detailed insights on sequential order contest, see F. B. Gershberg and A. P. Shimamura, 'Serial position effects in implicit and explicit tests of memory', *Journal of Experimental Psychology: Learning, Memory, and Cognition* 20/6 (1994), pp. 1370–1378; and N. Burgess and G. J. Hitch, 'Memory for serial order: A network model of the phonological loop and its timing', *Psychological Review* 106/3 (1999), pp. 551–581.

12 W. S. Harvey, 'Strong or weak ties? British and Indian expatriate scientists finding jobs in Boston', *Global Networks* 8/4 (2008), pp. 453–473, highlights that British and Indian migrating scientists had gains from both strong and weak ties in job searches; D. Z. Levin and R. Cross, 'The strength of weak ties you can trust: The mediating role of trust in effective knowledge transfer', *Management Science* 50/11 (2004), pp. 1477–1490, highlights that both weak ties and strong ties play an independent role in knowledge transfer within companies; D. W. Brown and A. M. Konrad, 'Granovetter was right: The importance of weak ties to a contemporary job search', *Group and Organization Management* 26/4 (2001), pp. 434–462, illustrates the benefits of weak ties over strong ties in job search and salary garnered, a stylized fact replicated in work by V. Yakubovich, 'Weak ties, information, and influence: How workers find jobs in a local Russian labor market', *American Sociological Review* 70/3 (2005), pp. 408–421. T. Elfring and W. Hulsink, 'Networks in entrepreneurship: The case of high-technology firms', *Small Business Economics* 21/4 (2003), pp. 409–422, emphasizes the gains from weak ties for emerging entrepreneurs in technology.

13 If you are interested in this topic there is a fantastic account of how women have a harder time in economics as compared to other disciplines. See S. Lundberg and J. Stearns, 'Women in economics: Stalled progress', *Journal of Economic Perspectives* 33/1 (2019), pp. 3–22.

1 The person I know who uses this adage the most is Professor Paul Dolan from the LSE. In fact, the name of the 'context matters' student prize on the executive masters in behavioural science came about from him saying those two words more than any other in his teaching. And there is lots of evidence in the behavioural science literature that illustrates this adage holds weight. For example, for a discussion on how environments can be used to change health-related behaviours, see G. J. Hollands et al., 'The TIPPME intervention typology for changing environments to change behavior', *Nature Human Behaviour* 1 (2017).

2 See A. North et al., 'The influence of in-store music on wine selections', *Journal of Applied Psychology* 84/2 (1999), pp. 271–276.

3 E. M. Altmann et al., 'Momentary interruptions can derail the train of thought', *Journal of Experimental Psychology: General* 143/1 (2014), pp. 215–226, found that interruptions less than three seconds long disrupted and caused more errors on sequence-based cognitive tasks in a lab experiment; G. Carlton and M. A. Blegen, 'Medication-related errors: A literature review of incidence and antecedents', *Annual Review of Nursing Research* 24/1 (2006), pp. 19–38, linked interruptions to medication-related errors in hospitals; A. Mawson, 'The workplace and its impact on productivity', *Advanced Workplace Associates, London* 1 (2012), pp. 1–12, argues that distractions bring individuals out of flow state.

4 Interruptions have been linked to lower levels of job satisfaction (for a study of nurses, see B. D. Kirkcaldy and T. Martin, 'Job stress and satisfaction among nurses: Individual differences', *Stress Medicine* 16/2 (2000), pp. 77–89), increased levels of irritability (for a study of call centre agents, see S. Grebner et al., 'Working conditions, well-being, and job-related attitudes among call centre agents', *European Journal of Work and Organiza-*

*tional Psychology* 12(4) (2003), pp. 341–365), and even depression (for a study of GPs, see study by U. Rout et al., 'Job stress among British general practitioners: Predictors of job dissatisfaction and mental ill-health', *Stress Medicine* 12/3 (1996), pp. 155–166).

5 For the link between airflow and productivity, see P. Wargocki et al., 'The effects of outdoor air supply rate in an office on perceived air quality, Sick Building Syndrome (SBS) symptoms and productivity', *Indoor Air* 10/4 (2000), pp. 222–236; and for a study that links air conditioning to sickness, see P. Preziosi et al., 'Workplace air-conditioning and health services attendance among French middle-aged women: A prospective cohort study', *International Journal of Epidemiology* 33/5 (2004), pp. 1120–1123.

6 For a study that highlights how indoor plants increase attention capacity in an office setting, see R. K. Raanaas et al., 'Benefits of indoor plants on attention capacity in an office setting', *Journal of Environmental Psychology* 31/1 (2011), pp. 99–105.

7 See M. Münch et al., 'Effects of prior light exposure on early evening performance, subjective sleepiness, and hormonal secretion', *Behavioral Neuroscience* 126/1 (2012), pp. 196–203; S. Joshi, 'The sick building syndrome', *Indian Journal of Occupational and Environmental Medicine* 12/2 (2008), p. 61; and V. I. Lohr et al., 'Interior plants may improve worker productivity and reduce stress in a windowless environment', *Journal of Environmental Horticulture* 14/2 (1996), pp. 97–100.

8 For a paper that links creativity to dim lighting, see A. Steidle and L. Werth, 'Freedom from constraints: Darkness and dim illumination promote creativity', *Journal of Environmental Psychology* 35 (2013), pp. 67–80; and for a discussion of bright lights and concentration, see H. Mukae and M. Sato, 'The effect of color temperature of lighting sources on the autonomic nervous functions', *The Annals of Physiological Anthropology* 11/5 (1992), pp. 533–538.

9 See L. Lan et al., 'Neurobehavioral approach for evaluation of office workers' productivity: The effects of room temperature',

*Building and Environment* 44/8 (2009), pp. 1578–1588; and L. Lan et al., 'Effects of thermal discomfort in an office on perceived air quality, SBS symptoms, physiological responses, and human performance', *Indoor Air* 21/5 (2011), pp. 376–390.

10 See H. Jahncke et al., 'Open-plan office noise: Cognitive performance and restoration', *Journal of Environmental Psychology* 31/4 (2011), pp. 373–382.

11 See S. Banbury and D. C. Berry, 'Disruption of office-related tasks by speech and office noise', *British Journal of Psychology* 89/3 (1998), pp. 499–517.

12 See P. Barrett et al., 'The impact of classroom design on pupils' learning: Final results of a holistic, multi-level analysis', *Building and Environment* 89 (2015), pp. 118–133.

13 See studies by A. S. Soldat et al., 'Color as an environmental processing cue: External affective cues can directly affect processing strategy without affecting mood', *Social Cognition* 15/1 (1997), pp. 55–71; R. Mehta and R. Zhu, 'Blue or red? Exploring the effect of color on cognitive task performances', *Science* 323/5918 (2009), pp. 1226–1229; S. Lehrl et al., 'Blue light improves cognitive performance', *Journal of Neural Transmission* 114/4 (2007), pp. 457–460; and Z. O'Connor, 'Colour psychology and colour therapy: Caveat emptor', *Color Research & Application* 36/3 (2011), pp. 229–234.

14 See Mehta and Zhu, 'Blue or red?' (2009), which summarizes studies on red versus blue.

15 See K. W. Jacobs and J. F. Suess, 'Effects of four psychological primary colors on anxiety state', *Perceptual and Motor Skills* 41(1) (1975), pp. 207–210. They considered the effects of red, yellow, green and blue on self- reported measures of anxiety, and found that higher anxiety scores were correlated with red and yellow, and conversely blue and green were correlated with lower scores. See also A. Al-Ayash et al., 'The influence of color on

student emotion, heart rate, and performance in learning environments', *Color Research and Application* 41/2 (2016), pp.196–205, which demonstrates that blue increases calmness as compared to red and yellow.

16 See Al-Ayash et al., 'The influence of color' (2016). They investigated the effects of six colours – vivid red, vivid blue, vivid yellow, pale red, pale blue and pale yellow – on reading task performance in students' private study spaces.

## *Chapter 7: Resilience*

1 See D. Laibson and J. List, 'Principles of (behavioral) economics', *American Economic Review* 105/5 (2015), pp. 385–390, which outlines some neat behavioural science factoids as a way to encourage innovative teaching of the subject in the classroom.

2 A. Killen and A. Macaskill, 'Using a gratitude intervention to enhance well-being in older adults', *Journal of Happiness Studies* 16/4 (2015), pp. 947–964, makes the link between practising gratitude and higher levels of self-esteem; F. Gander et al., 'Strength-based positive interventions: Further evidence for their potential in enhancing well-being and alleviating depression', *Journal of Happiness Studies* 14/4 (2013), pp. 1241–1259, makes the link between gratitude and lower rates of depression; and M. E. P. Seligman et al., 'Positive psychology progress: Empirical validation of interventions', *American Psychologist* 60/5 (2005), pp. 410–421, makes the link between gratitude and higher levels of happiness.

3 See N. Ashraf et al., 'Losing prosociality in the quest for talent? Sorting, selection, and productivity in the delivery of public services', LSE Research Online Documents on

Economics 88175, London School of Economics and Political Science, LSE Library (2018).

4 My own work with Paul Dolan shows that when it comes to intergenerational mobility, downward mobility deteriorates life satisfaction and mental health far more than upward mobility improves these life domains. We came to these conclusions when studying the British Cohort study in 1970, a fantastic UK data set that follows children born in 1970 throughout their lives.

5 See P. Grossman et al., 'Mindfulness-based stress reduction and health benefits: A meta-analysis', *Journal of Psychosomatic Research* 57/1 (2004), pp. 35–43, which combines the effects of a number of studies to illustrate the stress-lowering health benefits of mindfulness based on stress reduction therapy; and more recently M. Goyal et al., 'Meditation programs for psychological stress and well-being: A systematic review and meta-analysis', *JAMA Internal Medicine* 174/3 (2014), pp. 357–368. This was a meta-analysis of forty-seven randomized trials, which highlights moderate evidence of improvements in anxiety, depression and pain but no effect on mood, attention, substance use, eating behviour, sleep quality or weight.

6 G. Bonanno, 'Loss, trauma, and human resilience: Have we underestimated the human capacity to thrive after extremely aversive events?', *American Psychologist* 59/1 (2004), pp. 20–28, emphasizes hardiness as a pathway to resilience; S. Maddi, 'The story of hardiness: Twenty years of theorizing, research, and practice', *Consulting Psychology Journal: Practice and Research* 54/3 (2002), pp. 173–185, shows hardiness enhances resilience in the face of everyday stressors and demands; M. E. P. Seligman, 'Building resilience', *Harvard Business Review* 89/4 (2011), pp. 100–106, highlights enhancing mental toughness as a way to increase resilience.

7 See B. Smith et al., 'The brief resilience scale: Assessing the ability to bounce back', *International Journal of Behavioral Medicine* 15/3 (2008), pp. 194–200, which illustrates that resilience is positively correlated with social relations, physical health and mental health; Q. Gu and C. Day, 'Teachers' resilience: A necessary condition for effectiveness', *Teaching and Teacher Education* 23/8 (2007), pp. 1302–1316, for evidence that resilience makes teachers more motivated and committed; L. Abramson et al., 'Learned helplessness in humans: Critique and reformulation', *Journal of Abnormal Psychology* 87/1 (1978), pp. 49–74, which emphasizes that innovative thinking and resilience are correlated for college students.

# Bibliography

## *Books*

Annett, John, *Feedback and Human Behaviour: The Effects of Knowledge of Results, Incentives and Reinforcement on Learning and Performance* (Harmondsworth, Middlesex: Penguin Books, 1969).

Bandura, Albert, *Principles of Behavior Modification* (New York, London: Holt, Rinehart and Winston, 1969).

Cameron, Kim S., *Positive Leadership* (San Francisco, CA: Berret-Koehler Publishers, 2008).

Csikszentmihalyi, Mihaly, *Flow: The Psychology of Optimal Experience* (New York: Harper Perennial, 2008).

Dolan, Paul, *Happiness by Design: Finding Pleasure and Purpose in Everyday Life* (London: Penguin Books, 2014).

Dolan, Paul, *Happy Ever After: Escaping the Myth of the Perfect Life* (London: Allen Lane, 2019).

Dweck, Carol S., *Mindset: The New Psychology of Success* (New York: Random House, 2006).

Gladwell, Malcolm, *Outliers: The Story of Success* (New York: Little, Brown and Company, 2008).

Grant-Halvorson, Heidi, *Reinforcements: How to Get People to Help You* (Boston, MA: Harvard Business Review Press, 2018).

Hochschild, Arlie Russell, and Anne Machung, *The Second Shift: Working Parents and the Revolution at Home* (New York: Viking, 1989).

Kahneman, Daniel, *Thinking, Fast and Slow* (London: Allen Lane, 2011).

Knapp, Jake, and John Zeratsky, *Make Time: How to Focus on What Matters Every Day* (New York: Currency, 2018).

Page, Scott E., *The Diversity Bonus: How Great Teams Pay Off in the Knowledge Economy* (Princeton, NJ: Princeton University Press, 2017).

Smith, Emily Esfahani, *The Power of Meaning: Crafting a Life That Matters* (New York: Crown, 2017).

Sunstein, Cass, and Reid Hastie, *Wiser: Getting Beyond Groupthink to Make Groups Smarter* (Boston, MA: Harvard Business Review Press, 2015).

Thaler, Richard H., and Cass R. Sunstein, *Nudge: Improving Decisions about Health, Wealth, and Happiness* (New Haven, CT: Yale University Press, 2008).

Timmons, Jeffry A., *New Venture Creation: Entrepreneurship for the 21st Century* (Boston, MA: Irwin/McGraw-Hill, 1999).

Tracy, Brian, *Eat That Frog!: Get More of the Important Things Done Today* (London: Hodder Paperbacks, 2013).

Walker, Matthew P., *Why We Sleep: Unlocking the Power of Sleep and Dreams* (New York: Scribner, 2017).

## *Articles and papers*

Abramson, L., M. Seligman and J. Teasdale, 'Learned helplessness in humans: Critique and reformulation', *Journal of Abnormal Psychology* 87/1 (1978), pp. 49–74. https://psycnet.apa.org/record/1979-00305-001

Al-Ayash, A., R. T. Kane, D. Smith and P. Green-Armytage, 'The influence of color on student emotion, heart rate, and performance in learning environments', *Color Research and Application* 41/2 (2016), pp.196–205. https://doi.org/10.1002/col.21949

Almond, D., J. Currie and V. Duque, 'Childhood circumstances and adult outcomes: Act II', *Journal of Economic Literature* 56/4 (2018), pp. 1360–1446. https://doi.org/10.1257/jel.20171164

Altmann, E. M., J. G. Trafton and D. Z. Hambrick, 'Momentary interruptions can derail the train of thought', *Journal of Experimental Psychology: General* 143/1 (2014), pp. 215–226. https://doi.org/10.1037/a0030986

Aronson, J., C. B. Fried and C. Good, 'Reducing the effects of stereotype threat on African American college students by shaping theories of intelligence', *Journal of Experimental Social Psychology* 38/2 (2002), pp. 113–125. https://doi.org/10.1006/jesp.2001.1491

Ashraf, Nava, Oriana Bandiera and Scott Lee, 'Losing prosociality in the quest for talent? Sorting, selection, and productivity in the delivery of public services', LSE Research Online Documents on Economics 88175, London School of Economics and Political Science, LSE Library (2018). http://eprints.lse.ac.uk/88175

Banbury, S., and D. C. Berry, 'Disruption of office-related tasks by speech and office noise', *British Journal of Psychology* 89/3 (1998), pp. 499–517. https://doi.org/10.1111/j.2044-8295.1998.tb02699.x

Baron, J., and I. Ritov, 'Omission bias, individual differences, and normality', *Organizational Behavior and Human Decision Processes* 94/2 (2004), pp. 74–85. https://doi.org/10.1016/j.obhdp.2004.03.003

Barrett, P., F. Davies, Y. Zhang and L. Barrett, 'The impact of classroom design on pupils' learning: Final results of a holistic, multi-level analysis', *Building and Environment* 89 (2015), pp. 118–133. https://doi.org/10.1016/j.buildenv.2015.02.013

Bartels, M., V. Saviouk, M. H. M. de Moor, G. Willemsen, T. C. E. M. van Beijsterveldt, J.-J. Hottenga, E. J. C. de Geus and D. I. Boomsma, 'Heritability and genome-wide linkage scan of subjective happiness', *Twin Research and Human Genetics* 13/2 (2010), pp. 135–142. https://doi.org/10.1375/twin.13.2.135

Baum, J. A. C., and B. S. Silverman, 'Picking winners or building them? Alliance, intellectual, and human capital as selection criteria in venture financing and performance of biotechnology startups', *Journal of Business Venturing* 19/3 (2004), pp. 411–436. https://doi.org/10.1016/S0883-9026(03)00038-7

Bayer, P., R. Hjalmarsson and D. Pozen, 'Building criminal capital behind bars: Peer effects in juvenile corrections', *The Quarterly Journal of Economics* 124/1 (2009), pp. 105–147. https://doi.org/10.1162/qjec.2009.124.1.105

Bayer, P., S. Ross and G. Topa, 'Place of work and place of residence: Informal hiring networks and labor market outcomes', *Journal of Political Economy* 116/6 (2008), pp. 1150–1196. https://doi.org/10.1086/595975

Becker, S. O., A. Fernandes and D. Weichselbaumer, 'Discrimination in hiring based on potential and realized fertility: Evidence from a large-scale field experiment', *Labour Economics* 59 (2019), pp. 139–152. https://doi.org/10.1016/j.labeco.2019.04.009

Behavioural Insights Team, 'Applying behavioural insights to reduce fraud, error, and debt', Cabinet Office (2012). http://www.behaviouralinsights.co.uk/wp-content/uploads/2015/07/BIT_FraudErrorDebt_accessible.pdf

Bertaut, C. C., 'Stockholding behavior of US households: Evidence from the 1983–1989 Survey of Consumer Finances', *Review of Economics and Statistics* 80/2 (1998), pp. 263–275. https://doi.org/10.1162/003465398557500

Bertrand, M., and S. Mullainathan, 'Are Emily and Greg more employable than Lakisha and Jamal? A field experiment on labor market discrimination', *American Economic Review* 94/4 (2004), pp. 991–1013. https://doi.org/10.1257/0002828042002561

Bhattacharya, J., A. Garber and J. Goldhaber-Fiebert, 'Nudges in exercise commitment contracts: A randomized trial', *NBER*

*Working Paper Series* 21406 (2015). Retrieved from: https://www.nber.org/papers/w21406

Bohns, V. K., '(Mis)understanding Our Influence Over Others: A review of the underestimation-of-compliance effect', *Current Directions in Psychological Science* 25/2 (2016), pp. 119–123. https://doi.org/10.1177/0963721415628011

Bohns, V. K., and F. J. Flynn, '"Why Didn't You Just Ask?" Underestimating the discomfort of help-seeking', *Journal of Experimental Social Psychology* 46/2 (2010), pp. 402–409. https://doi.org/10.1016/j.jesp.2009.12.015

Bonanno, G., 'Loss, trauma, and human resilience: Have we underestimated the human capacity to thrive after extremely aversive events?', *American Psychologist* 59/1 (2004), pp. 20–28. https://doi.org/10.1037/0003-066X.59.1.20

British Business Bank, Diversity VC and BVCA, *UK VC & Female Founders* (2019). https://www.british-business-bank.co.uk/wp-content/uploads/2019/02/British-Business-Bank-UK-Venture-Capital-and-Female-Founders-Report.pdf

Brooks, P., and H. Zank, 'Loss averse behavior', *Journal of Risk and Uncertainty* 31/3 (2005), pp. 301–325. https://doi.org/10.1007/s11166-005-5105-7

Brooks, R., R. Faff, D. Mulino and R. Scheelings, 'Deal or no deal, that is the question: The impact of increasing stakes and framing effects on decision-making under risk', *International Review of Finance* 9/1-2 (2009), pp. 27–50. https://doi.org/10.1111/j.1468-2443.2009.01084.x

Brown, D. A., 'Pensions and risk aversion: The influence of race, ethnicity, and class on investor behavior', *Lewis & Clark Law Review* 11/2 (2007), pp. 385–406.

Brown, D. W., and A. M. Konrad, 'Granovetter was right: The importance of weak ties to a contemporary job search', *Group and Organization Management* 26/4 (2001), pp. 434–462. https://doi.org/10.1177/1059601101264003

Bruine de Bruin, W., 'Save the last dance for me: Unwanted serial position effects injury evaluations', *Acta Psychologica* 118/3 (2005), pp. 245–260. https://doi.org/10.1016/j.actpsy.2004.08.005

Burgess, N., and G. J. Hitch, 'Memory for serial order: A network model of the phonological loop and its timing', *Psychological Review* 106/3 (1999), pp. 551–581. https://doi.org/10.1037/0033-295X.106.3.551

Buttussi, F., L. Chittaro and D. Nadalutti, 'Bringing mobile guides and fitness activities together: A solution based on an embodied virtual trainer', *Proceedings of the 8th Conference on Human-computer Interaction with Mobile Devices and Services* (2006), pp. 29–36. https://doi.org/10.1145/1152215.1152222

Carlton, G., and M. A. Blegen, 'Medication-related errors: A literature review of incidence and antecedents', *Annual Review of Nursing Research* 24/1 (2006), pp. 19–38. https://doi.org/10.1891/0739-6686.24.1.19

Carrell, S. E., and M. L. Hoekstra, 'Externalities in the classroom: How children exposed to domestic violence affect everyone's kids', *American Economic Journal: Applied Economics* 2/1 (2010), pp. 211–228. https://doi.org/10.1257/app.2.1.211

Carrell, S. E., R. F. Fullerton and J. E. West, 'Does your cohort matter? Measuring peer effects in college achievement', *Journal of Labor Economics* 27/3 (2009), pp. 439–464. https://www.journals.uchicago.edu/doi/abs/10.1086/600143?journalCode=jole

Chambliss, H. O., R. C. Huber, C. E. Finley, S. O. McDoniel, H. Kitzman-Ulrich and W. J. Wilkinson, 'Computerized self-monitoring and technology assisted feedback for weight loss with and without an enhanced behavioural component', *Patient Education and Counseling* 85/3 (2011), pp. 375–382. https://doi.org/10.1016/j.pec.2010.12.024

Chandler, D., and A. Kapelner, 'Breaking monotony with meaning: Motivation in crowdsourcing markets', *Journal of Economic*

*Behavior and Organization* 90 (2013), pp.123–133. https://www.sciencedirect.com/science/article/abs/pii/S016726811300036X

Chen, L., J. Gordanier and O. D. Ozturk, 'Following (not quite) in your father's footsteps: Task followers and labor market outcomes', MPRA Paper 76041 (2017). http://dx.doi.org/10.2139/ssrn.2894978

Chernev, A., 'Context effects without a context: Attribute balance as a reason for choice', *Journal of Consumer Research* 32/2 (2005), pp. 213–223. https://doi.org/10.1086/432231

Cho, J. H., H. C. Lee, D. J. Lim, H. S. Kwon and K. H. Yoon, 'Mobile communication using a mobile phone with glucometer for glucose control in Type 2 patients with diabetes: As effective as an internet based glucose monitoring system', *Journal of Telemedicine and Telecare* 15/2 (2009), pp. 77–82. https://doi.org/10.1258/jtt.2008.080412

Chou, H. G., and N. Edge, '"They are happier and having better lives than I am": The impact of using Facebook on perceptions of others' lives', *Cyberpsychology, Behavior, and Social Networking* 15/2 (2012), pp. 117–121. https://doi.org/10.1089/cyber.2011.0324

Clark, A. E., and Y. Lohéac, '"It wasn't me, it was them!" Social influence in risky behavior by adolescents', *Journal of Health Economics* 26/4 (2007), pp. 763–784. https://doi.org/10.1016/j.jhealeco.2006.11.005

Cohen, G. L., J. Garcia, N. Apfel and A. Master, 'Reducing the racial achievement gap: A social-psychological intervention', *Science* 313/5791 (2006), pp. 1307–1310. https://doi.org/10.1126/science.1128317

Cohn, R. A., W. G. Lewellen, R. C. Lease and G. G. Schlarbaum, 'Individual investor risk aversion and investment portfolio composition', *The Journal of Finance* 30/2 (1975), pp. 605–620. https://doi.org/10.1111/j.1540-6261.1975.tb01834.x

Cooper, A. C., C. Y. Woo and W. C. Dunkelberg, 'Entrepreneurs' perceived chances for success', *Journal of Business*

*Venturing* 3/2 (1988), pp. 97–108. https://doi.org/10.1016/0883-9026(88)90020-1

Cucina, J., M. Vasilopoulos and N. Sehgal, 'Personality-Based Job Analysis and The Self-Serving Bias', *Journal of Business and Psychology* 20(2) (2005), pp. 275-290. DOI: 10.1007/s10869-005-8264-2

Davidai, S., and T. Gilovich, 'The ideal road not taken: The self-discrepancies involved in people's most enduring regrets', *Emotion* 18/3 (2018), pp. 439–452. http://dx.doi.org/10.1037/emo0000326

Davison, I. M., and A. Feeney, 'Regret as autobiographical memory', *Cognitive Psychology* 57/4 (2008), pp. 385–403. https://doi.org/10.1016/j.cogpsych.2008.03.001

De Neve, J.-E., N. A. Christakis, J. H. Fowler and B. S Frey, 'Genes, economics, and happiness', *Journal of Neuroscience, Psychology, and Economics* 5/4 (2012), pp. 193–211. https://doi.org/10.1037/a0030292

Di Stasio, V., and A. Heath, 'Are employers in Britain discriminating against ethnic minorities?' (2019). Summary of findings from GEMM project. Oxford: Centre for Social Investigation. Retrieved from: http://csi.nuff.ox.ac.uk/wp-content/uploads/2019/01/Are-employers-in-Britain-discriminating-against-ethnic-minorities_final.pdf

Dolan, P., and G. Lordan, 'Climbing up ladders and sliding down snakes: An empirical assessment of the effect of social mobility on subjective wellbeing', *Review of Economics of the Household* (May 2020). https://doi.org/10.1007/s11150-020-09487-x

Eckel, C., A. C. M. de Oliveira and P. J. Grossman, 'Gender and negotiation in the small: Are women (perceived to be) more cooperative than men?' *Negotiation Journal* 24/4 (2008), pp.429–445. https://doi.org/10.1111/j.1571-9979.2008.00196.x

Elfring, T., and W. Hulsink, 'Networks in entrepreneurship: The case of high-technology firms', *Small Business Economics* 21/4 (2003), pp. 409–422. https://doi.org/10.1023/A:1026180418357

Emmons, R. A., and M. E. McCullough, 'Counting blessings versus burdens: An experimental investigation of gratitude and subjective well-being in daily life', *Journal of Personality and Social Psychology* 84/2 (2003), pp. 377–389. https://doi.org/10.1037/0022-3514.84.2.377

Farmer, A., O. Gibson, P. Hayton, K. Bryden, C. Dudley, A. Neil and L. Tarassenko, 'A real-time, mobile phone-based telemedicine system to support young adults with type 1 diabetes', *Informatics in Primary Care* 13/3 (2005), pp. 171–178. http://dx.doi.org/10.14236/jhi.v13i3.594

Feinstein, B., 'The dynasty advantage: Family ties in congressional elections', *Legislative Studies Quarterly* 35/4 (2010), pp. 571–598. https://doi.org/10.3162/036298010793322366

Freund, P. A., and N. Kasten, 'How smart do you think you are? A meta-analysis on the validity of self-estimates of cognitive ability', *Psychological Bulletin* 138/2 (2012), pp. 296–321. https://doi.org/10.1037/a0026556

Friedman, S., D. O'Brien and D. Laurison, '"Like skydiving without a parachute": How class origin shapes occupational trajectories in British acting', *Sociology* 51/5 (2017), pp. 992–1010. https://doi.org/10.1177/0038038516629917

Galdi, S., M. Cadinu and C. Tomasetto, 'The roots of stereotype threat: When automatic associations disrupt girls' math performance', *Child Development* 85/1 (2014), pp. 250–263. https://doi.org/10.1111/cdev.12128

Gander, F., R. T. Proyer, W. Ruch and T. Wyss, 'Strength-based positive interventions: Further evidence for their potential in enhancing well-being and alleviating depression', *Journal of Happiness Studies* 14/4 (2013), pp. 1241–1259. https://doi.org/10.1007/s10902-012-9380-0

Gershberg, F. B., and A. P. Shimamura, 'Serial position effects in implicit and explicit tests of memory', *Journal of Experimental Psychology: Learning, Memory, and Cognition* 20/6 (1994), pp. 1370–1378. https://doi.org/10.1037/0278-7393.20.6.1370

Gilovich, T., V. Medvec and D. Kahneman, 'Varieties of regret: A debate and partial resolution', *Psychological Review* 105/3 (1998), pp. 602–605. http://dx.doi.org/10.1037/0033-295X.105.3.602
Gilovich, T., V. Medvec and K. Savitsky, 'The spotlight effect in social judgment: An egocentric bias in estimates of the salience of one's own actions and appearance', *Journal of Personality and Social Psychology* 78/2 (2000), pp. 211–222. https://doi.org/10.1037//0022-3514.78.2.211
Goldin, C., and C. Rouse, 'Orchestrating impartiality: The impact of "blind" auditions on female musicians', *American Economic Review* 90/4 (2000), pp. 715–741. https://doi.org/10.1257/aer.90.4.715
Goyal, M., S. Singh, E. M. S. Sibinga, N. F. Gould, A. Rowland-Seymour, R. Sharma, Z. Berger, D. Sleicher, D. D. Maron, H. M. Shihab, P. D. Ranasinghe, S. Linn, S. Saha, E. B. Bass and J. A. Haythornthwaite, 'Meditation programs for psychological stress and well-being: A systematic review and meta-analysis', *JAMA Internal Medicine* 174/3 (2014), pp. 357–368. https://doi.org/10.1001/jamainternmed.2013.13018
Grebner, S., N. Semmer, L. Faso, L. Lo, S. Gut, W. Kälin and A. Elfering, 'Working conditions, well-being, and job-related attitudes among call centre agents', *European Journal of Work and Organizational Psychology* 12(4) (2003), pp. 341–365. https://doi.org/10.1080/13594320344000192
Grossman, P., L. Niemann, S. Schmidt and H. Walach, 'Mindfulness-based stress reduction and health benefits: A meta-analysis', *Journal of Psychosomatic Research* 57/1 (2004), pp. 35–43. https://doi.org/10.1016/S0022-3999(03)00573-7
Gu, Q., and C. Day, 'Teachers' resilience: A necessary condition for effectiveness', *Teaching and Teacher Education* 23/8 (2007), pp. 1302–1316. https://doi.org/10.1016/j.tate.2006.06.006
Harvey, W. S., 'Strong or weak ties? British and Indian expatriate scientists finding jobs in Boston', *Global Networks* 8/4 (2008), pp. 453–473. https://doi.org/10.1111/j.1471-0374.2008.00234.x

Haworth, C., M. Wright, N. G. Martin, N. W. Martin, D. I. Boomsma, M. Bartels, D. Posthuma, O. S. P. Davis, A. M. Brant, R. P. Corley, J. K. Hewitt, W. G. Iacono, M. McGue, L. A. Thompson, S. A. Hart, S. A. Petrill, D. Lubinski and R. Plomin, 'A twin study of the genetics of high cognitive ability selected from 11,000 twin pairs in six studies from four countries', *Behavior Genetics* 39/4 (2009), pp. 359–370. https://www.ncbi.nlm.nih.gov/pmc/articles/PCMC2740717/pdf/nihms135626.pdf

Heckman, J. J., and T. Kautz, 'Fostering and measuring skills: Interventions that improve character and cognition' (No. 19656) National Bureau of Economic Research (2013). https://doi.org/10.7208/chicago/9780226100128.003.0009

Hellerstein, J., M. Mcinerney and D. Neumark, 'Neighbors and coworkers: The importance of residential labor market networks', *Journal of Labor Economics* 29/4 (2011), pp. 659–695. https://doi.org/10.1086/660776

Hollands, G. J., G. Bignardi, M. Johnston, M. P. Kelly, D. Ogilvie, M. Petticrew, A. Prestwich, I. Shemilt, S. Sutton and T. M. Marteau, 'The TIPPME intervention typology for changing environments to change behavior', *Nature Human Behaviour* 1 (2017). https://doi.org/10.1038/s41562-017-0140

Ioannides, Y., and L. Loury, 'Job information networks, neighborhood effects, and inequality', *Journal of Economic Literature* 42/4 (2004), pp. 1056–1093. https://doi.org/10.1257/0022051043004595

Jackson, C. K., and E. Bruegmann, 'Teaching students and teaching each other: The importance of peer learning for teachers', *American Economic Journal: Applied Economics* 1/4 (2009), pp. 85–108. https://doi.org/10.1257/app.1.4.85

Jacobs, K. W., and J. F. Suess, 'Effects of four psychological primary colors on anxiety state', *Perceptual and Motor Skills* 41(1) (1975), pp. 207–210. https://doi.org/10.2466/pms.1975.41.1.207

Jahncke, H., S. Hygge, N. Halin, A. M. Green and K. Dimberg, 'Open-plan office noise: Cognitive performance and restoration', *Journal of Environmental Psychology* 31/4 (2011), pp. 373–382. https://doi.org/10.1016/j.jenvp.2011.07.002

Johnston, D. W., and G. Lordan, 'Racial prejudice and labour market penalties during economic downturns', *European Economic Review* 84 (2016), pp. 57–75. https://doi.org/10.1016/j.euroecorev.2015.07.011

Joshi, S., 'The sick building syndrome', *Indian Journal of Occupational and Environmental Medicine* 12/2 (2008), p. 61. https://doi.org/10.4103/0019-5278.43262

Kahneman, D., and A. Tversky, 'Prospect theory: An analysis of decision under risk', *Econometrica* 47/2 (1979), pp. 263–291. https://doi.org/10.1142/9789814417358_0006

Khan, U., M. Zhu and A. Kalra, 'When trade-offs matter: The effect of choice construal on context effects', *Journal of Marketing Research* 48/1 (2011), pp. 62–71. https://doi.org/10.1509/jmkr.48.1.62

Killen, A., and A. Macaskill, 'Using a gratitude intervention to enhance well-being in older adults', *Journal of Happiness Studies* 16/4 (2015), pp. 947–964. https://doi.org/10.1007/s10902-014-95

Kirkcaldy, B. D., and T. Martin, 'Job stress and satisfaction among nurses: Individual differences', *Stress Medicine* 16/2 (2000), pp. 77–89. https://doi.org/10.1002/(SICI)1099-1700(200003)16:2<77::AID-SMI835>3.0.CO;2-Z

Kirkwood, J., 'Tall poppy syndrome: Implications for entrepreneurship in New Zealand', *Journal of Management and Organization* 13/4 (2007), pp. 366–382. https://doi.org/10.1017/S1833367200003606

Kirwan-Taylor, H., 'Are you suffering from tall poppy syndrome', *Management Today* 15 (2006). https://www.managementtoday.co.uk/suffering-tall-poppy-syndrome/article/550558

Kluger, A., and A. DeNisi, 'The effects of feedback interventions on performance: A historical review, a meta-analysis, and a preliminary feedback intervention theory', *Psychological Bulletin* 119/2 (1996), pp. 254–284. https://doi.org/10.1037/0033-2909.119.2.254

Koestner, R., N. Lekes, T. Powers and E. Chicoine, 'Attaining personal goals: Self-concordance plus implementation intentions equals success', *Journal of Personality and Social Psychology* 83/1 (2002), pp. 231–244. http://dx.doi.org/10.1037/0022-3514.83.1.231

Laibson, D., and J. List, 'Principles of (behavioral) economics', *American Economic Review* 105/5 (2015), pp. 385–390. https://doi.org/10.1257/aer.p20151047

Lan, L., Z. Lian, L. Pan and Q. Ye, 'Neurobehavioral approach for evaluation of office workers' productivity: The effects of room temperature', *Building and Environment* 44/8 (2009), pp. 1578–1588. https://doi.org/10.1016/j.buildenv.2008.10.004

Lan, L., P. Wargocki, D. P. Wyon and Z. Lian, 'Effects of thermal discomfort in an office on perceived air quality, SBS symptoms, physiological responses, and human performance', *Indoor Air* 21/5 (2011), pp. 376–390. https://doi.org/10.1111/j.1600-0668.2011.00714.x

Landry, C. E., A. Lange, J. A. List, M. K. Price and N. G. Rupp, 'Toward an understanding of the economics of charity: Evidence from a field experiment', *The Quarterly Journal of Economics* 121/2 (2006), pp. 747–782. https://doi.org/10.1162/qjec.2006.121.2.747

Latham, G. P., and E. A. Locke, 'Enhancing the benefits and overcoming the pitfalls of goal setting', *Organizational Dynamics* 35/4 (2006), pp. 332–340. https://www.sciencedirect.com/science/article/abs/pii/S0090261606000543?via%3Dihub

Lau, R. W. L., and S.-T. Cheng, 'Gratitude lessens death anxiety', *European Journal of Ageing* 8/3 (2011), pp. 169–175. https://doi.org/10.1007/s10433-011-0195-3

Lehrl, S., K. Gerstmeyer, J. H. Jacob, H. Frieling, A. W. Henkel, R. Meyrer, J. Wiltfang, J. Kornhuber and S. Bleich, 'Blue light improves cognitive performance', *Journal of Neural Transmission* 114/4 (2007), pp. 457–460. https://doi.org/10.1007/s00702-006-0621-4

Levin, D. Z., and R. Cross, 'The strength of weak ties you can trust: The mediating role of trust in effective knowledge transfer', *Management Science* 50/11 (2004), pp. 1477–1490. https://doi.org/10.1287/mnsc.1030.0136

Levin, I. P., S. L. Schneider and G. J. Gaeth, 'All frames are not created equal: A typology and critical analysis of framing effects', *Organizational Behavior and Human Decision Processes* 76/2 (1998), pp. 149–188. https://doi.org/10.1006/obhd.1998.2804

Locke, E. A., D. O. Chah, S. Harrison and N. Lustgarten, 'Separating the effects of goal specificity from goal level', *Organizational Behavior and Human Decision Processes* 43/2 (1989), pp. 270–287. https://doi.org/10.1016/0749-5978(89)90053-8

Locke, E. A., and G. P. Latham, 'Building a practically useful theory of goal setting and task motivation', *American Psychologist* 57/9 (2002), pp. 705–717. https://doi.org/10.1037//0003-066X.57.9.705

Lohr, V. I., C. H. Pearson-Mims and G. K. Goodwin, 'Interior plants may improve worker productivity and reduce stress in a windowless environment', *Journal of Environmental Horticulture* 14/2 (1996), pp. 97–100. https://doi.org/10.24266/0738-2898-14.2.97

Lundberg, S., and J. Stearns, 'Women in economics: Stalled progress', *Journal of Economic Perspectives* 33/1 (2019), pp. 3–22. https://doi.org/10.1257/jep.33.1.3

Lykken, D., and A. Tellegen, 'Happiness is a stochastic phenomenon', *Psychological Science* 7/3 (May 1996), pp. 186–189. https://doi.org/10.1111/j.1467-9280.1996.tb00355.x

Maddi, S., 'The story of hardiness: Twenty years of theorizing, research, and practice', *Consulting Psychology Journal: Practice and Research* 54/3 (2002), pp. 173–185. https://doi.org/10.1037/1061-4087.54.3.173

Mas, A., and E. Moretti, 'Peers at work', *The American Economic Review* 99/1 (2009), pp. 112–145. https://doi.org/10.1257/aer.99.1.112

Mawson, A., 'The workplace and its impact on productivity', *Advanced Workplace Associates, London* 1 (2012), pp. 1–12.

Mayo, M., 'If humble people make the best leaders, why do we fall for charismatic narcissists?' *Harvard Business Review* (7 April 2018). Retrieved from: https://hbr.org/2017/04/if-humble-people-make-the-best-leaders-why-do-we-fall-for-charismatic-narcissists

McElwee, R. O., D. Dunning, P. L. Tan and S. Hollmann, 'Evaluating others: The role of who we are versus what we think traits mean', *Basic and Applied Social Psychology* 23/2 (2001), pp. 123–136. https://doi.org/10.1207/153248301300148872

McFedries, P., 'Tall poppy syndrome dot-com', *IEEE Spectrum* 39/12 (2002), p. 68. https://ieeexplore.ieee.org/document/1088460

Megginson, W. L., and K. A. Weiss, 'Venture capitalist certification in initial public offerings', *The Journal of Finance* 46/3 (1991), pp. 879–903. https://doi.org/10.1111/j.1540-6261.1991.tb03770.x

Mehta, R., and R. Zhu, 'Blue or red? Exploring the effect of color on cognitive task performances', *Science* 323/5918 (2009), pp. 1226–1229. https://doi.org/10.1126/science.1169144

Miller, J., 'Tall poppy syndrome (Canadians have a habit of cutting their female achievers down)', *Flare* 19/4 (1997), pp. 102–106.

Morrison, M., and N. Roese, 'Regrets of the typical American: Findings from a nationally representative sample', *Social Psychological and Personality Science* 2/6 (2011), pp. 576–583. https://

journals.sagepub.com/doi/abs/10.1177/1948550611401756?journalCode-sppa

Mukae, H., and M. Sato, 'The effect of color temperature of lighting sources on the autonomic nervous functions', *The Annals of Physiological Anthropology* 11/5 (1992), pp. 533–538. https://doi.org/10.2114/ahs1983.11.533

Müller, K. W., M. Dreier, M. E. Beutel, E. Duven, S. Giralt and K. Wölfling, 'A hidden type of internet addiction? Intense and addictive use of social networking sites in adolescents', *Computers in Human Behavior* 55/A (2016), pp. 172–177. https://doi.org/10.1016/j.chb.2015.09.007

Münch, M., F. Linhart, A. Borisuit, S. M. Jaeggi and J. L. Scartezzini, 'Effects of prior light exposure on early evening performance, subjective sleepiness, and hormonal secretion', *Behavioral Neuroscience* 126/1 (2012), pp. 196–203. https://doi.org/10.1037/a0026702

Neumark, D., I. Burn and P. Button, 'Is it harder for older workers to find jobs? New and improved evidence from a field experiment', *Journal of Political Economy* 127/2 (2019), pp. 922–970. https://www.journals.uchicago.edu/doi/abs/10.1086/701029

Newark, D. A., V. Bohns and F. Flynn, 'The value of a helping hand: Do help-seekers accurately predict help quality?', *Academy of Management Proceedings* 2016/1 (2017). https://journals.aom.org/doi/abs/10.5465/ambpp.2016.11872abstract

North, A., D. Hargreaves and J. McKendrick, 'The influence of in-store music on wine selections', *Journal of Applied Psychology* 84/2 (1999), pp. 271–276. https://doi.org/10.1037/0021-9010.84.2.271

Novemsky, N., R. Dhar, N. Schwarz and I. Simonson, 'Preference fluency in choice', *Journal of Marketing Research* 44/3 (2007), pp. 347–356. https://doi.org/10.1509/jmkr.44.3.347

O'Brien, D., D. Laurison, A. Miles and S. Friedman, 'Are the creative industries meritocratic? An analysis of the 2014 British Labour Force Survey', *Cultural Trends* 25/2 (2016), pp. 116–131. https://doi.org/10.1080/09548963.2016.1170943
O'Connor, Z., 'Colour psychology and colour therapy: Caveat emptor', *Color Research & Application* 36/3 (2011), pp. 229–234. https://doi.org/10.1002/col.20597
O'Rourke, E., K. Haimovitz, C. Ballweber, C. S. Dweck and Z. Popovíc, 'Brain points: A growth mindset incentive structure boosts persistence in an educational game', *Conference on Human Factors in Computing Systems – Proceedings* (2014), pp. 3339–3348. https://doi.org/10.1145/2556288.2557157
Obermayer, J. L., W. T. Riley, O. Asif and J. Jean-Mary, 'College smoking cessation using cell phone text messaging', *Journal of American College Health* 53/2 (2004), pp. 71–79. https://doi.org/10.3200/JACH.53.2.71-78
Page, L., and K. Page, 'Last shall be first: A field study of biases in sequential performance evaluation on the Idol series', *Journal of Economic Behavior and Organization* 73/2 (2010), pp. 186–198. https://doi.org/10.1016/j.jebo.2009.08.012
Paunesku, D., G. M. Walton, C. Romero, E. N. Smith, D. S. Yeager and C. S. Dweck, 'Mind-set interventions are a scalable treatment for academic underachievement', *Psychological Science* 26/6 (2015), pp. 784–793. https://doi.org/10.1177/0956797615571017
Pinchot, S., B. J. Lewis, S. M. Weber, L. F. Rikkers and H. Chen, 'Are surgical progeny more likely to pursue a surgical career?' *Journal of Surgical Research* 147/2 (2008), pp. 253–259. https://doi.org/10.1016/j.jss.2008.03.002
Plomin, R., and I. J. Deary, 'Genetics and intelligence differences: Five special findings', *Molecular Psychiatry* 20/1 (2015), pp. 98–108. https://doi.org/10.1038/mp.2014.105

Preziosi, P., S. Czernichow, P. Gehanno and S. Hercberg, 'Workplace air-conditioning and health services attendance among French middle-aged women: A prospective cohort study', *International Journal of Epidemiology* 33/5 (2004), pp. 1120–1123. https://doi.org/10.1093/ije/dyh136

Quillian, L., D. Pager, O. Hexel and A. H. Midtbøen, 'Meta-analysis of field experiments shows no change in racial discrimination in hiring over time', *Proceedings of the National Academy of Sciences* 114/41 (2017), pp. 10870-10875. https://doi.org/10.1073/pnas.1706255114

Quoidbach, J., D. T. Gilbert and T. D. Wilson, 'The end of history illusion', *Science* 339/6115 (2013), pp. 96–98. https://doi.org/10.1126/science.1229294

Raanaas, R. K., K. H. Evensen, D. Rich, G. Sjøstrøm and G. Patil, 'Benefits of indoor plants on attention capacity in an office setting', *Journal of Environmental Psychology* 31/1 (2011), pp. 99–105. https://doi.org/10.1016/j.jenvp.2010.11.005

Riach, P. A., and J. Rich, 'An experimental investigation of sexual discrimination in hiring in the English labor market', *Advances in Economic Analysis & Policy* 5/2 (2006), pp. 1–22. https://doi.org/10.2202/1538-0637.1416

Riley, W. B., and K. V. Chow, 'Asset allocation and individual risk aversion', *Financial Analysts Journal* 48/6 (1992), pp. 32–37. https://doi.org/10.2469/faj.v48.n6.32

Roghanizad, M. M., and V. K. Bohns, 'Ask in person: You're less persuasive than you think over email', *Journal of Experimental Social Psychology* 69 (2017), pp. 223–226. https://doi.org/10.1016/j.jesp.2016.10.002

Rose, A., *The Alison Rose Review of Female Entrepreneurship* (2019). https://assets.publishing.service.gov.uk/government/uploads/system/uploads/attachment_data/file/784324/RoseReview_Digital_FINAL.PDF

Rosenthal, R., and L. Jacobson, 'Pygmalion in the classroom', *The Urban Review* 3/1 (1968), pp. 16–20. https://doi.org/10.1007/BF02322211

Rosso, B. D., K. H. Dekas and A. Wrzesniewski, 'On the meaning of work: A theoretical integration and review', *Research in Organizational Behavior* 30/C (2010), pp. 91–127. https://doi.org/10.1016/j.riob.2010.09.001

Rothbard, N., and S. Wilk, 'Waking up on the right or wrong side of the bed: Start-of-workday mood, work events, employee affect, and performance', *Academy of Management Journal* 54/5 (2011), pp. 959–980.

Rout, U., C. L. Cooper and J. Rout, 'Job stress among British general practitioners: Predictors of job dissatisfaction and mental ill-health', *Stress Medicine* 12/3 (1996), pp. 155–166. https://interruptions.net/literature/Rout-StressMedicine96.pdf

Rowe, C., J. M. Harris and S. C. Roberts, 'Seeing red? Putting sportswear in context', *Nature* 437/7063 (2005), p. 10. https://www.nature.com/articles/nature04306

Sacerdote, B., 'Peer effects with random assignment: Results for Dartmouth roommates', *The Quarterly Journal of Economics* 116/2 (2001), pp. 681–704. https://doi.org/10.1162/00335530151144131

Schmidt, U., and S. Traub, 'An experimental test of loss aversion', *Journal of Risk and Uncertainty* 25/3 (2002), pp. 233–249. https://doi.org/10.1023/A:1020923921649

Scoppa, V., 'Intergenerational transfers of public sector jobs: A shred of evidence on nepotism', *Public Choice* 141/1 (2009), pp. 167–188. https://doi.org/10.1007/s11127-009-9444-9

Seligman, M. E. P., T. A. Steen, N. Park and C. Peterson, 'Positive psychology progress: Empirical validation of interventions', *American Psychologist* 60/5 (2005), pp. 410–421. https://doi.org/10.1037/0003-066X.60.5.410

Seligman, M. E. P., 'Building resilience', *Harvard Business Review* 89/4 (2011), pp. 100–106. https://hbr.org/2011/04/building-resilience

Shaw, K. L., 'An empirical analysis of risk aversion and income growth', *Journal of Labor Economics* 14/4 (1996), pp. 626–653. https://doi.org/10.1086/209825

Simons, D., and C. Chabris, 'Gorillas in our midst: Sustained inattentional blindness for dynamic events', *Perception* 28/9 (1999), pp. 1059–1074.

Slovic, P., M. L. Finucane, E. Peters and D. G. Macgregor, 'The affect heuristic', *European Journal of Operational Research* 177/3 (2007), pp. 1333–1352. https://doi.org/10.1016/j.ejor.2005.04.006

Smith, B., W. Dalen, J. Wiggins, K. Tooley, E. Christopher and P. Bernard, 'The brief resilience scale: Assessing the ability to bounce back', *International Journal of Behavioral Medicine* 15/3 (2008), pp. 194–200. DOI: 10.1080/10705500802222972

Soldat, A. S., R. C. Sinclair and M. M. Mark, 'Color as an environmental processing cue: External affective cues can directly affect processing strategy without affecting mood', *Social Cognition* 15/1 (1997), pp. 55–71. https://doi.org/10.1521/soco.1997.15.1.55

Solnick, S. J., 'Gender differences in the ultimatum game', *Economic Inquiry* 39/2 (2001), pp. 189–200. https://doi.org/10.1111/j.1465-7295.2001.tb00060.x

Steidle, A., and L. Werth, 'Freedom from constraints: Darkness and dim illumination promote creativity', *Journal of Environmental Psychology* 35 (2013), pp. 67–80. https://doi.org/10.1016/j.jenvp.2013.05.003

Stinebrickner, R., and T. R. Stinebrickner, 'What can be learned about peer effects using college roommates? Evidence from new survey data and students from disadvantaged backgrounds', *Journal of Public Economics*, 90/8-9 (2006), pp. 1435–1454. https://doi.org/10.1016/j.jpubeco.2006.03.002

Stotts, A. L., J. Y. Groff, M. M. Velasquez, R. Benjamin-Garner, C. Green, J. P. Carbonari and C. C. DiClemene, 'Ultrasound feedback and motivational interviewing targeting smoking cessation in the second and third trimesters of pregnancy', *Nicotine and Tobacco Research* 11/8 (2009), pp. 961–968. https://doi.org/10.1093/ntr/ntp095

Stubbe, J. H., D. Posthuma, D. I. Boomsma and E. J. C. De Geus, 'Heritability of life satisfaction in adults: A twin-family study', *Psychological Medicine* 35/11 (2005), pp. 1581–1588. https://doi.org/10.1017/S0033291705005374

Sung, J., and S. Hanna, 'Factors related to risk tolerance', *Journal of Financial Counseling and Planning* 7 (1996), pp. 11–19. https://doi.org/10.2139/ssrn.2234

Tice, D. M., R. F. Baumeister, D. Shmueli and M. Muraven, 'Restoring the self: Positive affect helps improve self-regulation following ego depletion', *Journal of Experimental Social Psychology* 43/3 (2007), pp. 379–384. https://doi.org/10.1016/j.jesp.2006.05.007

Tiefenbeck, V., L. Goette, K. Degen, V. Tasic, E. Fleisch, R. Lalive and T. Staake, 'Overcoming salience bias: How real-time feedback fosters resource conservation', *Management Science* 64/3 (March 2013), pp. 1458–1476. https://doi.org/10.3929/ethz-b-000122629

Volpp, K., L. John, A. Troxel, L. Norton, J. Fassbender and G. Loewenstein, 'Financial incentive-based approaches for weight loss: A randomized trial', *JAMA* 300/22 (2008), pp. 2631–2637. https://doi.org/10.1001/jama.2008.804

Walton, G. M., and G. L. Cohen, 'A brief social-belonging intervention improves academic and health outcomes of minority students', *Science* 331/6023 (2011), pp. 1447–1451. https://doi.org/10.1126/science.1198364

Wargocki, P., D. Wyon, J. Sundell, G. Clausen and P. O. Fanger, 'The effects of outdoor air supply rate in an office on perceived air quality, Sick Building Syndrome (SBS) symptoms and productivity', *Indoor Air* 10/4 (2000), pp. 222–236. https://onlinelibrary.wiley.com/doi/pdf/10.1034/j.1600-0668.2000.010004222.x

Watson, J., and M. McNaughton, 'Gender differences in risk aversion and expected retirement benefits', *Financial Analysts Journal* 63/4 (2007), pp. 52–62. https://doi.org/10.2469/faj.v63.n4.4749

Yakubovich, V., 'Weak ties, information, and influence: How workers find jobs in a local Russian labor market', *American Sociological Review* 70/3 (2005), pp. 408–421. https://doi.org/10.1177/000312240507000303

Yeager, D. S., C. S. Hulleman, C. Hinojosa, H. Y. Lee, J. O'Brien, C. Romero, D. Paunesku, B. Schneider, K. Flint, A. Roberts, J. Trott, D. Greene, G. M. Walton and C. S. Dweck, 'Using design thinking to improve psychological interventions: The case of the growth mindset during the transition to high school', *Journal of Educational Psychology* 108/3 (2016), pp. 374–391. https://doi.org/10.1037/edu0000098

Zimmerman, D. J., 'Peer effects in academic outcomes: Evidence from a natural experiment', *Review of Economics and Statistics* 85/1 (2003), pp. 9–23. https://doi.org/10.1162/003465303762687677